Television and the

meaning of *live*

Television and the meaning of *live*

An enquiry into the human situation

Paddy Scannell

polity

First published in 2014 by Polity Press

Polity Press
65 Bridge Street
Cambridge CB2 1UR, UK

Polity Press
350 Main Street
Malden, MA 02148, USA

ISBN-13: 978-0-7456-6254-1
ISBN-13: 978-0-7456-6255-8(pb)

A catalogue record for this book is available from the British Library.

Typeset in 10.5 on 12 pt Plantin by
Servis Filmsetting Ltd, Stockport, Cheshire
Printed in Great Britain by Clays Ltd, St Ives plc

The publisher has used its best endeavours to ensure that the URLs for external websites referred to in this book are correct and active at the time of going to press. However, the publisher has no responsibility for the websites and can make no guarantee that a site will remain live or that the content is or will remain appropriate.

Every effort has been made to trace all copyright holders, but if any have been inadvertently overlooked the publisher will be pleased to include any necessary credits in any subsequent reprint or edition.

For further information on Polity, visit our website: www.politybooks.com

Contents

Acknowledgements

At the heart of this book is the concept of the care structure – the hidden creative input that goes into the making of any thing, any human institution, event or practice. How could I not be aware, then, of this book's care structure – the unseen unacknowledged labour of its production, all that has gone into its realization? It is this, of course, that must be properly and appropriately recognized in the act of acknowledging. It is a rather awesome responsibility and duty. There is so much to recognize, so many to remember – all those, who, on the one hand contributed to what went into the writing of this book; all those who have contributed to its production as a book.

I have paid my dues already to some of those whose work informs this book in its predecessor, *Media and Communication*, which contains accounts of the writings of David Riesman, Erving Goffman, Harold Garfinkel, Harvey Sacks, J.L. Austin, Paul Grice, Penelope Brown and Stephen Levinson. Their thinking has been formative for mine in the drawn out process of writing its successor. The extent of my debt of gratitude to Martin Heidegger will become apparent in everything that follows.

There are two key topics to the second part of this book: the study of live talk and of live events. I have thanks to pay in relation to both. In the first case to my friends and colleagues in the Ross Priory Group who have contributed so much, through the years, to my understanding of the workings of talk on radio and television.[1] They include Andrew Tolson, Joanna Thornborrow, Stephanie Marriott, Kay Richardson, Ian Hutchby, Trudi Harman and especially Martin Montgomery who introduced me to socio-linguistics (and sailing). The groundbreaking study of media events by Daniel Dayan and Elihu Katz was the initial inspiration for this book. As always, I have learned a great deal from the teaching situation through the years. All the programs discussed in part two have been used by me many times in the classroom. By dint of repeated viewings and discussions of them with students and colleagues, I have gradually come to see how they disclose the workings of live broadcasting and what is at stake in this.

On the production side, I must thank Andrea Drugan especially, my commissioning editor in Polity, and her colleagues Lauren Mulholland and Jonathan Skerrett. I confess I have lost track of all those colleagues whose friendship I have severely tested by asking them to read draft chapters at various points along the way. Rather than give offence to anyone by omission, I simply wish to thank them all – and especially the two reviewers for Polity who have read several iterations of the manuscript. Their patient advice and comments have been deeply helpful and taken into account. Dimitrios Pavlounis checked the references and compiled the bibliography, thereby sparing me a task I could hardly bring myself to do. Thanks, Dimitri – I could not have managed without your assistance. I have long ago acknowledged my debt to my wife and daughter, Suzi and Sonia, for their cheerful tolerance of 'the boringness of Heidegger'. For their continuing forbearance towards him and their loving support of me, I continue to be more grateful and thankful than I can possibly say.

Preface

I would like to think of this enquiry into radio and television as a contribution to what might be called third-generation media studies. It follows on directly from *Media and Communication* (Sage 2007) which was written as a textbook to introduce students to the academic study of media and communication. In my accounts there were two key moments: the formation of a sociology of mass communication at Columbia in the 1930s, and of media studies at Birmingham in the 1970s. The book's focus was *not* in the first place on media and communication but throughout on how academics engaged with and thought about the media and why. As I will shortly argue, academics go about their task by producing their object of enquiry as an academic object. But radio and television, the internet and mobile phones are simply *not* academic things – and in fact are resistant to being thought of as such. My aim and purpose here is an attempt to think of radio and television in their terms rather than in academic terms. This means to think of them *in situ*: as everyday worldly phenomena, as part and parcel of ordinary existence. In what follows, I set aside all *critical, theoretical* and *political* approaches in my enquiry into television as disclosive of the human situation today. In so doing I am, to put it another way, bracketing the discourses of sociology and cultural media studies – the first two generations of academic enquiry – of which I gave accounts in *Media and Communication*.

The provocation of this book is that it sets aside one of the most taken-for-granted, normal and normative assumptions of modern academic thought – namely, the explanatory power of sociology. I do so in order to resuscitate something that it has smothered out of existence and which yet underpins all its discourses. Anthony Giddens has argued, rightly I think, that sociology is perhaps *the* discipline of modernity: it is 'the most generalised type of reflection upon modern social life

[. . .] Modernity is itself deeply and intrinsically sociological' (Giddens 1991: 41, 43). We have all learnt to think sociologically. It has become a second nature to us. In today's common-sense self-understanding, human being is being social. This book is an enquiry into the meaning of the word 'life' and whatever that means it is surely something more than the *merely* social. Its problem, however, of which I am vividly aware, is that can no longer be taken as a *serious* question. It has dwindled to the status of an Oxbridge undergraduate joke (*Monty Python and the Meaning of Life*). The question of existence is, I have come to think, a limit question for the humanities and social sciences today, since it is nowhere recognized, acknowledged or addressed by them – in the fields in which I read, at least. The meaning of 'the social' marks the limits of their thinking and, by extension, the limits of modernity's self-understanding if (as I take it) that question is indeed modernity's ownmost topic and concern, as Anthony Giddens has argued. It is a foundational assumption of this book that what lies outside 'the social' (what determines it)[1] is 'existence'; life itself, life as such.

I begin with a sketch of phenomenology as an interdisciplinary way of thinking, and go on to a consideration of its distinctive, distinguishing topic, as worked out by Martin Heidegger, namely the question of existence, the meaning of (the word) 'life'. This was the focal concern of *Being and Time* (hereafter *BT*), one of the seminal texts of European thinking in the last century. But it was written nearly a hundred years ago, and the world today is not as it was when Heidegger published his life-defining work in 1927. If we are to benefit from its thinking, it must be re-thought in light of its relevance in and for our own times and this is what I try to do. I have undertaken a summary best reading of *Being and Time* which I hope is true to its central project, while critiquing it at certain points and trying to retrieve its integral unity. For it must be emphasized that it was hastily written (in order to get tenure!) and remains incomplete. In particular, it fails to deliver on what its title promises – namely a clear account of the relationship between the two components of its title – 'being' and 'time'.

The standard introduction to *BT*, in America especially, is *Being-in-the-world*, by Hubert Dreyfus. It was first published in 1991 and has since gone through dozens of reprints. By now it has become the classic *vade mecum* and guide to *BT* for English-speaking readers. Yet it is *only* about Division One, the first part of the book. Division Two is ignored. In his preface, Dreyfus tells us that he considers Division One to be 'the most original and important section of the work'. Division Two, he goes on, has two separate and somewhat independent themes. The first is the 'existentialist' topic of resolute, authentic being in face of existential anxiety, guilt and death. The second is the temporality of human existence and of the world, in which Heidegger tries to retrieve an originary 'ecstatic' temporality that goes beyond time as succession (the movement from past to present to future). On this Dreyfus comments:

> Although the chapters on originary temporality are an essential part of Heidegger's project, his account leads him so far from the phenomenon of everyday temporality that I did not feel I could give a satisfactory interpretation of the material. Moreover, the whole of Division II seemed to me much less carefully worked out than Division I and, indeed, to have some errors so serious as to block any consistent reading. (Dreyfus 1991: viii)

I agree. Division One has an integral unity, a clear narrative direction to it and a remarkable focused intensity of purpose in pursuit of its goal – the truth of what it is to be, what in fact we are, namely human. It can be read as a stand-alone text, and in many ways it is. But it is incomplete. The topic of the book as a whole, as given in its title – Being *and Time* – simply has not yet appeared. Division One was intended as a preparation for that topic. It is a long time coming in Division Two, and by the time he gets there Heidegger has lost his way. The topic of temporality is not properly reconnected with the topics of Division One. But without it we cannot grasp the overall unity of the work. This can be summarily stated. It is a fundamental enquiry into the human situation.[2] It has three irreducible components: people, place and time. Division One explicates the first two topics (place and people) in preparation for the third: time, the 'lost' topic of Division Two.

Dreyfus unerringly identifies the great theme of Division One as being-in-the-world. This has two components. The first (and it is the key to everything that follows) is the being *of* the world: the ordinary everyday human world of material things, the immediate environment, the *umwelt* (the topic of place). This is explored in chapter three, the magnificent cornerstone of the whole of the first part of the book. It is followed immediately by the obvious next most relevant topic, namely the being *in* this ordinary everyday world of *ordinary everyday people* (the pivotal second component of the human situation). This, the topic of chapter four, is the crux of Division One, and it is at this point, as I will shortly argue, that Heidegger takes a wrong turn that distracts him from his overall project. Nevertheless, the first two components of the human situation are convincingly established in Division One; the being-there of the ordinary everyday world and the being-in-it of ordinary everyday human beings. But the project is radically incomplete without the absolutely crucial question of time. Being-in-(the time of)-the-world: *that* was the projected but not fully realized integral theme of Heidegger's exploration of the human situation and its inextricably connected elementary components – place, people, time *and in that order*.

The world of the 1920s, in Division One, is always the *umwelt*; the immediate environment in which any individual life is unavoidably situated. But nearly a century later the world today, for anyone living in a post-modern society, is both their own immediate environment (the place where they live) *and* the world-as-a-whole. This is the world as routinely and daily disclosed by all tele-technologies of communication and, centrally, I will argue, by the two key technologies of radio and television taken together under the rubric of broadcasting. As anyone at all familiar with Heidegger knows, he was, in his later years, much vexed by the question of technology and, as an aspect of his general distaste for its frenzied dominion, he was none too fond of either radio or television. Radio broadcasting, he declared in 1949, 'has interfered with the essence of the human' (Figal 2009: 278). As television spread through Germany in the next decade, Heidegger publicly deplored its impact on his fellow Germans while occasionally enjoying watching live TV coverage of soccer (of which he was passionately fond).

Human technologies are world disclosing. So Heidegger argued in his much discussed lecture on 'The question concerning technology', the first version of which was given in Bremen in 1949, in a country shattered and ruined by a worldwide war of its own making. What was that war if not the first total global war on land, sea and air in which technologies of mass destruction put to the slaughter over sixty million people. The apotheosis of all these technologies was the atomic bomb – modernity's technological sublime. It was with all this in mind that Heidegger thought and spoke of the question of technology.[3] But in our world today, technologies no longer appear as an overwhelming threat to human life as such. They are rather, in many respects, our essential everyday life support systems. It is another fundamental assumption of this book that we now live in a totally technologized world. To understand *our* 'conditions of existence' demands that we address the question of technology as constitutive of the world we live in.

Television is, like any complex technology, a continuously evolving, changing historical thing. When I began work on it back in the late 1970s, I thought of it in two related ways. There was the TV set in the living room, and what we (in Britain) watched on it – namely the BBC and ITV. It was natural for me to think of TV and radio as more or less synonymous with the BBC – with *British* television. It was the only television I knew (apart from American shows, restricted to no more than 15% of total output). Television was experienced, thought and studied at first within the frame of the nation-state. It is no longer possible to think within this frame. Today, we must think of television *as such*: not this or that television – American, British, Japanese or whatever – but simply, *television*. To be sure, when I try to show how it works, in what follows, I take particular cases and these, naturally enough, turn out to be drawn from the televisions that I know – British and, to a lesser extent, American. But the programs I examine have no privileged status by virtue of their being American or British. When dinosaurs were first discovered, all over the world, they were not thought of as *American* or *British* dinosaurs when their remains were discovered in those places. Old programs, wherever they were made, are now part of the accumulating common global fossil record of broadcasting. What follows is an effort at re-thinking the initial terms in which I thought of radio and television as I encountered them back in the 1970s. Such an effort is a necessary response to two basic facts – one great, one small. The world has changed in the last 40 years – and so have I.

I began this book as a contribution to the study of media events, inspired by the seminal work of Daniel Dayan and Elihu Katz. They understood media events within the frame of a Durkheimian sociology of ritual. I was particularly taken by their subtitle, 'The live broadcasting of history', and that was and remains a focal concern of the second half of *Television and the Meaning of 'Live'*. It is a study of what is at stake in live-to-air radio and television broadcasting. This is a rather peripheral topic in Media Studies as Jerome Bourdon (2000) has noted, and there is, at best, only a scattered literature on it.[4] It took quite some time for me to discover it as the crux of my own concerns in the two related topics of part two; talk on early radio and television and the coverage of media events and news. I gradually came to see them both as inseparable and basically to do with the *management of liveness*, more exactly the problems broadcasting unavoidably confronts in managing the immediate *now* of speech (talk) and action (events) in live-to-air transmission. On the one hand, there is the ever-present risk and danger of technical error and performance failure that is intrinsic to live situations in public; on the other hand, the potential triumph of what Hannah Arendt calls 'great deeds and words' in the unforgiving light of publicness. The breakthrough into what the book is now about came when I saw that these issues were in no way peculiar to broadcasting – that they are, in fact, the issues that all of us confront in the management of our own daily lives and concerns. The issues posed by live broadcasting, I began to think, tell us something of the nature of the everyday human situation that all of us are unavoidably in. I mean we, the living, who must always speak and act in the immediate now-of-concern in the course of an unfolding life. In so doing we confront the same possibilities and dilemmas – whether at the level of individual lives or of high politics – that broadcasters face anywhere in the world. There is no more guarantee of success for broadcasters in *any* live broadcast situation than there is for any of us in any real-time life situation in which we find ourselves – the issues in both circumstances are the same. The question of the meaning of live broadcasting had grown into the meaning of life as we, the living, encounter it – and at this point I realized the book needed a complete rethink!

I therefore wrote what is now part one of the book as a preliminary exploration of the human life situation as we the living encounter it, in preparation for the study of the live situation in broadcasting as encountered by both parties to it – the broadcasters on the one hand, listeners and viewers on the other. Each part is, I hope, reciprocally illuminating of the other. Heidegger provided the essential framework of part one as the prelude to part two, but I had to wrestle him into shape. I have *re-thought* Heidegger in light of my concerns. Rooted out of my accounts are Heidegger's dubious notions in *Being and Time* on the masses (the They) and authenticity. His later jeremiads on technology are discarded, while hanging on to the key point that the essence of technology is nothing technological.[5] I have re-thought the question of being-in-the-world – the great theme of *Being and Time* – as being-(*alive and living*)-in-(*the time of*)-the-world. Unless the question of being is made fully explicit as being alive in time, there will always be the danger of lapsing into what Heidegger himself labels onto-theology, the cloudy realms of metaphysics. The underlying concern of *Being and Time* is one that I unreservedly share – to salvage and redeem the lost topic of existence, the meaning of 'life'. But to bring that question back to life requires tact in getting the balance and tone right, in raising the question again in an appropriate and timely way that makes it fresh and relevant to our world, our lives and our concerns today. This I have tried to do through an enquiry into live radio and television because that seems to me to be precisely the right way back to the question. Broadcasting is part of the taken for granted fabric of the world as a whole and speaks to the everyday life concerns of peoples situated in their own life world everywhere. In its management of live-to-air talk and events on radio and television, broadcasting unobtrusively reveals something of itself and of the world-historical situation of human life today, as I at last discover.

Part one

An introduction to the phenomenology of television

Prologue: Heidegger's teacup

By way of a beginning here are three stories about Heidegger and television. Martin Heidegger's life spanned most of the last century. He was born in Messkirch in 1889 and died in 1976. Messkirch, at the time of Heidegger's birth, was a village with a population of around 2,000, situated in south-west Germany, just north of Lake Constance and the Swiss border. He grew up in a deeply rural, traditional Catholic environment; his father was a craftsman, a master cooper and the sexton of the parish church. His mother's family were small tenant farmers.[1] In 1961, Messkirch celebrated the 700th anniversary of its founding and it invited its most famous son, the now world renowned philosopher, Martin Heidegger, to join in the festivities and give a talk.

Heidegger's talk, appropriately enough, was on the meaning of 'home', and, he remarked, coming home to Messkirch today, the first thing one notices is the forest of television and radio aerials on every roof-top. He saw in this a potent symbol of what the future held in store for Messkirch and the world. The TV aerials showed that human beings were, strictly speaking, no longer 'at home' where, seen from outside, they lived. The people of Messkirch might be sitting in their living room, but really, thanks to television, they were in the sports stadium or on a safari or being a bystander at a gunfight in the Old West (Pattison 2000: 59–60). The 71-year-old Heidegger was deeply suspicious of the intrusive, alien presence of television in people's homes.[2] It was part of the domination of mankind by modern technology.

That is the first story. Here is the second. Heidegger, for sure, did not have a television set. And yet, in his later years, he would regularly go to a friend's house to watch television. All his life Heidegger had been a keen sportsman. He was an excellent skier and would head for the snow-covered slopes whenever he could in the winter. He had always been fond of football and in his youth he was, Safranski tells us, a useful performer on the left wing. In his later years he became an enthusiastic follower of the European Cup on television and, 'during one legendary match between Hamburg and Barcelona, he knocked over a teacup in his excitement' (Safranski 1998: 428). This match took place in the 1960–61 season, the same year in which Heidegger gave his talk in Messkirch.[3]

And lastly, another football story – as told in English by Friedrich Kittler before an English audience.[4] Heidegger is now an old man in his eighties and his death is less than two years away.

Back in 1974 when Germany's football team won the title of World Champion – for the second time – the philosopher Martin Heidegger happened to take a train from Heidelberg back to Freiberg [. . .] and since in city trains at that time there were dining cars Germany's greatest thinker had the chance to make the acquaintance of Freiberg's theatre director:
'Why didn't we meet before?' was the director's urgent first question. 'Why don't you ever show up at the dramatic performances I give?'
Heidegger's answer was simple:
'Because on your stage they're just actors whom I'm not at all interested to see.'
'But dear Professor, I beg you, what else could we in the theatre possibly do?'
'I'd rather like seeing and hearing not actors but heroes and gods.'
'Impossible. Heroes don't exist and gods even less.'
'So haven't you watched our recent world championship on TV? Although at home my wife Elfride and I don't have one, I visited some nearby friends in order to watch. And for me the most obvious thing to remark was the fact that Franz Beckenbauer, the hero of the German team, was never fouled or wounded – he's proven to be invincible and immortal. Now you can see, even amongst us, there are heroes and gods!'

What do these stories tell us? Like any good tale they point to a moral which I take to be something about academics and how they think as academics on the one hand, and how they act when, on the other hand, they stop being academic. In his public role of mystic sage, Heidegger deplores television. When he gets home and hangs up his professional hat, he becomes ordinary like the rest of us, and does what the rest of us do ordinarily. He watches television and is absorbed by it. What needs serious consideration is not what Heidegger *thought* about television, but what happened to him when he watched it. Heidegger's spilt teacup is what calls for explanation. How could he be so excited? By the end of this book I hope to have offered some answers to that particular question. Here at the beginning I want to note the problems of academic thinking, particularly when it engages with the ordinary world of everyday life which for all of us today includes something that we speak and think of as 'television'.

1

What is phenomenology?

Phenomenology is a logos (a discourse) of the phenomena (the things that are visible). It is distinct from and in opposition to what we might call noumenology – the logos of the noumena: the invisible things, the things that belong to *nous* (the mind, consciousness, logos itself). Since Plato, the distinction between the visible things of the human world and the invisible things of the human mind has been a polarizing philosophical crux. What is the relationship between them? Plato was suspicious of phenomenal reality (the world as it appears to us) and privileged ideas (the ideal forms of thought/consciousness) over the appearances of things. Since then, in the Western tradition, consciousness (introspective mental acts of cognition) has been taken as the basis of what it is to be human: *cogito ergo sum*. It is the *cogito* (the 'I think') that grounds the *sum* (I am). Phenomenology is firmly committed to a view that thinking begins by looking outwards not inwards. In an originary sense we are moved (are summoned) to thinking by looking at the world, the alpha and omega of all thought – where thinking begins and ends. The point is not to contemplate the world, still less to presume to change it – but perhaps, at last, to recognize, acknowledge and try to understand it. This is what phenomenology essays. Its motto is given by Edmund Husserl (who gave phenomenology its name within philosophy): 'To the things themselves'. This means to attempt to think of things in *their* terms in the first place: not what *I* might think they are but what, in fact, *they* are. In phenomenological thinking, what a thing *is* (its truth; what it 'means') is immanent in the thing as it appears to us and as we encounter it. Things are disclosive of what they are; they reveal themselves *as* what in fact they are in the ways in which they appear and present themselves. For this way of thinking truth is revelatory: the immanence of truth in the world as the truth of the world.

At the end of the introduction to *Media and Communication* (*M&C*),

I offered a preliminary succinct definition of phenomenological thinking as 'an effort at an understanding of the world uncluttered by the usual academic baggage' (Scannell 2007: 6). I meant this as a provocation, but also exactly. An initial formulation of phenomenology might be that it is a way of thinking situated in academia that serves in part to put in question the taken for granted assumptions that underpin academic disciplines and their frames of thinking. In particular, it is a critique of the way in which academic thought invariably works to produce the objects of its thinking as academic objects. This point has been made most pungently by Michel Foucault's concept of the 'discursive formation'. A discursive formation is the product of institutional discursive regimes of truth (law, medicine, psychiatry, sociology) with the power to objectify that of which they speak. What is criminal and what is not, what is health and what is not, what is sanity and what is not, what is the social and what is not – positively and negatively the truth of what these things 'are' is the effect of self-validating, self-legitimating, self-regulating discourses that produce them as such. Outside of the university, there is no such thing as Literature – I mean Literature as the academic thing that is taught at universities, with degree courses and graduate programs and a forest of learned books and journals going back a century or more which collectively combine to produce the thing that is known and understood by all concerned (not without occasional challenges) as Literature. The truth of what this thing is, is the effect of institutional realities that produce and reproduce it as such – as a purely academic object. In the world outside the institutions of higher education, there are books of all sorts and there is a complicated publishing business and there are (or were) bookshops and there are readers . . . but all this goes on outside of the university and is not studied within it. Literature is not, in the first place, a worldly thing. It is an academic thing – objectified as such by the internal institutional processes that produce it as such.

The disciplines that constitute the humanities and social sciences (I leave the natural sciences out of these considerations) are all, in Foucault's terms, discursive formations: Literature, linguistics, anthropology, history, sociology, psychology. They are, in the first and last instance, all the effects of institutional modes of thought that produce them as institutional realities. And there is no necessary correspondence between any of them and what lies outside the university itself – namely the non-academic world of everyday life. Phenomenology is of course a hideously academic word – who outside the university would ever use the word in ordinary, non-academic conversation? But it wants to escape from the world of the university and reconnect with the world outside its lecture theatres and seminar rooms. It aspires to engage with the ordinary everyday world without preconceptions, theories or prejudices; without thinking in advance that it knows what it thinks about it.

Phenomenology does not belong to any single discipline – it is not simply or only a sub-field of philosophy for instance. It is a way of thinking that is cross-disciplinary and inter-disciplinary. Let me take two instances of phenomenological thinking from different disciplines by way of illustration; one from the UK, one from the USA. They occur more or less at the same time yet independently of each other. The first example is 'linguistic phenomenology', the second is ethnomethodology. I have given summary accounts of both in *M&C*. Linguistic phenomenology is the phrase that J.L. Austin used to describe what he did (Austin 1961: 182). His approach is more usually described as ordinary language philosophy. It is an essentially pragmatic view of language that asks what we do with words and tries to answer that question by carefully exploring how we use them. It is a view of language that is poles apart from language as conceived by linguists – by structural linguistics from Saussure to Chomsky. Linguistics produces language as an academic object and proceeds to study it scientifically (objectively). In so doing, it has transformed ordinary language that anyone and everyone can and does use into a technical, specialist object that only experts can understand. Austin's approach privileges the non-academic, ordinary worldly phenomenon of language-in-use as used by anyone and everyone (in Saussurean terms he is concerned with *parole* rather than *langue*). It endorses phenomenology's motto – to the things themselves. In this case ordinary (non-academic) words and what we do with them – how we put them to use, in what circumstances and for what practical worldly purposes.

Ethnomethodology is the term coined by Harold Garfinkel to describe the new kind of radical sociology that was emerging in the USA in the 1950s. His work, and that of Erving Goffman and Harvey Sacks, marked a sharp break with mainframe American sociology,[1] which thought of society in terms of large-scale institutional structures (the state, the economy, the culture industries) whose continuing existence demanded the production and reproduction of individuals adjusted to their systemic requirements. This modernist macro-sociology was challenged by the new postmodern sociology of the 1950s which took the micro-social as its domain of enquiry. For Garfinkel, the kind of sociology he had learned at Harvard under Talcott Parsons had the effect of reducing individual social members to judgemental dopes who 'function' to maintain the stable features of the social order by acting in ways that serve to reproduce it. This disciplinary model of society presumes that individuals left to their own devices (i.e., without the control of social institutions) would, in a state of nature, act solely in their own interests and against each other. 'Society' acts as an external constraint that imposes and maintains social order. The new sociology sharply disagrees with this. If there is to be such a thing as society, there must be individuals predisposed to cooperative action and interaction with each other. Collaborative behaviours are not the effect of a mysteriously pre-existing social order that imposes itself upon individuals. Rather, the orderly interactions of individuals oriented to cooperation (working together) produce and maintain a social world. At stake in this difference between the old and the new sociology is the relationship between structure and agency (Giddens 1984). Ethnomethodology attends to the reasonable accountable methods of *ethnos* (social members) in interaction with each other and the ways in which they thereby sustain an intelligible, workable, meaningful world-in-common.

The philosophy of ordinary language and the sociology of interaction appear in different places at the same time and both, I have argued, are in response to the structural transformation of the world that becomes visible in the 1950s and which I have described as the transition from the time of the masses (the modern era that ends in 1945) to the time of everyday life – the post-war, post-modern era of today. Both are instances of what I think of as the phenomenological turn: the turn to the things themselves – language as such, the social as such. Let me summarize their similarities as a preliminary sketch of what I mean by the phenomenological orientation to things:

- Both take a pragmatic approach to their object (language, society) that is distinctly parsimonious in respect of theory.
- Each asks 'How does it work? What can we do with it?' Both presume the usability, the workability of their object domain. Both conceive of it as a practice. Each explores how the practice works, in what ways and under what situational constraints.
- Each is oriented towards action rather than contemplation (theory). It is a mistake to think of Austin's work as speech act theory – that term was introduced by his student, John Searle (1969). Austin's thinking is profoundly resistant to theorizing. And likewise, the sociology of interaction – the interactive order that Goffman made his life's work.
- Each presupposes that the practice has an implicit logic-of-use: i.e., that language-in-use, interaction-in-action have reasonable, accountable and justifiable features that are taken as given and oriented to by participants.
- These logics are not in any way external to the practices: they are what constitute their possibility. They are the structuring features that produce the practices (of conversation pre-eminently) as essentially reasonable (accountable, justifiable) and thereby workable.

- In all this, the object domains are viewed from the perspective of the ordinary and mundane – the routine practices of everyday activities (such as talking) in practice, in use, in action. This perspective is thus oriented to the point of view of the laity and not that of the sociologist, the philosopher, the priest or the professor.
- The phenomenological perspective is aligned with that of ordinary social members. Both are oriented to a hermeneutics of trust that takes things at face value in the first instance. In this way the phenomenological position is sharply at odds with the dominant sceptical hermeneutic perspective of academia which is oriented to suspicion.

Phenomenology's topic

Phenomenology, then, is a way of thinking that can be applied to any academic field of enquiry. It functions negatively as a critique, or reality check, on the taken-for-granted assumptions that constitute the disciplines in the humanities and social sciences. Positively, it has its own object domain – one that is largely absent from almost all the dominant discursive fields of academic enquiry today. Its project is, in this respect, redemptive: to breathe life into a lost, abandoned topic – the question of existence, the meaning of 'life'.[2] Once upon a time human beings were moved to wonder at the question of existence when they looked up at the stars and contemplated the heavens. In the totally human world of today, in which the natural world is no more than an occasional disastrous intrusion, the question of existence has become mundane. In our world, the meaning of 'life' is disclosed by the liveness of television and other electronic media of everyday communication.

The question of existence – the meaning of 'life' – is everywhere present and nowhere considered in the field in which I work – namely media and communication studies. It is there most visibly in that well-worn expression: 'everyday life'. I have shown, in the long narrative of *Media and Communcation*, that 'everyday life' achieved recognition across a range of academic fields of enquiry and in different countries in the 1950s. It was, in all sorts of ways and for all sorts of reasons, a post-war phenomenon first explored by Henri Lefebvre in his remarkable *Critique de la vie quotidienne* in 1947. It became a central concern of American sociology in the 1950s. *Personal influence* (Katz and Lazarsfeld 1955) was a study of the ways in which ordinary American women made decisions – about what to buy in the supermarket, what movie to go and see, what fashion to follow, what their opinions were about current events. And these opinions, tastes and choices were shaped in interaction with others, in conversation with friends and relations, family members, colleagues in the routine contexts of their daily lives. The new post-war sociology of social interaction pioneered by Erving Goffman, Harold Garfinkel and (a little later) Harvey Sacks, took mundane existence as its core problematic. In Britain the redefinition of culture brought about by Richard Hoggart and Raymond Williams re-specified it as the ordinary way of life of the working class (Hoggart [1957] 1992) or of a whole society (Williams [1958] 1965). The philosophy of ordinary language taking shape at Oxford in the 1950s was in tune with this cross-disciplinary concern with the ordinary and the everyday developing in different countries in the course of the decade – an emergent structure of thinking in response to a newly visible worldly phenomenon that hitherto had been off the radar of academic enquiry. I am not of course suggesting that everyday life was invented by academics, still less that it did not exist before the 1950s! Rather that it became salient in a quite new way in that key post-war decade. Academics began to attend to it because it was the moment in which ordinary mundane existence entered into publicness and history and as such it came to their notice. And one thing that made this double process visible was that then very new (and desirable) everyday technology – the TV set. Television itself is both a formal indication of the entry into history of everyday life and a key means whereby it became publicly visible and historical . . . a claim to be explored and justified in what follows.

The question of existence then, is to be considered in a particular way (as ordinary, everyday existence) and through one historically particular formal indication of it, namely television. The justification for treating the question of existence (the meaning of 'life') from an ordinary perspective is set out in detail by Martin Heidegger in Division One of *Being and Time*, and I will come to this in a moment. But it is the absolutely crucial starting point. It rescues the question from the blight of irrelevance into which it had long since lapsed. No longer some vague metaphysical, theological question of the Meaning of Existence (God, the Universe and Everything), it is posed by Heidegger concretely and directly and in ways that anyone can connect with and understand (if you stay with him long enough to get used to his inimitably tortured prose). The question now becomes that of the life that is, in each case, mine and the world in which I, in each case, am – the *umwelt*, the roundabout-me-world of everyday existence. This is the starting point of a fundamental enquiry into the meaning of 'life' (being)[3] in terms of its fundamental components: place, persons and time, the irreducible components of any actual, concrete existential situation. My 'self' in relation to others and their 'selves' in the places where I live in the times of my life – this, concretely and matter of factly, is the life-situation in which all of us find ourselves to be. A crucial question, of course, is 'Who is this "me"?' Further, 'What is the nature of my existential situation – my being in time and place?' And 'what kind of world is it that "gives" the very possibility of my being in it and how?' This is the domain of enquiry that properly belongs to phenomenology: it is in exploring the mundane world of everyday life that we begin to get to grips with the question of existence; the meaning of life.

But why might television be a way into this question? We live in a totally technologized world – 'we' being the privileged members of post-industrial societies. 'We' are not the rural poor of other parts of today's world. Such people do not (yet) live in a world that has things like television sets in it. Our world is one that is no longer defined and driven by necessity and whatever kind of thing television might be, it is not a necessary thing. The world that we (post-industrial people) inhabit is one in which we are totally dependent on the humanly created infrastructure that gives unceasingly, from moment to moment, hourly and daily, day in day out, the taken-for-granted conditions of our lives – in just about every conceivable way. By the infrastructure, I mean the global transport and communications networks that underpin today's global economy and the common world to which it gives rise and of which we (post-modern people) are the most privileged beneficiaries. This world is without precedent. Now at last, really and truly, all the world's a stage and all its men and women are its players. To say we live in a totally human world means that we live in a totally technologized world. If the infrastructure should collapse, the common world collapses. We are wholly dependent, in every aspect of our lives, on the harnessed energies of the petro-electro-chemical industries and the infinite supply of commodities generated by the global economy. The meaning of life today is a technological question, if by that is meant 'the conditions of existence today'. Heidegger's generation was much concerned with this question and he himself pointed out that the essence of technology is nothing technological. One way into the meaning of life today is through the question of technology precisely because it defines our conditions of existence.

Raymond Williams has argued that the 'long revolution' in Britain (the agonized, conflicted working through in time of industrial modernization) was, in the long run, a force for the good and that, by the 1950s, the mass of the population was directly benefiting from it (Williams [1961] 1965). Rising standards of living, increased material goods, gave the majority of people more control over their own lives, more choice in the disposition of personal time and income than had ever been possible for the hitherto but now no longer silent (silenced) masses. Television in the fifties, we might say, paraphrasing Williams, was and remains a significant index of the emergence of a post-modern, post-industrial culture of everyday life: an inter-personal culture oriented to leisure, material goods, conversation and enjoyment in the context of day-to-day existence. From its earliest days, television has been the expressive register, in the totality of its output, of the emergence of a post-war way of life oriented more towards communication than conflict. This transition took place throughout North America and Europe, though at different rates in different countries, in the transformed post-war world. The majority of people today, in the advanced economies of the world, enjoy a standard of living, a level of material abundance and well-being, that was scarcely imaginable in my childhood (the late 1940s). A key indicator of this is the quite remarkable expansion of life expectancy for men and women since the fifties. On present demographic trends it has been predicted that between one in four and five people alive in Britain today may live to be a hundred. Of course not everyone has benefited in the general extension of material well-being, and the gains are most certainly not evenly and equally distributed. A culture of affluence creates quite new kinds of moral problems and ethical dilemmas for its populations. But by and large and on the whole the members of post-war post-industrial societies today lead lives no longer dominated and defined by primary poverty, immediate material necessity. Freedom means, in the first place, freedom from necessity. Only when the necessary conditions of material existence have been secured can the enjoyment of unnecessary things begin. Television is one such unnecessary thing: one significant material good that is surplus to requirements. It is not for nothing that it has been conceived of and used, from the start, as a new form of everyday entertainment in societies oriented to leisure and free time.

The acknowledgment of the goodness of material things is a key theme of this book, and expressed in its central concept of the care-structure. If we live in a world that we can take on trust, it is only because we have faith in all the things of the world that allow us to be about our daily concerns in hopeful ways that are not essentially problematic. The workability of worldly things – each and all, separately and together – is the mark of the workability of the world – its enabling power that grants its inhabitants, the generations of the living, to be about their daily lives in manifold taken-for-granted ways. The gift of things is that they allow us to take them for granted. I wish to make a strong claim for the goodness of the world as immanent in the things of the world, a goodness that can be determined exactly by the measure of unthinking and unconditional trust that we are able (or not) to invest in it. The natural attitude towards the everyday world is one of faith and hope in its ordinary unremarkable workability – for by and large and on the whole, in common experience, things work pretty well all the time for all of us. Not now and then, or when they're in the mood, or only on Tuesdays – but always and everywhere and unceasingly. Television is like this, when you think of it. The TV set does what I want it to do. It turns 'on' whenever I press the button on the RCD (remote control device), if I can find it. And whenever I turn it on, I find there is always something to watch – all the usual programs on the usual channels at the usual times on the usual days. The trick is to see just how utterly astonishing and amazing this entirely unremarkable fact, in fact, is. But, of course, ordinarily, that is just what we never see. It is a focal concern of this phenomenological enquiry not simply to make visible what the world conceals about itself, but to explain it. The concept of the care structure both accounts for and justifies the invisibility of what is hidden but immanent in the everyday material world of things.

2

Available world

The care structure

What then is the *care* structure of things – of any and every thing, of any and every human practice and institution? It is nothing more or less than the human thought, effort and intention that has gone into producing the thing *as* that which it is. This care, of course, disappears into the thing, is subsumed by the thing, which stands independent of all the creative labour that produced it. We can never see what went into the making of any thing, whose hidden meaning is the starting point of Marx's celebrated analysis of the commodity and its secret. At first glance commodities are just ordinary trivial things and yet they contain, Marx argues, all sorts of subtle metaphysical niceties. They are social hieroglyphs that do not come to market with their meaning branded on their forehead. The task of analysis is to expose what commodities conceal about themselves – and the truth that they hide is the exploitative character of the human labour that produced them.

The character of labour under the then new conditions of factory capitalism in nineteenth-century Britain is the great theme of Marx's defining masterpiece, *Capital*. The factory worker is alienated from his or her labour in every way and at every level of the production process. In the first instance, the so-called 'free wage bargain' between the capitalist and the worker is the moment in which the labourer is alienated from his own self: in exchange for a subsistence wage he has exchanged his freedom for bondage and become subject to the will of the other who employs him. The factory worker has no control over the conditions and terms of work: he has no say in where he works or at what times. He does not define what he does or how he does it. At all points he works to the bidding of others. There is no creative satisfaction in his work as a hired hand. His work is repetitively monotonous, physically exhausting and very often dangerous and damaging to health. He clocks on in the morning, clock watches through the working day and clocks off when the factory whistle blows in the late afternoon. What he does is meaningless to him. He works only because he must in order to secure a basic living for himself and his dependants – the dull compulsion of economic necessity. In the end he does not own the fruits of his labour, nor realize its value. Commodities go to market where they exchange against the commodity of all commodities, money (pure value). What is realized in exchange, the *exchange value* of commodities, is profit, or surplus value. This surplus value – created by the labour process, realized in exchange – is expropriated by the capitalist. Thus what is concealed in the exchange value of commodities is the rate of exploitation of the hidden human labour that produced it.

Marx distinguished between exchange value and use value. His analysis is hugely tilted in the direction of the former to the exclusion of any real consideration of the latter. Because the labour that produced commodities is exploited (and it really is), Marx seemed to think that the products of this labour must themselves be contaminated; corrupted, as it were, by the process of their manufacture. He saw industrial society as one in which relations between things had come to dominate relations between human beings. And he clearly regarded the falling value of relations between people and the rising value of things (what he called commodity fetishism) as morally offensive. Lukacs drew the obvious conclusion: the commodity was not simply the enigmatic product of alienated labour; it was the mark of a reified society in which all social members were estranged from themselves and each other. The members of the Frankfurt Institute for Social Research took this one stage further in their mordant critique of mass culture. The music, radio and film industries of the 1920s and 1930s were part of the logic of domination inscribed in factory capitalism. The false pleasures they offered were a new form of soft power whose siren songs bound the masses to their fate. Mass culture was a masquerade of mass deception. Its effect was to emasculate the revolutionary potential of the masses and reconcile them to their situation as the exploited majority in an intrinsically unfair, unjust society.

Now there was and there remains an essential truth in all this. But by now, at the start of the twenty-first century, it is at best a half truth, for who would seriously argue against the material benefits of the post-modern world in which we live today? It is a fundamental issue about which we must be clear. The end of scarcity, the overcoming of subsistence forms of life is an unmitigated good; an unequivocal historical gain. To be free from necessity is the material basis of freedom. This is the meaning of the post-modern world in which we live today. If it has a rational basis, it must be found in its material base: the taken-for-granted, fully technologized world of everyday things upon which our everyday lives today depend. This world has come into being at a huge price: the immense suffering, over centuries, of countless lives caught up in and consumed by the convulsive transformation of the world brought about by industrial capitalism. And yet, in the long run, its benefit – a world that has overcome necessity – is beyond price. We, post-modern peoples today, are all the beneficiaries of the working through in time of world modernization, driven now, as then, by the capitalist mode of production – and we have an incalculable debt of gratitude to the generations of the dead who suffered the consequences of that long revolution, whose promise began to be delivered through all sections of society in the transformed post-war world of the last century.

Thus, in thinking today about what is hidden in the things that make up the everyday environment in which we live we must always take into consideration *both* aspects of what they conceal; the exploitation of the labour that produced them *and* their care structures. The relationship between the two is contradictory, but they do not cancel each other out. Each has a different hermeneutics – one of trust, the other of suspicion; a sceptical view of hidden exploitation, a trusting view of hidden care. One is not truer than the other. Both are true. But ultimately, of course, one must ask whether one outweighs the other. In my view, we should not be so overwhelmed by the exploitative character of labour in the capitalist mode of production as to reject the mode of production itself. The question of labour is at the heart of the politics of any industrial or post-industrial society. It concerns the political struggle over the distribution of the social surplus that the mode of production creates. Should the state intervene to redistribute the social surplus throughout society in the interests of social justice and the common good? Since the Second World War, democratic societies have swung back and forth in being more or less in favour of distributive social justice.

It is not an incorrigible matter, and the politics of distributive justice is the potential, if not always actual, solution to the exploitation of the labour that is hidden in things.[1] The care-structure is the measure of their goodness. Good for what?, we might ask. Good for the purposes for which they were made, we might reply. That is to say, they work: they really and truly deliver the goods that they promise. They are technically efficient, usefully useable, handy kinds of things. They offer themselves as utilities and, insofar as I or anyone can put them to good use, they are, in their own small ways, good things. Now it is clearly the case that things may be made for good or ill. They may be technically efficient and well made but harmful in their application and use. I address this crucial issue later when I make a historical case for the atomic bomb as modernity's technological sublime and the mobile phone as today's post-modern world-defining technology. One is a thing oriented to killing people. The other is oriented to talk between people. One is so terrifyingly destructive that today's global politics is committed to putting this particular technological genie back in its bottle so it can do no harm. The other is a force for the good, insofar as it is preferable for people to be talking to, rather than killing, each other.

Marx saw the commodity as an enigma, a riddle whose secret was the hidden reality of its conflicted relations of production. The concept of the care-structure likewise acknowledges that things have a hidden reality – in this case the creative thoughtful labour that produces any thing as a human good that is fit for use. In either case, the key question is: why (and how) is it hidden? Ideology critique was the answer to the secret of the commodity. It conceals its exploitative character by presenting itself as an innocent, ordinary, trivial kind of thing. In so doing, it draws the ideological veil over its real meaning – exploited labour. The same criticism was made of television in its early days. Television seemed to present a transparent window on the world, as if what it showed were somehow natural, self-evident and obvious. Television, it was argued, concealed its own mode of production. It concealed its own work of selecting and framing what it showed in ways that (secretly) favoured the interests of those with economic and political power – the dominant ideology thesis, in short. The hermeneutics of suspicion regards what is hidden in things as the deceptions of power which it is its critical duty to unmask.

Now it is not that this is wrong. But it is certainly not all there is to say on the matter, and the very same phenomena can be interpreted in ways that flatly contradict the sceptical interpretation of what is hidden in things. In all that follows, I too recognize that television characteristically conceals its own mode of production – it quite deliberately hides its own work in the production and presentation of its program output. But, as we shall see, in my accounts, it does so not in order to deceive, but rather to produce guarantees of reality-and-truth as the basis of genuine experiences for viewers. In this hermeneutics, television works, by and large, for and in the interests of its viewers rather than against them. The hermeneutics of trust proceeds from a wholly different standpoint from that of the hermeneutics of suspicion – one that is struck by and seeks to account for the goodness of things and the wonder of the ordinary everyday world. It has, however, the same problematic: namely, that things conceal their goodness every bit as thoroughly as the ideological veil is drawn in the critical paradigm. What, then, is the riddle of the ordinary and the everyday? It can be simply put. There is nothing to say about it. It is banal, obvious, boring, uneventful and, in short, if not meaningless then at the very least not very meaningful. And everybody knows this. And we all know that television is like this precisely because it is such an everyday thing: it is trivial, a waste of time, boring, bad for the kids, etc. Are we not amusing ourselves to death in today's banal everyday world – and does not television confirm this, especially in its latest incarnation as Reality TV?

The opaqueness of the everyday was a crux for the sociology of interaction, especially for Harold Garfinkel, who struggled valiantly with its impenetrable character. Austin and Grice were both convinced of the fine-grained and precisely meaningful character of ordinary talk. And this in face of the prevailing scepticism in Oxford at that time which regarded ordinary talk as useless for any philosophical purpose because it was unfit for conceptual analysis on account of its 'ambiguity, misleadingness, vagueness and the incorporation of mistakes and absurd assumptions' (Grice 1989: 176–7). And the banality of the ordinary world was an unresolved crux in Martin Heidegger's enquiry into being and time. The tranquillized obviousness of everyday life (Heidegger [1927] 1962: 359) was something to be overcome by authentic, resolute being in resistance to its stultifying complacency.

The hermeneutics of facticity

Reading *Being and Time* was a transformative experience from which it has taken me a good few years to recover – to recover that is, an adequate, critical perspective on its astonishing achievement. So I want to start by acknowledging just how much I learnt from reading Heidegger and the extent to which I am forever in his debt. I now think – and it has taken me a dozen years at least to come round to seeing this – that Heidegger was, in writing his defining work, already beginning to lose the freshness of the original view of the world that inspired it. It is that freshness of vision that I took from reading him and which has remained with me ever since. The revisionist account of *BT* that follows is, I would like to think, an effort to redeem the original project that begins to go awry in Division One and is not successfully retrieved in Division Two. What was the project? It was a basic enquiry into what it is to be human. Heidegger called it fundamental ontology – a logos of *ontos*,[2] a discourse of being. We must remember, though, that it was an incomplete project – 'a magnificent torso', as someone has called it, rather than a finished work. What we have is what was published in 1927: two parts of a three-part first volume to be followed by a second volume, also in three parts. Divisions One and Two of the first part are all that we have, and it must be said that their quality is uneven and the relationship between them less than clear.

The key to Heidegger's project is the way that he raises the question of being: not being-in-one's-head (the philosophy of consciousness) but being-in-the-world, as Hubert Dreyfus's commentary on Division One makes abundantly clear (Dreyfus 1991). The starting point for trying to understand what it is to be what we in fact are (namely human) is to look outwards not inwards. We discover ourselves in what we have made of things – more exactly we find (and lose) ourselves in the world of our making. Most immediately, what Heidegger means by 'world' is the environment, the *umwelt*. *Um* means around or about: the roundabout-me-world, the ordinary world of everyday existence in which I, in each case, am. It was the discovery of *this* world that so excited the young Heidegger. 'Living in an environment, it signifies to me always and everywhere, it has all the character of world. *Es weltet* (it worlds)' he told his class in a lecture from 1919 (Figal 2009: 35). He had found a new way of 'seeing' it, which he called 'the hermeneutics of facticity', the topic of a course of lectures he gave at Freiburg in the summer semester of 1923. The course title was, simply, 'Ontology'. But Heidegger begins by claiming that traditional ontology cannot get to grips with its question – that of 'being'. A new approach is needed and he calls it 'the hermeneutics of facticity'. In the course of the lectures, Heidegger develops a concrete, matter-of-fact account of the human situation. Being human means being here in the world, the ordinary world in which each and every *Dasein*[3] is situated. Towards the end of the course, Heidegger discusses two different ways in which we encounter everyday things – a table, say:

> In *the* room there at home stands *the* table (not 'a' table among many other tables in other rooms and houses) at which one sits *in order to* write, have a meal, sew, play [. . .] Its standing-there in the room means: Playing this role in such and such characteristic use. This or that is 'impractical', unsuitable. That part is damaged. It now stands in a better spot in the room than before – there's better lighting for example. Where it stood before was not at all good (for. . .). Here and there it shows lines – the boys like to busy themselves at the table. These lines are not just interruptions in the paint, but rather [it means]: it was the boys and still is. This side is not the east side, and this narrow side so many cm. shorter than the other, but rather this is the side at which my wife sits in the evening when she wants to stay up and read; there at the table we had such and such a discussion; there that decision was made with a *friend*; there that *work* written that time; there that *holiday* celebrated that time. (Heidegger [1923] 1999: 69)

In *Being and Time* Heidegger gives formal accounts of the two different ontologies that are concretely indicated in this description: the objective world of object-Things (ontology A), and the meaningful world of significant things (ontology B). The fundamental difference between them shows here in the difference between the indefinite and the definite article. *A* table . . . any table, a table Thing. Any table (as a universal) can be *objec*tively described and defined in terms of its objective observable and determinable properties. It (any table) is made of such and such materials. It stands so high. It is *x* centimetres long and *y* centimetres wide and it weighs so much. On the other hand, *the* table (*this* table) is a particular thing. Heidegger clarifies the significance of the table (what it *means* as distinct from what objectively it is) as part of a world for those for whom it matters. Its significance lies in the ways that it matters. It is significant because it is put to significant use. *This* is what we do at the table, Heidegger says: I write; my wife reads or sews; my young sons play and (literally) leave their mark upon it. They have scored its surface with their pencils so that whenever he sees those marks, Heidegger is reminded of their presence. The table is marked with their being. They have impressed themselves upon it in their own small way. Such are the everyday structures of significance in and for which the table is a part.

Everyday things are everywhere imbued with the presence of particular some ones. Any thing can be transformed to appear as some thing: a transformation brought about by some one impressing upon the thing the mark of their being. You can tell that a living room bears the mark of the people that live in it. You see this without noticing it really in the things that show as theirs – mementoes, keepsakes, ornaments and souvenirs – in all the bric-a-brac, the seen but unnoticed clutter in the room. A room stripped of such stuff is not a homely (lived in) room.[4] Some years ago I stood in the empty living room of the house in which my mother had lived for so many years; the house in which I and my brothers and sisters grew up, and from which she had moved because now, in old age, it was too difficult living there alone. Stripped of all its familiar things – these photographs of the family on the mantelpiece, that set of china in the corner cupboard (a wedding present), the three piece suite of furniture chosen after much deliberation – the room (the house itself) no longer bore the marks of her presence. The house, which *was* her life, *upon which* she had impressed her being there, was no more so. Her being which once was there was now gone and would not return. Places stripped of the presence of particular someones may have an aesthetic purity. They may be technically efficient. But they are strictly impersonal, as are so many public, institutional rooms . . . lecture and seminar rooms for instance.

Heidegger goes on to imagine the 'awhileness' of the table in his living room:

> That is *the* table – as such it is there in the temporality of everydayness, and as such will it perhaps be encountered again after many years when, having been taken apart and now unusable, it is found lying on the floor somewhere, just like other 'things', e.g. a plaything, worn out and almost unrecognizable – it is my youth. In a corner of the basement stands an old pair of skis, one of which is broken in half – what stands there are not material things of different lengths, but rather the skis from that time, from that adventure with so and so. [. . .] These are characteristics of the world's being encountered. What now needs to be enquired into is how *they constitute the being-there of the world*. (Heidegger [1923] 1999: 69–70; translation slightly modified and final emphasis added)

The table ('now') and the old pair of skis ('then') are part of Heidegger's youth. It is not just we ourselves but our things too (the things we care for) that change *in* time. In our living room, there in a basket covered over by a jumble of other things, is a small stuffed pony made of wool. This is – or, rather, was – Nitty; Princess Nitty Noy of Noyland, in the imaginary world created by my daughter when she was a little girl. This world once was for her (and for me) real, true and alive. It is so no longer because my daughter is now in her twenties and has long since grown out of the games of her childhood. But it is hard to imagine throwing Nitty away even though she no longer has any 'use'. This small thing is full of memories. In it I still see (I still hear) the traces of my daughter as she once was, when she was five or six.

This is something of the significance of everyday things. But surely such meanings are purely personal and subjective? Is not Nitty just 'in fact' a mass-produced consumer good for kids onto which one particular child has projected her own particular childish fantasies? Maybe. But is it not rather that my daughter put the thing (the toy) to use in an appropriate way? Any toy has 'to-be-played-with' as its for-the-sake-of-which, and this is inscribed in its design, in the materials from which it made, its shape and size and so on. Just as the table elicits a wide range of involvements – eating, sewing, reading, playing, talking – and is 'for' these things, so too a small fluffy toy elicits a range of behaviours that are appropriate to it, and my daughter found one. She discovered (invented) an appropriate thing to do with it. She 'created' Nitty. She brought her into being. For a while at least, Nitty was not an imaginary projection onto what was 'in fact' just stuff (material) put together in a particular way. Nitty was real and alive for my daughter and for me too. She was, for a while, part of both our lives. Nitty was designed 'as' a toy and as such embodied the care-structure of a toy. A toy 'is' a meaning structure. This meaning structure *is* the relational totality of involvements that the toy elicits. To this care-structure my young daughter brought her self and her concerns and impressed them both upon the toy in her own small and unique way.

Thus what intersected in the play of the game (the created world of Noyland) was the impersonal care-structure of a mass-produced thing and the personal care-and-concern that my daughter brought to it. It would be wholly wrong though to imagine that the former is the actual and objective 'reality' while the latter is 'just' a subjective, imaginary projection upon it. My daughter did indeed project her self upon the fluffy toy. But her particular 'upon which' (*her* game) was, in a general sense, anticipated and allowed for, in the toy's design and manufacture, as an appropriate appropriation of it. Everyday things have a 'they' structure (they are for anyone) but upon such structures we impress our selves and in so doing transform them and make them part of our lives. As such they accompany us through life and are the placeholders of meaningful events, places, moments and relationships in the course of a life time. *This* was given me by my wife at the beginning of our relationship before we married. *That* I bought on a particular journey abroad. When I listen to *this* song I remember a particular time, a place, a person. These are the structures of significance in which we dwell for a while in the round-about-me world of everydayness.

Brief though it is, Heidegger's account of the existential situation in his lectures of 1923 has a vivid immediacy that is fading if not lost in *Being and Time*. 'The hermeneutics of facticity' course brought together, in an integral unity, the fundamental components of the human life situation: people, place and time. Being in the world is always being in a world with others (the *umwelt* is a *mitwelt*) in some particular place at some particular time. These three themes are there in *BT*, but they no longer hold together, and that beautiful, clear and non-judgemental vision of the miraculous facticity of the ordinary world has clouded over. There are major gains, however, in the formal clarification of the underpinnings of the new hermeneutics of facticity and in particular of the ways in which the built environment (the *umwelt*) gives itself in such ways that I or anyone can matter-of-factly *be* in a world that allows me to be about my everyday concerns, whatever they may be, in ways that are essentially unproblematic. This is 'the ordinary effect' (it's natural; it's obvious) which a sceptical hermeneutics regards with suspicion. The task of a hermeneutics of trust is to account for the same phenomenon, but in a precisely different way. Heidegger's analysis of the worldliness of the world (the topic of Chapter 3, Division One) is a stunning account of how things give themselves as things-for-use and this leads on to a consideration of the spatiality of the *umwelt*, the ways in which all things in any particular place constitute the conditions of *being there* for any and every one. It is a remarkable and profound enquiry into the fundamental meaning of being *in* and leads to the great discovery that 'being in' most radically means *being-in-concern*; care as the foundational definition of what it is to be human, alive and living with others in a common world of concern.

Consider, by way of illustration, an ordinary academic situation in which teachers and students often find themselves: the seminar.[5] All of us in the seminar can say two things that are true for each and all who are present. 'I am in the seminar': 'I am in the seminar room' – two ontological claims to the basic existential situation of being 'in'. It is not immediately obvious, however, that these are two essentially different ways of being-in: that one exemplifies ontology A, the other ontology B.

I am in the room. The chair, the table, the projector, the black (or white) board is in the room . . . It makes sense to say these things and thus, in this ontology, my way of being in the room is the same as that of every other thing in the room. I am in the seminar. The chair, the table, the projector is in the seminar? It makes no sense to say such things. This mode of being is particular only to the human beings present in the room and no thing else.

Describe being in the room. The chair in the room, say. It stands so high it weighs so much; it is light it is heavy; it is brown or black or gray. It weighs so much; it has such and such dimensions. It has arms and legs. Describe the human being in the room in the same way: it stands so high; it weighs so much; it is light or heavy; it has grey hair and blue eyes. Its dimensions are such and such. It has two arms and two legs. This is ontology A: the discourse of beings: the universe of material things: things as objects with objective properties that can be objectively observed measured and described. In this ontology, each of us is a material thing like every other material thing in the room. We are indeed in this ontology not just *like* things, but in fact *are* things just like all the other things in the room.

Describe being in the seminar. I am interested in the seminar. I am very interested, I am fascinated, excited and enthralled by it. Or maybe not. I am bored by the seminar. I am irritated by it. I am wondering whether it will ever end. I am thinking about other things – what I will do when at last I escape from the seminar . . . All these are possible ways of being in the seminar and each of us doubtless is in the seminar in a way that differs slightly or greatly from other people from moment to moment, from start to finish. But irrespective of how I in each case am subjectively in and experiencing it, the seminar is unavoidably that with which each and all who are there are dealing *now*, coping with *now*, engaging with *now*, whether positively or negatively or neither as in the case of bored withdrawal. But disengagement from the situation is still an active way of being in the seminar. In short, being in the seminar is unavoidably an involvement, a commitment to *being in* it and that means being concerned with it one way or another. And this is Heidegger's amazing discovery of what it is to be human. Being human is being in concern always and unavoidably in whatever waking situation we are in. We are always in a situation that calls upon us to cope with it, to manage it, to deal with it somehow or other. *Mea res agitur.* I am my concerns (Heidegger [1924] 1992: 8E). Being alive and living in the world is being in concern. Care is the foundational ontological condition and structure of the being of human beings.

But what gives the possibility of my concerns? What gives the possibility of being in the seminar? What are the care structures that allow us to be there together in the immediate now-of-concern, caught up in the care-structure of the seminar to which all are, by virtue of being there, unavoidably committed? What is the seminar? It is in the first place an event – a mundane kind of event to be sure, but an event in the way that Dayan and Katz conceive of media events. For the seminar to happen it must have had a fore-structure whose care-and-concern was to make it happen. For the seminar's participants to be gathered together in order to be in it, each individual has routine daily care-structures already in place in order to be there.[6] And for all concerned to be gathered in by the gathering power of the event's fore-structure, there must be in place the care-structure of the dedicated place in which all are gathered, the utterly familiar known-and-taken-for-granted room in which the seminar takes place.

Under the aspect of ontology A (the being of things), chairs and tables and desks and projectors and lap-tops and things are all just that – each with its own stand-alone existence as a thing-in-itself, with its own observable, measurable and describable properties which define it in its material objectivity. As such, each thing has no connection with any other thing. Each object is intelligible in its own observable and measurable objective terms but, strictly, meaning-less. But under the aspect of ontology B, *every* thing in any room has an intentional purpose or reason for being there and, as such, is strictly meaning-full. They are there in the room not just as naturally occurring objects but for good and practical human means and ends. To enquire into the care-structure of a chair is to set aside the objective question 'What is it?' and to ask 'What is it (meant) for?' What is its point or purpose, its raison d'être, its reason for being? It is for sitting on or in. But the way of sitting *on* the chair at the seminar is not the same way as sitting *in* the chair at home watching television. The chair in the seminar room is a sit-up-and-pay-attention chair. It is designed to make us do just that. It is not meant to be comfortable; it is not easy to fall asleep in. It is not an easy chair for lazing about in and eating potato chips and laughing at the TV (like Martin Crane's La-Z-Boy recliner which his fastidious son, Frasier, so dislikes).

The care-structures of the chair in the living room and the chair in the seminar room are different and indicate different involvement-wholes, different concerns. Moreover, the chair's care-structure in either setting makes sense only in relation to all the other things in the living room or the seminar room that separately and together combine to give the relational totality of involvements, the particular care-structures of the activities they are specifically designed to support in the particular places in which they are situated and for which they were made. Such is the spatiality of the everyday human world, the first fundamental existential component of the human situation.

It is the mark of Heidegger's genius to have started with this powerful and persuasive analysis of the immediate everyday world in which each of us unavoidably 'is'. The concept of the care-structures of the things of the wholly human world, which is always already 'there' before and after every encounter with it in any actual situation any where any time, explains how it is in fact possible for each and all 'to be' in any kind of real-world situation at all while justifying (accounting for) the ways in which this 'care' is concealed from us. It is concealed in order to 'let us be' – to let us be ourselves and to be about our ordinary but always particular concerns in ways that are essentially unproblematic. That we do not see this – that we do not have to care about our ordinary being in the world (that it is not in any essential way a problem, an issue) – is the transcendent gift of the enduring human world to the human beings who dwell in it at any time. As such, it is a seen but unnoticed formal indication of the radical historical transcendence of the human world (and historical humanity itself) that is always, and necessarily, hidden from the radically non-transcendent generations of the living who inherit the world from the generations of the dead who were there before them and in which they, the living, now dwell – for a while.

This preliminary account of the care structures *as such* is by way of an introduction to the more particular technological and production care-structures of radio and television. I wished first to establish what it means to think of the care-structures as a dialectical synthesis of Marx and Heidegger. In my discussion of the application of the concept to radio and television I add a third key component, namely the rational (reasonable, accountable) conditions of their logic-of-use, which draws on H.P. Grice's theory of communicative intentionality. But for now I want to add one last proviso to this initial opening-up of the concept. If we focus on exchange-value, we see only the conflicted relations of production that are hidden in things. If we focus on their use-value, we see only the care structures that produce things as material goods. It is like the glass of water: one sees it half empty, the other sees it half full. It is not an either/or – the glass most certainly is either and both. Each perception is true; neither cancels the other. But they *are* contradictory ways of seeing and it is not possible, at one and the same time, to see it as both. You can only occupy one or other, but not both, at any moment in time. The hermeneutics of trust and suspicion must both be acknowledged and recognized if we are to confront with clarity the moral choices and ethical dilemmas with which we are endlessly confronted by the material things of our world. I buy a pair of shoes. They are good. They are stylish. They fit me. They are comfortable. They are well made and will serve me well for quite a while – in short I like them. But it may be that the shoes are the product of indentured child labour in another part of the world. Does that fact destroy its use-value? No. But it most certainly follows that I should care, that it must matter, how they are made.

In any democratic economy of abundance, there must necessarily be a politics of care about all aspects of material things – how they are made, their usage, impact and effect. Hidden in the care structure is not *just* the immediate labour that produced it. There is the long historical struggle over the terms and conditions of labour: the length of the working day and week; the abuse of child labour; health and safety in the workplace – all this and more. It is *all* the hidden concern that produced it as what it is – and this is a continuous historical process, because the things themselves have continuously evolving life histories as they enter into use and thereby the life of the societies of which they become an integral part. The care-structures of complex things like TV sets or cars have complicated evolving histories. Cars are intrinsically dangerous things as David Blanke makes clear in his vividly scary account of the mass uptake by Americans of the automobile in the first four decades of the last century (Blanke 2007). Improved car safety evolves in time as part of the public politics of care that includes consumer lobby groups, activists, legislation and regulation. Ralph Nader's polemical indictment of the American automotive industry, *Unsafe at Any Speed* (1965), triggered widespread public concern at the time and led to the introduction of seat-belts and air bags by an initially reluctant car industry. The concept of the care structure is the place-holder for all that contributes to the production of things as things-for-use, including continuing public and political debate about all aspects of their social impact and regulation. The crucial, defining characteristic of the care-structure is its invisibility in the things themselves: how *that* is understood is the hermeneutic question.

3

Available self

The 'who' of everyday existence

What next? Heidegger turns immediately to the question of 'the "who" of everyday existence'. It is a good and relevant next question. The question of the self is central to the thinking of Divison One and is the crux of the pivotal fourth chapter whose rather clunky title is: 'Being-in-the-world as being-with and being-one's-self. The "They"'. We move from the *umwelt* to the *mitwelt* which is, as such, disclosive of *mitsein* (being-with). The social character of the care-structures of the everyday world points to the social character of those who made it and who dwell in it. The ontology of the social is the theme of the chapter and the ways in which sociality is an integral component of the ontological structures of the self. What then, or 'who' is the self in everyday life? Heidegger's answer to his question is: 'The Self of everyday Dasein is the *they-self*' (*BT*: 167). What does this mean?

In everyday life I am not 'me'; I am not *my* self. I am an anonymous instance of *das Man*. The rendering of this untranslatable term in English is a crux. Macquarrie and Robinson, who have given us the standard English translation, go for 'the They'.[1] Hubert Dreyfus, in his excellent commentary on Division One of *Being and Time*, prefers to translate it as 'the One' (the oneself) which – like the French *On* (*comme on dit*) – captures the idiomatic use of the impersonal in English: 'it's what one does', 'it's the way one does things' (Dreyfus 1991: 151–2). There is, then, in idiomatic English a 'oneself' – an impersonal self – that does 'the done thing' and that can think and talk of itself imper-sonally, as if it were someone else. But such a formulation misses the force of 'the They' as an anonymous collectivity of which 'one' is a part. Heidegger's key perception is that the possibility of individual 'sub-jectivities' is always already given by the play of prior anonymous and public social processes. The problem is that, rather than exploring the ontology of 'the They', Heidegger jumps ahead to his own existential*ist* interpretation of the phenomenon. It is at just this point, I now think, that he takes a wrong turn[2] from which his project never recovers:

> In utilizing public transport and in reading newspapers, every Other is like the next. The Being-with-one-another dissolves one's own Dasein completely into the kind of Being of the Others, in such a way, indeed, that the others, as distinguishable and explicit, vanish more and more. In this inconspicuousness and unascertainability, the real dictatorship of the 'they' is unfolded. We take pleasure and enjoy ourselves as *they* take pleasure; we read, see, and judge about literature and art as *they* see and judge; likewise we shrink back from the 'great mass' as *they* shrink back; we find shocking what *they* find shocking. The 'they', which is nothing definite, and which all are, though not the sum, prescribes the kind of being of everydayness. (Heidegger [1927] 1962: 164)

In this passage the lineaments of a 'mass society' are described. The masses travel by public transport, read newspapers, share the same enjoyments and have the same opinions about everything. Each of us is one of the masses, while not recognizing that we are: 'we shrink back from "the great mass" as *they* shrink back; we find shocking what *they* find shocking'. But rather than analyzing the significance of this, it is simply judged and condemned. The dictatorship of the They is thought of as a form of collective domination over the individual Authentic self, the realest 'me'. It is 'a falling', a 'disburdening of one's Being' a 'surrendering' to 'distantiality, averageness, leveling down, publicness' (166). It is the mark of 'inauthenticity and failure to stand by one's Self' (166). It is a way of being that 'misses itself and covers itself up' (167). But what Heidegger misses – and it is essential to his whole thesis – is anything like an adequate analysis of the *necessarily* anonymous character of social life as that into which *any* individual is thrown and *in* which individuality is formed. The ontology of being-with as *such* is simply not undertaken. The nature of the social – which is what is at issue in the phenomenology of being-with – remains undeveloped in Heidegger's analysis. I have tried to develop, thinking with but against Heidegger, a more adequate formulation of the phenomenology of the self in everyday life, taking as my starting point the 'who' of everyday broadcast media. Who is the listener or viewer addressed by daily radio and television output?

The media are part of anyone's life in a post-traditional society. In the USA or Britain just about everyone makes use of them on a daily basis. An obvious conclusion to draw from this is that the media must be organized in such ways that anyone and everyone can use and understand them. This does not necessarily mean that everyone will like them (will want to read this or that newspaper, watch this or that program). But it must mean that newspapers, radio and TV programs are so designed as to be intelligible to just about everyone. To whom then, do the media 'speak'? Who do they address, and how? If, say, a TV program is watched by twenty million people, how is watching that program experienced by all those millions? Do they find that they are addressed as a multitude? As all those millions? As 'the masses'? The answer is surely, no. Each viewer finds that what they see and hear seems to speak to them directly and individually.[3] If this is so, then broadcast programs and daily newspapers appear to have a peculiar communicative structure. They are heard, seen or read by millions (by anyone and everyone) and yet, in each case, it seems, they speak to listeners, viewers or readers personally, as individuals. They are, it could be said, for me or anyone. I have called this a *for-anyone-as-someone* structure (Scannell 2000). We get a clearer picture of what it means if we begin by considering the two other such structures that are implicated in it, namely *for-anyone* structures and *for-someone* structures.

For-anyone structures

A for-anyone structure is something which, in its organization and design, presents itself as useable and useful for anyone (no matter who). What we call mass-produced goods have such a structure. The critics of mass culture condemned mass-produced goods for their standardized, uniform character. They imposed the stamp of sameness on everything and this, they argued, tended to the liquidation of individuality and difference (Adorno and Horkheimer [1944] 1979). Well, maybe. But suppose we turn this round and see that this uniform and standardized character is a very useful feature of many kinds of manufactured thing. I want, say, a toaster that toasts. It doesn't have to do this for me personally. It does have to be designed in such a way that anyone can figure out what it is for and how to use it and in fact do so easily and quickly. It will also be important that the toaster works every time it is used – not just now and again. Given that a toaster, to do its job, must have certain basic design features, it is not surprising that toasters (when you go to choose one) turn out to be pretty similar. There will be some differences (can it cope with muffins and bagels as well as sliced bread? How many slices can it toast?) but not much. It simply doesn't matter whether or not the toaster is 'for me' personally. Personally I don't care what kind of toaster it is so long as does its job every time and doesn't burn the toast.

Mass-produced goods may be anonymous, impersonal things. But why should they be anything other than this? Their standard, uniform, repeatable character is precisely the mark of their usefulness for anyone and everyone, any time any where. What of mass communication? Is it appropriate to call newspapers, radio and TV, the *mass* media? In one obvious way it does seem so. When people all over the world watch the same movies or TV programs, they can surely be described as mass media. But the crucial question is, 'How are these countless millions spoken to?' Our experience of newspapers, radio and TV programs is that they speak to us as persons not as members of a crowd or mass. Early thinking about new media of communication thought of them as mass communication, attributing to them the characteristics of existing dominant forms of public address which set aside the individual face needs of audience members, and treated them impersonally as anonymous (faceless) members of a crowd (or mass). Such a definition was appropriate to the communicative practices of public oratory at the historical moment when film, radio, mass circulation daily newspapers and television became part of the social fabric of western twentieth-century societies. But it is not appropriate to those media themselves and their communicative practices. The mass media address many millions simultaneously, but they do not speak to multitudes as the masses but to individuals as persons.

For-someone structures

As the polar opposite of for-anyone structures, for-someone structures bespeak things made for use only by particular individuals; glasses, dentures, made-to measure clothes or cars, for instance. Cars for the mass market are mass-produced for anyone and everyone. But the Formula One racing car driven by Michael Schumacher was custom-built for him and no-one else. What of for-someone communicative structures? These are not so much useable by as meaningful only for a particular someone. We can most readily see their significance when we think of the meaning of photographs or, more exactly, snapshots. A snapshot is what you or I take with a camera and almost always as a matter of personal record: of babies and children as they grow up, of holidays or of significant family events such as birthdays, weddings, graduation day and so on. These are purely personal things and are quite distinct from 'photographs' by professionals as 'art' or for publication in magazines or advertising or whatever. Photographs have a public significance, and they proclaim their 'publicness' (as art or advertising or social comment) in their form and content. A snapshot in its content and form (its lack of composition, its fuzziness, etc.) proclaims its 'privateness'. It is not for public consumption. In a beautiful essay on photography, Roland Barthes describes looking through some old family photos shortly after the death of his mother. He is looking for a photograph that will bring to life for him the spirit and being of his mother: the one in which he recognizes 'the truth of the face I had loved'. At last he finds it:

> The photograph was very old. The corners were blunted from having been pasted into an album, the sepia print had faded, and the picture just managed to show two children standing together at the end of a little wooden bridge in a glassed-in conservatory, what was called a Winter Garden in those days. My mother was five at the time (1898), her brother seven. He was leaning against the bridge railing, along which he had extended one arm; she, shorter than he, was standing a little back, facing the camera; you could tell that the photographer had said, 'Step forward a little so we can see you'; she was holding one finger in the other hand as children often do, in an awkward gesture. The brother and sister, united, as I knew, by the discord of their parents, who were soon to be divorced, had posed side by side, alone, under the palms of the Winter Garden (it was the house where my mother was born, in Chennevieres-sur-Marne). I studied the little girl and at last rediscovered my mother . . . In this little girl's image I saw the kindness which had formed her being immediately and forever, without her having inherited it from anyone . . . (Barthes 1984: 68–9)

This is something of what Barthes sees in the faded old photograph of his mother. He can tell us what he sees in it, what it means to him. But you or I cannot, nor ever could, see it as he sees it. The photograph is not reproduced in the book. For Barthes himself it is everything. 'For you, it would be nothing but an indifferent picture, one of the thousand manifestations of the "ordinary"' (Barthes 1984: 73). For-someone structures point to the incommunicable self and the incommunicability of experience. Each one of us has an inner (an ownmost) self that is inexpressible to others. This inexpressible self is a cumulative thing that is formed by the gradually unfolding story of a life as lived, of cherished and cherishable moments, people and places. At most this self is share-able with intimate others. It finds objective expression in great art and literature. But ordinarily and for the most part it is not sayable or share-able. I understand what Barthes sees in the photograph of his mother. I understand it because I know what it is to feel such things. There are people in my life who have such significance for me. But to understand and accept the truth of what he sees in this particular photograph is not to share it. All I would see was something that said 'History' (that's an old photo) and 'Culture' (what funny clothes she's wearing, and what's that conservatory thing she's standing in?). The Winter Garden photograph is meaningful for Roland Barthes and no-one else. Thus, for-someone communicative structures point to the inwardness of a personal life as experienced by someone with the attributes of a unique person; someone-in-particular.

For-anyone-as-someone structures

To understand this structure, we must constantly keep in mind its double character that operates at two levels simultaneously: it is always, at one and the same time, for me *and* for anyone. It thus is an intermediary structure that mediates between the utterly impersonal for-anyone structure and the utterly personal for-someone structure. As such, the for-anyone-as-someone structure expresses and embodies that which is between the impersonal Third person and the personal First person, namely the Second person (the me-and-you). The for-anyone-as-someone structure expresses 'we-ness'. It articulates human social sociable life. One pervasive way in which this structure shows up on radio and television is in the mode of address they routinely employ. The mode of address of radio and television shows in two interconnected ways. Most basically it is manifest in ways of saying. To this is added, in television, ways of showing. Saying and showing – letting things be heard and seen – these are the two fundamental communicative acts of broadcasting and are discussed in some detail in part two of this book.

Television's mode of address is underpinned by the way in which its constructs its 'look', how its speakers are presented to viewers, how they appear to us when we turn on the set. It is, for instance, an entirely unremarkable, taken-for-granted thing that when I watch the news on TV it seems that the newsreader in the studio is speaking directly to me, as I watch. I know, of course, that the newsreader is in fact reading the news. I don't suppose that he or she is an accomplished actor who has learnt a script by heart and produces a word-perfect performance each night. Nor does it appear that the newscaster 'ad-libs' the news. It is not a brilliant, spontaneous improvisation that is routinely produced for TV viewers. Given that news is read, why do we not see the newsreader reading the news from a script in front of her or him? Why should it matter that he or she appears to be addressing the viewer (who turns out, in every case, to be 'me') directly? Why, indeed, bother to have a visible newsreader at all? It makes no difference to the actual content of what is being said.

The direct look-to-camera of the newsreader is a technological effect of the autocue or teleprompter, whose significance I will return to. It is a

deliberately sought-for, constructed and concealed look that is directed
'out' of the studio. It implicates a someone someplace to receive it who
turns out to be, in each case, 'me'. And it begins to establish what's
happening (namely the newscaster reading the news) as a real-time,
real-world interactive occasion in which I, in each case, am directly
implicated. Thus I find, when I turn on the news, that I am spoken to
while knowing that millions of others are watching at exactly the same
time and seeing and hearing exactly the same things. In each case the
experience is the same. In each case it is 'for me'. This is the characteristic effect of a for-anyone-as-someone structure. The news is, in each
case, appropriated by me as an aspect of my experience[4] and yet at the
same time this experience is shared by countless others.[5] It is thus an
experience that I share with others and as such is, in principle and in
fact, talkable about by me with anyone else who has watched the same
news program. And so it is more generally in respect of the daily output
of radio and television. For-anyone-as-someone structures in principle
create the possibilities of, and in practice express, a public, shared and
sociable world-in-common between human beings.[6]

The communicable self in everyday life

Heidegger missed the foundational significance of the 'They' as the
basis of the phenomenology of the 'self'. Just when he should have
opened up what it means, he closes it down. He sets up a false opposition between two integral aspects of the structure of the being that each
of us has; namely that each and all are, at one and the same time, just
like everyone else (and necessarily so) *and* a uniquely particular person
– the one and only, genuine 'me'. In Chapter 3 he has shown how the
umwelt 'works': how all things in any particular where (the bedroom, the
bathroom, the airport, the highway . . . *every* particular 'there' in which
I or anyone am at any time) combine together as a relational totality
of available resources to facilitate whatever it is that I am doing there.
This is the immediate everyday world and as such it has a necessarily
anonymous and public character. It is not there just for 'me', and to
suppose for a moment and act as if it were would be a certifiable delu-
sion. It is there for any and everyone, each and all, and in the same
way. The implication is surely clear. If this world is made by human
beings, and if it has an anonymous collective and public character as
the foundational condition of its availability for use by everyone – then
this must be a foundational characteristic of the beings who made it.
The anonymous public character of the ordinary world is disclosive of
the utterly impersonal and transcendent collective genius of a common

humanity working in and through deep historical time. That is just what the everyday things of the world conceal from us (otherwise we would be dumbstruck in amazement all the time) and which it is the hermeneutic task to unconceal as the truth of worldly things and the human world itself. The they-self is a formal indication of the utterly impersonal aspects of the being that 'I' in each case have in common with all other beings like 'me'. A common world and a common language must have, as the conditions of their possibility, the same fundamentally impersonal common characteristics as their creators and users, and vice versa. That is why, rightly, Heidegger takes 'the They' as the starting point for the topic of Chapter 4.

Why then does he go wrong? At this point we need to bring in the third component of the existential situation which I will come to next – namely time. It is evident (now) reading something written in the 1920s, that Heidegger's anxieties about 'the They' are a product of his time – the time of the world in which *Being and Time* was written. There is nothing personal, still less original, about Heidegger's worries about the domination of individual life and experience by anonymous, impersonal social forces. It was, perhaps, the defining anxiety of the culminating moment of high modernity, the two decades of the twenties and thirties, caught between two world wars. The high anxieties of Heidegger's generation were not imaginary. They were part of a pervasive structure of feeling on both sides of the Atlantic, and present as much in the popular culture of the time as in the lucubrations of the intellectuals. It really did then seem as if impersonal social forces threatened to overwhelm individual life and experience, and in the end they did. Mass society (the Modern era) self-destructed in the Second World War.

In his concern to protect the integrity of the authentic self, Heidegger slides rapidly into an attack on the everyday social world as inauthentic – given over to gossip and idle talk and dominated by the They. In so doing he undermines the extraordinary clarification he has just achieved of the anonymous public everyday world in which all individuals are situated. And indeed, from now on, through to the end of Division One and well into Division Two, Heidegger is preoccupied with individual experience. It is widely recognized that *Being and Time* is, inter alia, a devastating critique of the Cartesian philosophy of consciousness (or transcendental subjective rationality). But a recurring mantra in *BT* is 'the being that is, in each case, mine' and a concern for the possibility of its being authentic against the dictatorship of *das Man*. The brief sketch of the phenomenology of the self that I have just outlined proposes that 'the realest who of everyday existence' is neither the inauthentic They-self (as Heidegger thought) nor its opposite, the ownmost authentic self (as he would wish) but an intermediary *communicative* self that is betwixt and between the other two: the self in interaction with others, the *sociable* self of everyday life. In putting it like this, there are clear dangers of making the phenomenology of the self seem more abstractly schematic than I intend. So I want immediately to say that the three-part structure I have proposed is no more than a heuristic device for clarifying an emergent historical phenomenon. The communicative self, the sociable self-in-everyday-life, only becomes visible and recognized as such in the post-war decade. That is what, in part, my analysis of the transition from the time of the masses to the time of everyday life was at pains to track in academic writings across several disciplines on both sides of the Atlantic.

And if there was one book that clarified my understanding of this historical restructuring of the self it was the pivotal American sociological text of the mid-century, *The Lonely Crowd* by David Riesman. The 'self' is not a fixed and given thing. It is shaped by social and cultural factors, as these are determined in and by time. Charles Taylor has argued that the concept of the 'self' is the basis of modern identity, a historically formed and by now deeply taken for granted way of understanding what it is to be a distinct individual with the attributes of a person (Taylor 1992). Riesman's argument is more particular: he is concerned with the restructuring of the American soul, a transformation that is becoming visible in the immediate post-war moment in which his book was written. An older 'ideal type' is being replaced by a new and quite different personality type – in short, what he calls the 'inner-directed' individual is giving way to the 'other-directed' individual in post-war America. The sociological source of the inner-directed type is, as Riesman acknowledges, Max Weber's famous interpretation of the connections between the Protestant ethic of seventeenth-century Europe and the rise of capitalism.[7] This by now old early-modern middle-class type is figured in the banker, the tradesman, the entrepreneur, the engineer. However, on the cusp of the mid twentieth century a new post-modern type[8] begins to appear: the other-directed individual who takes her norms not from her own inner compulsions but from external social pressures, the 'primary group norms' of those she encounters in her daily life. Riesman stresses that this is a very recent development, a newly emerging social phenomenon that is not restricted to, but is most advanced in, the USA. The 'new' middle-class type is figured in the bureaucrat, the salaried employee in the large firm. What produces conformity in this kind of individual is not some inner self-regulating device, but the values and attitudes of others: 'either those known to him or those with whom he is indirectly acquainted, through friends and through the mass media' (Riesman [1950] 2001: 21). The post-modern individual, unlike his rugged go-it-alone modern predecessor, is exceptionally sensitive to others: he is shallower, freer with his money, friendlier, less certain of himself, more dependent on the approval of others (ibid.: 19).

This transformation of the structure of the self is understood firstly, in Riesman's account, as an adjustment to the changing nature and experience of work and the workplace, and secondly to the growing priority of leisure in people's lives. The nineteenth-century workplace (typically the factory) had a clear managerial hierarchy of authority and status, was governed by impersonal relationships between masters and men, and driven by a concern with the management of the technical, productive aspects of the work process. Life was work-determined and most people had little surplus income or free time at their disposal. The mid-twentieth-century workplace (typically, the office) has a flatter, less hierarchic structure, is less command-driven and more concerned with people-management and good working relationships in the workplace. There is more time and money available to spend on something hitherto reserved for the rich and privileged – namely, leisure – as more free time becomes more available for more and more people.[9] Relationships, at work and play, are now defined by *sociability*.

This new social type did not suddenly spring from the ground fully formed from dragons' teeth. It was long in the making,[10] but finally became visible in the key decade of the 1950s because this kind of personality was ultimately an effect of the transition from an economy of scarcity to one of plenty – and the defining characteristic of 1950s America and Britain was a continuously rising standard of living for the majority of people in both countries. The post-war, post-modern sociable self is a communicative soul unlike the strong, silent uncommunicative inner-directed modern individual of the pre-war era who didn't say much. He didn't need to. He *knew* who he was. But post-modern types don't know who they are, and take comfort in conversation in which they find their selfhood affirmed in talk with others.

In sum: The second topic in this enquiry into the basic components of the life-situation that each and all of us are unavoidably *in* is the question of the self, the 'who' of everyday existence: the question of place, followed by the question of the persons in place, in Heidegger's account. I have tried to correct his astigmatic vision of the ordinary self in everyday life, in order to reclaim his original clear and non-judgemental vision of the question of existence in terms of ordinary everyday life. I am concerned to validate the category of the ordinary person as a historical phenomenon and to rescue it from academic condescension. The ordinary person is one who has a differentiated life that allows for the discovery of a differentiated self – a self with its own opinions, values, attitudes, preferences, tastes, etc. (to all of which it is entitled) and who forms these opinions and values and so on in interaction with similar selves. This differentiated self is indicative of the fading of the time of the masses who led an *undifferentiated life* defined and dominated by work under the dull compulsion of economic necessity.

The communicative, communicable self in everyday life is the *available* self – available as its self to other similar selves. Heidegger's analysis of the everyday world was in terms of its availability: the ways in which everyday things that make up the immediate environment 'give' or make themselves available as things-for-use. So likewise with the everyday self. A more than instrumental social world requires that its members be sociable. Sociability – the *ability* to be at ease in the society of unknown others and to interact with them without (too much) anxiety in the many and varied social situations of everyday life is not a naturally occurring phenomenon. It was the defining characteristic of an emergent, other directed individual in the mid twentieth century, and how to be this kind of person was something that had to be discovered and learnt. The universal medium of communication in everyday life is talk. Talk serves many immediate instrumental purposes. But talk for talk's sake – ordinary, non-instrumental talk for the simple sociable pleasure of it – is the mark of sociable social life. You may call it idle talk or gossip, if you will, but that is simply to pre-judge it; no more than an academic prejudice. And it depends on people who are able and willing to make themselves available to each other for the sake of the interaction itself, for the simple enjoyment of being-with-one-another. This is the measure of ordinary sociable existence which depends upon a certain kind of person: the available, communicative self whose historical formation and appearance I have briefly hinted at.

A key topic in the second half of this book is how to talk – on radio and television. I show how this was something that had to be worked out. It was not a natural thing, nor was it obvious at first how to do it – either for the producers or the participants in the programs I discuss. The idea of talk-in-public as an entertainment for absent viewers and listeners was a discovery of radio and television in their early years and specific to each as a then-new everyday medium of public communication. Television did not create the sociable, communicative other-directed self of everyday life. But it required and encouraged it and quickly came to depend upon it. The latest re-incarnation of this dependency is, of course, the ubiquitous genre of Reality TV, so popular in every corner of today's world. Less than 60 years after its entry into publicness and history on American and British television, the communicatively available self in everyday life has gone global. Today, of course, it is no longer just on television that the post-modern self is found in interaction with others like itself. The astonishingly rapid uptake of the aptly called new *social* networks – Facebook and Twitter – is the latest proof (if it were needed!) of the essentially communicative character of today's world and the communicatively oriented, other-directed people who inhabit it.

4

Available time

The times of everyday life

Dasein is da-sein, there-being. Being there in the world (its spatiality); being there as someone (its personhood); being there for a while (its temporality) – these are the three basic existential components of the human situation. The third and last of them is the most determining, the most enchanting and the most elusive. It is the great theme heralded in the title of *Being and Time* – a topic that is a long time arriving and curiously disappointing when it does. The coherence of the overall project has collapsed, derailed by the distracting intrusion of the existentialist theme of Authentic being in face of the inauthenticity of the everyday life world.[1] Five lengthy chapters intervene between Chapter 4 of Division One (the who of everyday existence) and Chapter 4 of Division Two, whose topic is 'the temporality of everydayness'. It is resumed in light of a lengthy discussion of authenticity and being-towards-death. Frankly I find it confused and confusing – and mainly because by now the passionate energy and clarity with which the theme of Division One was so heroically pursued (care as the truth of what we are) has dissipated. There is much authorial muttering in Chapter 4 of Division Two – the author in conversation with himself as he tries to sort out what he's thinking. So rather than stay with Heidegger as he flounders with the meaning of 'time' in the closing sections of *BT*, I want to attempt a synthesis of his thinking, from that time, on the topic and from there to segue into some considerations of my own on time and television.

The meaning of (the word) 'time' was a central concern in the early 1920s. The beautiful motif of 'awhileness' underpinned the course on the hermeneutics of facticity in the summer of 1923. But the remarkable lecture on 'The concept of time', given to the Theology Department at Marburg the following year, provides the clearest and most succinct summary of Heidegger's thinking on the topic in those years. 'I *am* my time' was its keynote theme (Heidegger [1923] 1999: 22E). What time is that? Time is the horizon of being. All *living* things are in time. The time that is closest to, in each case, 'me' is the time of my life and the life and times of the world in which I am. The life that is mine – my *life time* – has a definite ontological-existential structure: it starts some particular time; it goes on for an indefinite but certain stretch of time, and ends some particular time. Life time has an unfolding, irreversible momentum: it is, in fact, always unavoidably moving forwards and thus each individual life has a particular temporal ontology. The fundamental orientation of human temporality is being-towards-the-future, my being futural (Heidegger thinks of this as being-towards-death, and it inspires his existentialist resoluteness in confrontation with mortality). The living thing that is 'me' evolves, grows, matures, ages, fades and dies. 'I' have no say in this. Life itself, life *as* such, is not 'mine'. I do not own it, although it defines me. It is in each case given at birth and taken (or given) back in death. I did not choose my life and though I might, by nip and tuck, try to hide its incremental impact in time from myself and others, I cannot arrest or defer its implacable momentum forward. It is a journey down a one-way street. There is no 'time-out' from life – we can never stop the clock for a bit of respite from it. It has a foregiven existential structure: a beginning, an in-between and end. As such, it has a clear story structure (the 'story' of my life) that is in principle narratable – but not by 'me'. I may be said, in some respects, to be the author of the life that is mine, but I am not (nor can I be) its narrator.

The time that I am 'in' (my being *in* time as distinct from the time *of* my being) is the life and times of the generations of the living and the life and times of the world of the present in which I am with others. The world in which I have my life with others is always only and ever the living world in its unfolding phenomenal now: *this* now, the time *now*, the time of my being-in-the-world-with-others, the *hic et nunc* (the here-and-now) in its moment by moment coming-into-being – *being* – and passing. This is the *awhileness* of the being of the living world and all living things: of the floral kingdom, of the animals, of human beings and the things that are theirs – Heidegger's table and skis. The living are always and unavoidably *in* the present: our present situation, the life and times of the present. The present is a stretched temporality (the span of my life; the time of my presence in the world) that spans the generations of the living. Its focal moment is always (all ways) 'now', the *immediate* present. 'What is this now, the time now as I look at my watch? [. . .] Am I myself the now and my existence time? Or is it time itself that procures for itself the clock in us?' (Heidegger [1924] 1992: 5E). I look at my digital watch and say: 'Now it is 8.50 a.m. Now it is 9.10 a.m. I look at my analogue watch and say: 'Now it is ten to nine. Now it is ten past nine'. Again (as with being *in* space and place), it is perhaps not immediately apparent that these are two fundamentally different ways of reckoning time, of being *in* time. The immediate present has two temporal as well as spatial ontologies: the punctual now (ontology A); the phenomenal now (ontology B) – numbered time and experiential time. Each is disclosed in the two different ways of displaying the immediate now on clocks and watches.

The digital clock tells me the exact time *now*: 9.11, 9.12, 9.13, 9.14 . . . an infinitely recurring sequence of now points. In this method of numbering time there is always only and ever the immediate punctual now. The analogue clock displays the time *now* in terms of a before and after. Now it is ten *to* (before and towards) nine; now it is ten *past* (and after) nine. I hear myself, now as I write, learning to chant this time in my Infant School of more than 60 years ago: 'The little hand points at the nine. The big hand points at the three. It is a quarter past nine' the chorus of little voices chirrups in my ears. The digital clock tells the time but the analogue clock does not. It shows it in a way that must be learnt and interpreted. It displays the now as a situated moment in a time that has a future (yet to come) and a past into which it is departing. Numbered time is the time of the lifeless infinite-eternal time-space universe (ontology A). Phenomenal time is the time of the life of the living world (ontology B). The punctual now knows no before or after: it is always only and ever the *now*; a frozen perpetual now; time at a standstill; time as an infinite-eternal numbered sequence of zero or null points. On the great digital clock of the universe, the time is forever *n*(ow)+1; the infinite time of the eternal-punctual now, time out of time. It is the wondrous but strictly meaningless order of time that is brought into being and rendered intelligible by mathematics. It is utterly distinct from all the orders of meaningful time that are gathered in the phenomenal now of immediate experience: the now in the immediacy of my concern. This now, the situational now that I am *in* (the *now* of my being in the seminar, for instance), is time in motion, time passing.[2] It is both coming and going: coming into being and, in its moment of *being*, becoming past. It is the *living* moment, the meaning of *live*. In ordinary time we are absorbed in the moment without noticing it, without experiencing it. We encounter the moment *as such* only occasionally in the ecstatic *now!* of being – *die Augenblick*, 'the twinkling of an eye', in which everything is transformed.[3] I discuss this moment later in relation to Heidegger, television and football. It is the key to an understanding of the meaning of the event, the topic of the final section of this book. And it is the clue to an understanding of the meaning of *live* and why this topic not just *might* but perhaps *must* be approached through television.

So now for the meaning of (the word) 'live'. Let us start by noting that it is an odd word because, when used alone, it seems to need to be put in quote marks to disambiguate it from the ordinary verb whose pronunciation is the same as 'give' (note that when used as an adjective – live performance, live concert, etc. – the meaning is clear). I usually italicize or parenthesize the stand-alone word (an odd usage after all) to avoid confusion. What does the dictionary tell us of the meaning of live?

> **Live/***adjective***. M16**
> **[ORIGIN. Aphet. from ALIVE, repl. earlier LIVES** *adjective.***]**
> **1 a** That is alive; living as opp. to dead. Chiefly *attrib.* **M16. b** Actual, genuine; not pretended or pictured or toy. Chiefly in *a real live.* Usu. *joc.* **L19. c** Corresponding to actual facts. **E20. d** Of a performance etc.: heard or watched at the time of its occurrence, as opp. to recorded on film, tape, etc.: given in front of a public audience as opp. to in a recording studio etc. Also (of a recording, a film etc.) made of a live performance. **M20.**
>
> **a** P. THEROUX We got used to father looking like a live scarecrow. **d** A. ROAD Recording.. can never be quite as nail-biting as live transmission. *Guardian* No doubt the video is not quite the same as watching the race live. [Shorter Oxford English Dictionary, 6th edition 2007]

One of the beauties of the OED is the way in which it captures, so succinctly, the evolving life histories of words. Live is aphetized from alive (it drops the preliminary vowel) in the mid sixteenth century and that is its core modern meaning. We see clearly that the word acquires a new range of meanings (**d**) in the early and mid twentieth century and that these are to do with the experience of performances (events, etc.) as they happen in real time for audiences who are present at them. Live performance requires an audience, as distinct from performances in recording studios which do not. Live performances before audiences are opposed to recordings on film or tape. But note also that recordings can be made of live performances which are described as 'recorded live' (the third variant meaning of **d**). Thus live is understood as especially related to technologies that permit both the transmission *and* recording of events, performances, speech, music and song in the enunciatory now of their happening, the living moment in which they unfold. The exemplary quotations (**d**) show that in common ordinary usage, the meaning of live is understood in relation to broadcast media. Both contrast the recording of the event with the experience of it in live transmission. The first claims that the experience of a recording *after* the event is not quite the same as watching or hearing it in live transmission (by implication on radio or television). The second says the same thing with specific reference to the *video* (recording on tape or disc) in contrast with (by implication) watching it (the race) live-and-in-real-time on TV.[4] Both quotations treat the recorded version and the live transmission as similar but *not quite* the same – a crucial consideration for later. The meaning of 'live', then, concerns what it is to be alive and this question is raised, in our kind of world, in relation to technologies for the transmission and recording of events and performances as they happen 'live and in real time' and the experience of this. To enquire into the meaning of 'live' is to be drawn perforce into a consideration of the essence (the essential meaning) of radio and television both of which began as live *broadcast* media.

We should remember that 'broadcasting' is an old, rural term that found a new technological application and meaning in the early twentieth century. It was used to describe the transmission effect of wireless telephony, a technology that extended wired telephony by providing links between two transmission-reception points without the necessity of lines (above or below ground or water) to make the connection. In point-to-point communication – the original intentional application – the side-effect of transmission (that anyone else within range of reception and with adequate receiving equipment could also pick it up) was a minus rather than a plus. The general social application of the technology for informational and entertainment purposes was discovered in the 1920s when wireless *broad*casting began. John Durham Peters has reminded us of the true force and significance of this word by reconnecting it to the Parable of the Sower as told by Jesus, which he takes as the paradigm for communication as *dissemination* in contrast with the other great communicative paradigm of *dialogue*, exemplified by the discourse and method of Socrates (Peters 1999).

Historically, it is clear that radio was conceived as a technology for extending dialogue, but discovered its true communicative potential as broadcast dissemination. Dialogue is a personal two-way interaction between people. Dissemination is an impersonal one-to-many one-way system of communication. To broadcast, before radio, meant to scatter seed abroad. Jesus stands before a large anonymous crowd, gathered on the shore of the Sea of Galilee and tells them a story. The sower goes out one day to scatter his seed: some falls on stony ground and is pecked up by the birds of the air; some falls among thorns and is choked as soon as it springs up; some falls on shallow soil, springs up quickly but soon withers and dies. And some (but only some) falls on fertile soil and yields a good harvest; thirtyfold, sixtyfold, a hundredfold. The story is, of course, Jesus' discourse on his own method as a teacher, on what he is doing even as he speaks to the assembled crowd.

Socrates, Peters tells us, argued for insemination as more virtuous than dissemination. Insemination is to implant the seed in another where it will bear fruit. Dissemination is like the sin of Onan who spilled his seed upon the ground. It is a wasteful scatter for there is no guarantee that the seed will, in due course, bear fruit. Put like this, Jesus' method of communication is scandalously inefficient. But that, Peters stunningly argues, is its disinterested kindness and generosity. The Parable of the Sower makes manifest, in its form as much as its message, that the love of God (*agape*) is indiscriminately available for all, not just the few that are open and receptive to the Word. Broadcasting is a fundamentally democratic form of communication. But more than this, and crucially, it is like the love of God in that it is non-reciprocal. It gives without any expectation of a return. It neither expects nor requires acknowledgement and thanks. It is one-way and unconditional and for anyone *as someone* anywhere anytime. It *cannot* be reciprocated. This is the gift of broadcast communication and its indiscriminate availability. It enters into countless lives day by day and everyday and becomes, in every instance, part of the life that is mine.

Today we live in what Sylvie Agacinski has called the time of the media.

> We cannot speak of *the* time, as if it were homogeneous, unifiable by a single measure and a single history. There are different orders of temporality (corresponding to the *tempos* of various events) just as there are different orders of historicity.
>
> Today, the universal clocks are the audio-visual media, and the *clock-radio* is the object that best represents the takeover, the makeover, of the clock. Indeed, this object is not a simple means for being awoken by music or the morning news; it is the concrete sign that we live *in the time of the radio, in the time of the media* and their programs.
>
> (Agancinski 2003: 46–7, paragraphs re-arranged; original emphases)

Agacinski contrasts the time of the media with older historical temporalities – the rhythm of the sun, the seasons, the harvest. But really the time of the media stands in contrast with the time of the masses. The time of the media means, in the first place, time *for* the media: *available* time. Societies of which daily radio and television services are an integral part have risen above subsistence economies and the realm of necessity. They bespeak a world in which the 'silent majorities' have at the very least a marginal surplus of money and time to spend on the purchase and use of radio and television sets as pastimes. The time of the media, long in coming, was decisively established in the 1950s. This was the beginning of 'the age of television' in which time no longer dominates and oppresses individuals but begins to be something that they manage and enjoy as part of their ordinary, everyday life. The meaning of *live* broadcast radio and television is intimately entwined in the historical emergence of everyday life as a particularizing order of historical time. We experience the liveness of broadcasting in the immediate now of the particular program; the soccer match, say, or the news. But that is an effect of the intercalation of the times of the media with the times of everyday life. In what ways are the media available *in what orders of time*? Three different cases of the temporal availability of television today will be briefly considered: video on demand, 24/7 news channels and, finally, the schedules of central broadcasting institutions (the likes of CBS, NBC and the BBC).

The times of television

My time is the time of the life that is mine, but within that, what is the time that is at my disposal, for use at my discretion, my *free* time? Available time is what is left over, each day when other times have made their prior demands. In determining rank order, there is *necessary* time, *coercive* time and *free time*. Necessary time is that which is needed for the restoration and renewal of my body; the utterly determining time of sleep which takes up about a third of the time of human days. In my waking hours, time is taken up with other necessary things to do with the care and maintenance of my body: washing, cleaning, combing, brushing, eating. Coercive time is the time of labour: the time I *must* spend at work whether at home or at school, at the office or in the factory. And when the prior demands of these two orders of time have been met, what remains (the marginal surplus) is for me – the time that is for me to do with as I please, free time, *my* time, available time, time for television. But what determines the availability of personal discretionary time and why does it matter?

In a major study of the time budgets of individuals in six different countries, Robert E. Goodwin and his colleagues show that in some countries individuals may be rich in disposable personal income but poor in disposable personal time. They argue that discretionary time is crucial to the well-being of individuals and their self-realization in the course of an unfolding life. To have more or less of it is consequential in this respect and what determines its availability is partly to do with external social factors and partly with individual life choices. Some countries have more generous allowances for holiday time than others. Some have more public holidays, others have less. The length of the working day and week varies and is partly determined by government regulation, or not. These extrinsic factors are indicative, in a very general sense, of the cultural ethos of time in any particular society and how it is thought of, valued and experienced. Attitudes to time (notions of punctuality, for example) are cultural variables and affect such basic everyday matters as to how much time should be spent on eating, for instance (the midday meal in Southern Italy is a wonderfully leisured, sociable affair that can last a couple of hours at least). At the level of personal choice, the study finds that discretionary time varies markedly in the course of a lifetime. The amount of time committed to work and leisure is partly determined by the culture, but is also a matter of personal choice. Some prefer to work harder (longer) for monetary reward. Others want more time for themselves and work less, accepting a trade-off between gains in disposable time and income. The authors of the survey wryly conclude that if you want a generous amount of personal discretionary time in your life, don't get married. If you do, don't have children, and if you do, don't get divorced. And, if possible, live in Sweden where the state provides generous time benefits for parents with children (Goodwin et al. 2008: 263).

The times of television are attuned to the available times and time of individual lives. Video on demand (VOD) is a time-storage system, the temporal equivalent of the convenience store or supermarket where you can get what you want any time at your convenience. For a store to be convenient, things must be conveniently available. The thousands of different in-store goods are not a great random jumble of stuff: they are carefully arranged – dairy produce down this aisle, fresh meats here, fish there and so on. Things arranged in this way are thereby easily available for any one any time they choose to come along. And so too with video on demand. In the early years of satellite television (the 1990s in Europe) you could access lots of different channels, but they came up randomly and you had no idea what you were looking at or what their schedule was. You would hit many channels that were either a snow-blizzard or encrypted so you hadn't a clue what they were (apart from the heavy breathing). Watching satellite television was a frustrating hit and miss experience to which the electronic program guide (EPG) was the brilliant technological solution. The EPG functions like a home-shopping catalogue. It provides clear, easy and fast access to any of the thousand or more television and radio channels that it makes available. The many hundreds of channels have been sorted and stacked. Sport, music, movies, sex, shopping, God – all these generic channels dedicated to a single theme or topic, and much more, have been conveniently grouped together. Once you get used to the EPG, just as once you know where things are in the supermarket, browsing through them is a comfortable and familiar experience. Video on demand offers a customized convenience conception of the meaning of choice attuned to twenty-first-century lifestyles in which more and more is available from any where for any one at any time.

24/7 news is another product of the telecommunications revolution of the late twentieth century. It started in 1980 with Ted Turner's Cable Network News (CNN) service, the first all-news station in the USA and at the same time the first 24-hour continuous never-ending news service. At first it seemed a curiosity, one more indication of the emergence of new niche markets as the impact of the multi-channel TV environment created by cable and satellite delivery systems took off in the eighties. Its real significance only became apparent in the first Gulf War (1991). CNN was the only news station with three of its journalists already in Baghdad when the war began and they were able to transmit riveting eyewitness accounts of the bombing of the city from the moment it started. For the first time CNN overtook the three long-established networks as the prime site to which viewers turned for continuing live coverage of a major breaking news story. The importance of 24-hour news in the new world of global television was suddenly apparent to everyone. Within a couple of years there was much talk of 'the CNN effect' – the impact and effect of continuous live news coverage on international diplomacy and politics in relation to two kinds of inter-twined event – war and humanitarian crises caused by natural disasters or human conflict in any part of the world. In light of continuing news coverage, governments and their military were faced not simply by new security issues, but by a general speeding up of their responses to crisis situations. Especially when humanitarian issues were raised by unanticipated crises, the 24/7 international news agenda seemed to demand of governments more immediate and decisive responses than hitherto.

Today politics, diplomacy and war around the world is played out in the floodlight glare of unending live news coverage. The straplines on the screens of 24/7 news stations tell of *breaking news* and its *live* coverage. In this, news time is always only and for ever *now*: the immediate present in which news is or is about to happen. It is news on demand as always available for anyone anytime now. Two different orders of available time intersect in the immediate present of 24/7 news: the time that is mine (which is strictly personal) and the utterly impersonal global time of the human world. The one is private (for someone time) the other, public (for anyone time) and both are reflective of polar, dialectical aspects of the human self and the human situation. The available now has, as we have seen, two distinctive temporal ontologies. On demand television exists in and as the eternal now (ontology A), while broadcast television exists in and as the phenomenal now of ontology B.

Broadcasting is the ur-form of radio and television. It was discovered in the 1920s as a derivative of wireless *tele*phony, which in turn was an extension of wired telephony, with telephony as an improvement on the earliest electric tele-technology,[5] wired and then wireless *tele*graphy.

The most basic characteristic of all these tele-technologies is live, immediate connectivity between spatially distant points (*tele* (Gk) = distant or far). They are all *live* technologies, technologies of liveness, which facilitate live interactive connection between people through the immediacy of living speech. The communicative common denominator of all tele-technologies is talk, the universal medium of communication in everyday life anywhere anytime. The aliveness of tele-technologies is the effect of the power (energy) source that is the condition of their possibility; namely electricity. There has been much talk of the power of broadcast television since it began some 60 or more years ago and very little of the energy source that powers television itself and without which it could not possibly exist. The discovery of electricity as a natural form of energy, of how to capture, generate, store and distribute it as the fundamental technological infrastructure upon which today's world depends (along with oil and its derivatives) – all this was and remains quite invisible, a vast hidden techno-scientific industrial care-structure that holds our world in place through time.

In essence tele-technologies of communication are about time. It is time that is consumed in phone talk, listening to radio or watching television. In all actual applications and uses of these intricately connected technologies, the question of the meaning of time lies at the heart of the existential-ontological question, 'What *are* they?' What are the times of broadcast radio and television? They are quite distinct from 24/7 time and they are manifold: the time of day, of weeks and months; of the seasons and years; public time (the time of the world) and private time (*my* time), and now, perhaps, above all, historical time – the final theme of the second part of this book.

The day is a natural order of time in the living world (it is not a human invention like hours and minutes). Day time, night time – each day has an immanent structure, rhythm and tempo around which human life, even today, remains adjusted. Light and darkness; waking and sleeping; morning, noon and night: a natural order of time that is both linear and irreversible through the day and infinitely cyclical and repetitive from one day to the next. Each day goes through the same cycle as every other day. Human life is 'naturally' in the first place and historically and culturally in the second place adjusted to the rhythm and cycle of days. The days of our lives have a natural arc of morning, noon and night which is the storyable arc of our own existence too. Life and days are inextricably folded into each other and show up in the schedules of the broadcast day in which the *historical* and *future* present show up in relation to each other in the *immediate* present of live-to-air transmission.

The future present shows up as a set of expectations at the beginning of each day. Start-of-day news and indeed all early morning live-to-air programs on radio and television are not just *at* that time but *for* that time. In all sorts of ways they are concerned with the day ahead and all the upcoming and ongoing issues that will mark this 'today' as this day in particular. The routine, recurring time-checks, weather and traffic reports provide relevant data that allow listeners and viewers to orient themselves to and prepare for the day ahead. This is the *future present* of the day today; what lies ahead. End-of-day news broadcasts (BBC1, *News at Ten*, in the UK for instance) look back on what was anticipated in start-of-day news. They bring the events of the day-now-past into the present in live-to-air reports and interviews. This is the retrospective *historical present*, concerned with what has just-now happened and what it meant and means. It too exists in and for its own and particular time-of-day. It summarizes, assesses and, where appropriate, brings closure to the now-ending day. The weather reports that immediately follow nightly news are oriented to tomorrow. News junkies in the UK, who switch to *Newsnight* (BBC2: 10.30pm) after the News at Ten, know that they will get further discussion and comment on the events of the day. The program always ends with a brief look at tomorrow's newspaper headline stories, thereby indicating closure and renewal – back to the future!

Thus routinely, day by day, the broadcasting schedule articulates and expresses each day in its prospective and retrospective character – its ontology of expectations, its assessments of whether they were met – in the live momentum of the phenomenal now from morning through to night. At the waking break of day, time is all before us and as we move through the day (as we move through life) there is less of it before and more of it behind us. At close of day we can only look back on the day-now-past and look forward to the day-to-come as we prepare for sleep. It is this existential structure of the temporality of dailiness to which broadcast services on radio and television are always and everywhere attuned: to our sense of mornings (and what the cares and concerns of the morning are) and of evenings and their concerns and cares: to the weekend and things to do on Saturdays (watch sport, for instance); to the seasons of the year and what to do in winter and in summer time. If we can meaningfully speak of broadcast radio and television as part of our lives, it is because (and only because) their services are attuned[6] to the existential structure of the days of our lives while at the same time connecting each and all of us, day in day out, to the life of the world in its manifest, manifold diversity. This double articulation of life (my life and its times linked to the life and times of the world) is endlessly reiterated in the schedules of every-day broadcasting through the day from morning to night.

Television and historical time

The dailiness of broadcasting was a central motif of *Radio, Television and Modern Life* (Scannell 1996). The culminating theme of this book is the world-historical character of life today as disclosed by the historicality of radio and television broadcasting. The earlier book was a product of research and writing in the 1980s. At that time the question of television and history was simply not visible because television then had not yet entered into history, thereby becoming historical. Time has passed since then and now, today, a quarter of a century later, broadcast television has begun to have a history and thus what has begun to appear is its role in the historical process as such. What then is the historical process? How do things become historical and what kind of historicality is shown in and by television? What *is* historical time?

> For nothing is more important, nothing comes closer to the crux of social reality than this living, intimate, infinitely repeated opposition between the instant of time and that time which flows only slowly. Whether it is a question of the past or of the present, a clear awareness of this plurality of social time is indispensable to the communal methodology of the human sciences. (Braudel [1969] 1980: 26)

In the late 1950s, the eminent French historian Fernand Braudel drew a distinction between two different orders of time; the short and the long term. The former he called *histoire événementielle* and the latter, the *longue durée*. The short term is the time of everyday life, the life and times of the present, full of noise and bustle, movement and activity. The long term is the past, receding back, further and further, into remote, inaccessible pre-historic time. In sharp contrast with the noisy changing present, it becomes increasingly silent, unchanging, motionless and fathomless. How are the two connected? It is rather like the surface and depths of the sea. The surface, endlessly ruffled by wind and weather, is in perpetual, restless motion. But beneath it lies the deep, and the more you descend into it the more you encounter its dark and motionless silence. Braudel thought the *longue durée* was the proper object of historical enquiry. He dismissively compared *histoire événementielle* with a candle flame whose 'delusive smoke, fills the minds of contemporaries' but quickly flickers and dies, leaving no lasting trace (Braudel [1969] 1980: 27). For Braudel, as for many intellectuals of the last century, the eventful time of everyday life was the sphere of illusion, deception and ideology. The historian's proper concern was with the unchanging, underlying, structural determinants of the everyday for these were what shaped and defined it. This 'structuralist turn' was by no means confined to historians at the time. In France and elsewhere structuralism was becoming the new big idea in the humanities and social sciences of the sixties and seventies.

Well this was a while ago, from the short-term perspective of our own day, and the tide has gone out on the moment of structuralism. But the distinction Braudel drew, if we re-think it carefully, helps us understand the dialectics of historical time. Let us accept as valid the distinction between the short and the long term. But it is not a matter of preferring one to the other. Rather it is a question of how the two are inextricably interconnected. The endless interplay between past and present, properly understood, is the dialectic of history, if by that is meant the play of the past as it acts upon the present and of the present as it acts upon the past in order to bring on the future. History is indeed 'made' in the present (where else?) but is not visible as such to those who dwell in it, the generations of the living in any present time. History only appears *as* history as it exits from the restless, noisy present and enters the silent and unchanging past. The present, in which we live, is indeed the time and place of action, in which decisions are made and courses of action committed to with fateful consequences for a future made possible only by what is done in the here and now. But we, who are caught up in the present, can never foresee, in spite of our best efforts, the actual long-term consequences of what we do. These *only* become apparent with the wisdom of hindsight, which is the effect of the passage of time from the present into the past. The owl of Minerva takes flight at dusk.

Academic engagement with media has always been concerned with the shock of the new and successive generations have grappled with the impact of new media in their times. In America in the thirties and forties, the then very new medium of radio provoked high anxiety. It could stimulate widespread panic (Cantril et al. 1940), persuade the masses to part with their money (Merton [1946] 2004) and was, as someone put it at a conference attended by Paul Lazarsfeld, 'as powerful as the atomic bomb' (Lazarsfeld and Merton [1948] 2004) – a frankly incredible view today, but evidently not so then. Forty years ago, when the new medium of television became the focus of study for an emergent 'media studies', it too was seen as a powerful 'ideological state apparatus'. Nowadays radio and television are thought of, by those who pursue today's 'new media', as 'old' or 'traditional' compared with shiny new things like the internet, cell phones, iPods, Facebook, YouTube, Twitter and so forth. In all three moments, academic engagement with the new media of the day has been absorbed in and by the politics of the present and its unavoidable concern with events and happenings in the immediate now of the contemporary world. The study of media effects is necessarily concerned with the short term, with the immediate impact of broadcast output on its audiences. It must treat this as a matter for empirical investigation by trying to find out how real people, one way or another, respond to media and how they use them. Media studies and the sociology of mass communication confront the politics of the present, the play of *histoire événementielle* (of 'media events') while being themselves caught up in the historical process whose lineaments they struggle to perceive.

The new, by definition, has no history as it enters into the life of the present. Its newness is its strangeness. What *is* it? Who can say? The long-term effects of new media can only be, for all of us caught up in the immediate present and its politics, a matter of, at best conjecture, for their long-term effects are yet to come. They lie ahead and all attempts to 'read' the future are, at best, no more than prophecy. Long-term effects, which arise in the present, only become visible as such in the journey into the darkness and silence of the *longue durée*. In this transitional passage of time, the essence of history is disclosed, for it contains the dialectic of long-term temporal continuity and short-term temporal change. How then does this process work – more exactly, *when* does the present become the past? What is the transitional order of time in which the long term begins to appear out of the short-term present? It is *generational* time, the time of generations, in which the fundamental historical work of regeneration (of change and renewal from one generation to the next) is enacted in the present by the generations of the living. The historian's task, Braudel thought, was to be concerned with the silent, imperceptible movement of slow time, while the sociologist attended to the noise of history in the making, the bustling life and times of the present. The study of television, and of media in general, requires that we attend to both, but it is only now that the historical study of television is becoming possible, for only now do we begin to see its recession into the past and the working through of generational time in its output.

Thus, for instance, as feminist scholarship has shown so clearly, changing social attitudes to family, marriage and gender relationships in the USA over the last 60 or more years, can be explored through popular TV fiction, decade by decade, from the fifties to the present. The idealized white middle-class family (dad, mom, three kids) of the 1950s is exemplified by *Father Knows Best* (CBS 1953–9). But patriarchal authority (naturalized, knowingly but without irony, in the show's title) is about to be shaken and stirred. In her scintillating reading of *Bewitched*, Susan Douglas has shown how, in the sixties, as the Women's Liberation Movement begins to get under way, a popular TV show of the day could handle the idea of the empowerment of women and their representation as smarter than men, but only magically – as a fantasy.

Samantha is a clever witch who actually *wants* to be a dumb human housewife (Douglas 1994). In the seventies things have really begun to shift. In *The Mary Tyler Moore Show*, Mary has left home after breaking up with her boyfriend to take a job in the city working for a TV station – but it's Minneapolis St Paul not Manhattan, and it's the local rackety news channel, not one of the metropolitan networks. Mary herself was seen at the time as a charming, quavery representation of 'the new woman' – a young single working woman in her early thirties, rather than the traditional married mom. In the 1980s the demands of liberal feminism for equal working rights with men appear to have been met and are explored in *Cagney and Lacey*, which challenged the traditional male-dominated police drama genre by placing two women (Christine Cagney, played by Sharon Gless and Mary Beth Lacey, played by Tyne Daley) as working cops and buddies in a predominantly male inner city police station. It was a deliberate political intervention, intended by its creators (Barbara Avedon and Barbara Corday) to challenge the ways in which women were portrayed on mainstream television (D'Acci 1994). By the nineties it is now a given, on American TV, that women can have successful careers and work along with men. And yet the new 'post-feminist' woman of the nineties is curiously dissatisfied: *Ally McBeal* works for a prestigious Boston law firm, yet her sexual relations with men are problematic and she is still fantasizing about finding Mr Right – to the dismay of an older generation of women who struggled to escape the marriage trap (Lotz 2006).

The generation that grew up in and was radicalized by the sixties (in reaction to their parent culture of the fifties) in time becomes the parent generation to children born in the eighties. The relationship between older and younger generations, parents and children, mothers and daughters – the politics of re-generation – is vividly apparent in the tensions between second wave feminism of the seventies and third wave, or 'post' feminism, of the nineties (Douglas 2010). And this is seamlessly displayed in television's fictional output, which is naturally and rightly treated by critical feminist television studies as a key historical resource for the exploration of changing social relations within and between the sexes. Such work has only recently become possible. All the programs I have mentioned were made in and for their own time with no thought for a future in which they would become the past. It is that guileless innocence (the lack of any ambition to be anything more than in and for the present in which they were made) that guarantees the truth of these popular fictions as authentic testimonies to their times. Only as the programs of today disappear from the schedules do they enter into the past, becoming part of the historical record through recording technologies that preserve them as such. Season by season, year by year, today's output begins to settle as sedimented time strata silently bedding down, layer by layer, on the ocean floor of the *longue durée*. As these sedimentary deposits build up, it becomes possible to see the long-term effects of the politics of the present. Television shows of the nineties take for granted what women of an earlier generation had to fight for. They also forget that what they are able to presume is the gift of the politics of the present in the past. And all this depends upon technologies of record without which history cannot appear. Recording is not the opposite of 'live' in broadcasting. Rather, as we shall see, it records the life and times of the present and preserves it in a time-capsule which miraculously comes to life once more each time we press 'play' on the DVD remote. The archives of radio and television are only now beginning to be seen and understood for what they are, an archive, as Derrida puts it, of life itself[7] – an astonishing and very different historical repository from what historians have traditionally thought of as their primary source, namely written texts.

The final theme of this book is the world-historical character of life today and the role of television not simply in displaying this but as a key player in the making of history in the enunciatory now of the immediate, living present. Television today is not what it was back in the 1970s when I first began work on the historical development of broadcasting in the UK. Its spatial horizon has been transformed as its time horizon has imperceptibly extended. The central broadcasting institutions of particular countries no longer define for their viewers what TV 'is' via the world-view they offer. I now think of the BBC and the American networks as instances of television world-wide – still important, for sure, in their respective countries, but indicative of something much larger. For a while, back in the 1970s and 1980s, it seemed as if an early, emergent sense of TV beyond the nation-state, a glimpse of globalized television, would be dominated by the entertainment produced by the American networks. The British sociologist, Jeremy Tunstall, wrote a book called *The Media Are American* that came out in 1977. At the same time, in the USA, Herbert Schiller published *Communication and Cultural Domination* (1976) in which he argued that the American entertainment industries were dominating the whole world (the cultural imperialism thesis). This seemed, for a while, nothing less than the obvious truth. The global success of *Dallas*, which played in over 150 countries around the world, appeared as the conclusive ocular proof of American cultural hegemony in the 1980s (Ang 1985, Liebes and Katz 1990). But today this is evidently no longer the case and in 2006 Tunstall published a follow-up called *The Media Were American*. In our times it is not so easy to say what television is. It seems to be everywhere and nowhere. We all know and understand that we live in a single,

common world; that what happens any where is consequential everywhere else; that all our lives are interconnected economically, politically
and culturally. We know that this in itself is an effect of the continuously
evolving global infrastructure that began to emerge many centuries ago
but which now, uniquely, is in plain sight and for all to see, thanks to
the extraordinary developments in tele-technologies of communication
of the last 30 years or so.

The world in Heidegger's accounts was the immediate life-world in
which I-or-anyone am situated. That was and remains the primary way
of encountering the world in the existential situation that each and all
are always and inescapably *in*. But the spatial horizon of immediate
individual existence has changed beyond recognition since the time of
its writing, and this as a result of mediated forms of communication
and mass travel underpinned by rising living standards across the last
century. The earliest study that I know of on the impact of broadcasting
on everyday life was conducted by Winifred Gill and Hilda Jennings
for the BBC in 1939. Their small-scale study of a working-class district
in Bristol showed clearly that the coming of radio had quite literally
transformed the horizon of people's existence and given them new
things to talk about. All the evidence, from every country, confirms
that for most people in the early twentieth century the horizon of their
lives, in comparison with ours at the start of the twenty-first century,
was extraordinarily limited. Mass air travel, as we now know it, was
then unimaginable. People stayed where they lived and a journey of
more than a few miles was always a major excursion. On the whole,
they knew no more than what was happening in the street where they
lived, or in their neighbourhood or town at most. What was everywhere
longed for by everyone was contact with that great and public world,
over the hills and far away, that lay beyond the horizon of immediate existence. Raymond Williams acutely characterized the European
drama of the late nineteenth century (the plays of Ibsen and Chekhov
in particular) as seeming to consist of people staring out of windows
in provincial drawing rooms 'waiting anxiously for messages, to learn
about forces "out there", which would determine the conditions of
their lives' (Williams 1974: 27). The transport and communications
infrastructure of the modern world that began to be put in place in the
late nineteenth century was intended to facilitate the management of
economic, political and military life. But Williams draws our attention,
at the same time, to the hesitant discovery of wider social and cultural
applications for the emergent global communications infrastructure in
the era of high modernity. That is what we see taking place in radio's
'utopian moment' in the early 1920s when its form and content had
yet to be discovered and it seemed, on first contact, like a magic carpet

transporting astonished listeners to far away places and peoples and happenings with which they had had no previous possible connection.

Live connectivity and its meaning is an underlying motif of this book; the quite extraordinary transformations in the communicative horizon of life across the last century directly linked to tele-technologies (telephone, radio, television and beyond) as these have evolved in time through to now, the endlessly talkative world of the early twenty-first century. Today instant connectivity with the whole world is a taken-for-granted aspect of everyday life for most members of post-modern societies that is readily and continuously available through a bundle of related technologies, with central radio and television services as their hubs. But what this means, or how to understand it, is beyond the grasp of the politics of the present in which we are all (academics included) unavoidably caught up. We can only ever grasp the consequences of our actions in the here and now as they disappear into the past, and only then insofar as we have a preserved record, an archive, from which to recall what was once the present. The meaning of history, more exactly, of historical time, as disclosed by broadcast media, is the final theme in all that follows.

The question of truth

I have attempted a summary 'best reading' of what I take to be Heidegger's project in *Being and Time* while at the same time re-interpreting it. I have tried to recapture the project as a whole, which entails re-uniting the question of time with the ordinary everyday human world and the ordinary human beings who dwell in it every day. I have made some key adjustments to Heidegger's thinking and each is connected to the other. In the first place, I have treated the question of care as immanent in the humanly made material things of the everyday world and not, in the first place, as an aspect of *Dasein* itself. What being human 'means' is something to be inferred from the human world, not from the individual human subject. Secondly, I have 'corrected' his interpretation of the everyday self. And thirdly, I have reconnected 'world' and 'self' to the third and final component of the human life-situation, namely time. The order in which these three integrally connected components of the human situation are raised is crucial. It was a brilliant stroke to begin with the question of the being there of the everyday human world before turning to the question of the self in this everyday world. And these two components needed to be 'in place' before turning to the question of time, in which both world and self are situated. The pivotal second component (the existential structure of the self) is the crux of the whole project. For Heidegger it was 'obvious' that the self in everyday life was inauthentic. If I can *now* see certain blindnesses in his thinking on this, it is not because I am smarter than him but because time has passed and what it is like to be in the world today is not as it was in the time when *Being and Time* was written. It follows, obviously, that there are blindnesses in my own thinking that I cannot possibly grasp because there are things about my world, my self and my times that can only become apparent to future generations in the fullness of time. These reflections take us directly to the central problematic of Heidegger's project of which he was fully aware: namely that the world both reveals and conceals what it is from those who dwell in it at any time. Its essential meaning never is nor ever could be fully available to the generations of the present who live in it. The phenomenological task is most basically the work of unconcealment – of discovery and disclosure, of uncovering what is covered over (Wrathall 2011).

Heidegger thinks of unconcealment as the literal translation of the ancient Greek word *aletheia*,[8] which is usually translated as 'truth'. His project was a quest for truth: the truth of what it is to be what in fact we are. We are the being for whom being itself is an issue. The question of being is uniquely human because we alone confront the question of what it is to be alive and living in the world. Other intelligent living species *are* and indeed have their concerns. But human beings not only *are* but know and understand that they are. And that is why the question of existence (the meaning of 'life') belongs to us. We own it as our ownmost concern. For Heidegger, truth lives and dies with a common humanity that dwells in truth and error. And this presupposes certain fundamental human capabilities that are thematized in Chapter 5 of Division One. Having shown how the everyday world makes itself available to the ordinary everyday self, the question arises as to the conditions of the possibility of being in concern *as such*. What capacities does a world-creating, world-sustaining being have to have? Heidegger identifies three related capabilities: affectedness,[9] understanding and speech. They are all immanent, interdependent pre-linguistic, pre-cognitive human capacities whose combined effect is to lay us open to the experience of the living world and all other living beings, to an intuitive grasp or understanding of what it means to be alive and living in the world and, finally, to be able to make this experience and understanding communicable and sharable through speech. Affectedness is the capacity for direct and immediate responsiveness to being in the world. It is to be open to the experience of being *as such*. This interactive responsiveness between world and self, self and world shows up as mood – the immediate live and direct experience of *being open* to being in the world. The phenomenology of mood is one of Heidegger's most brilliant insights and a key consideration in my later discussion of the meaning of events. To this elemental capacity of openness to being, we must add that understanding which stands under all experience and grasps (pre-linguistically, pre-cognitively) what it is to be alive and living in the world as such. And both these capabilities achieve articulation in the capacity to communicate with others that is manifest in and as talk – the universal medium of meaningful, purposeful interaction between our selves about our selves and world. Together these three capabilities are the indexical markers not just of our openness to existence (which we share with other animals) but our unique grasp of the *fact* of life, the being there of the living world and our being in it. Our openness to this question – life *as* a question, our being in question – is the essence of the dialectic of truth, the meaning of 'life', which is immanent in the living world, endlessly manifest and endlessly concealed. Unconcealment, as *the* phenomenological task, consists in trying to open up what is always in plain sight yet seldom seen.

The standard view of truth, in the Western tradition, is that it lies in the correspondence between well-formed linguistic statements or propositions and worldly states of affairs or 'facts'. Heidegger acknowledges this, but argues for an earlier understanding of truth from which the correspondence theory of truth is derived (Wrathall 2011). There are two kinds of truth and they underpin the two ontologies. Epistemological truth (truth as knowledge) belongs to ontology A: it is mathematical and scientific truth whose domain is the time-space universe of matter. Here truth is (and must be) a matter of factual correctness. But the truth of ontology B is not like this. It is not the objective truth of matter, but the matter of existence, of being alive and what this means as it becomes available through our empathetic understanding of the question and our ability to speak of and discuss it.

> The thought of unconcealment [. . .] holds that we encounter entities [things] as being what they are only in virtue of the world within which they can be encountered and disclosed. But these worlds are themselves subject to unconcealment – they emerge historically and are susceptible to dissolution and destruction. Thus being itself must be understood not as something determinate and stable, but in terms of the conditions for the emergence of entities and worlds out of concealment into unconcealment.
> (Wrathall 2011: 1)

The truth of ontology B is historical. It concerns the life and being in the world of a common humanity as it unfolds in the present through deep historical time projecting forwards into a limitless future. This truth is not relative. It is and must be, in the long run, one and indivisible. But we, the living, are always and unavoidably situated in a position that is fundamentally relative to the working through in time of human history. For how can any of us – in our radically finite and fallible mortal state of being – ever hope to grasp what it is that unfolds in the surpassing human world through deep historical time? The transcendent truth of history (history *as* truth) is of necessity forever out of reach.

The question of transcendence and non-transcendence is everywhere implicit in everything this book is about, but I defer reflection on it to *Love and Communication*, the final volume in this trilogy. The question to be uncovered here is the truth of television: what, in fact, it was, is and could be. To hold the question in this existential-temporal frame requires us to try to grasp what a world without television (the world before television) was like and how it prepared in advance the conditions of possibility for a world with things like television in it. This is what Wrathall means by the emergence of things and worlds out of conceal-ment into unconcealment. The conditions of possibility for television had once to be uncovered and discovered. It had then to be brought to presence, realized and actualized – but how, and in what ways and why? As it entered into existence (that is to say, as it came to life), television, like any living thing, grew, spread, developed and changed continuously. And what it was, at first, was far from clear. Television is a technology – but not just a technology. It is a central political and cultural institution within nation-states – but not just that. It is an everyday resource for modern and post-modern peoples. It is all this and more. In being all this, it is disclosive of (it reveals or unconceals) a world of which, in a very short space of time, it has become an integral component. It is time now to turn from this preliminary sketch of phenomenological enquiry to the phenomenology of television as indicative of the human situation today. I begin with the worldliness of television as disclosed in and by the everyday act of turning on the TV set.

5

Turning on the TV set

Heidegger makes a crucial distinction between the ways in which we encounter everyday things: they are either *zuhanden* (ready-to-hand) or *vorhanden*, present-to-hand.[1] Everyday things have both characteristics, which correspond to the fundamental ontological distinction between beings (things) and their being. Heidegger's well-known example of an everyday thing is a hammer (Heidegger [1927] 1962: 98). As a present-to-hand (*vorhanden*) thing, I see it objectively; an object with objective properties. It weighs so much. It is made of such and such materials. It is large. It is small. I can measure its dimensions. Thus I perceive the hammer as an observable, measurable, material thing-in-itself unconnected to anything else in the environment. There it is, present to my sight, lying on the material surface of the table-Thing whose objective, physical properties I can equally well and similarly describe. As a ready-to-hand (*zuhanden*) thing-for-use, however, in ontology B, I pick it up and start hammering. In this ontology I know what a hammer is by using it properly; by putting it to proper use. If I grasp the hammer by its shaft and try to write with it, I have misunderstood its *what* (what it's for). If I grasp it by the head and try to hammer with the shaft, I have misunderstood its *how* (how to use it).

Any handy (*zuhanden*) thing, or piece of *equipment*, is for use by any body. As such it implicates in its what and how an activity of some sort of which it is a part. Any activity is an involvement-whole. *With* the knife and chopping board I prepare the vegetables, *in order to* make the soup, *towards* the preparation of the meal, *for the sake of* the satisfaction of a daily human need. Things implicate an action which in turn presupposes an activity-structure: with which > in order to > towards > for the sake of – an involvement-whole. But what gives the possibility of the activity as an involvement-whole? How, more exactly, do I encounter things? We do not encounter things any-old-how, any-old-where. They have their whereabouts. I do not keep the pots and pans in the bedroom, nor my clothes in the kitchen cupboards. The kitchen is a *region* in which all necessary and relevant things are to hand (handy) for the activities that are relevant and appropriate to it. And so it is, more generally, in respect of the environment. Wherever I am – on the motorway, at the airport, at my office, in the pub, in bed – the immediate environment *pre-assigns* the possibility of whatever I am doing (or not doing). Every thing in any particular worldly whereabouts has its being there in relation to everything else. That is how we encounter the world. That is how we are able to – and in fact do – go about our ordinary daily concerns. That is what it begins to mean to speak of the world as *a relational totality of involvements* which is Heidegger's formal definition of it:

> The 'for-the-sake-of-which' signifies an 'in-order-to'; this in turn, a 'towards-this'; the latter, an 'in-which' of letting something be involved; and that, in turn, the 'with-which' of an involvement. These relationships are bound up with one another as a primordial totality; they are what they are as this signifying in which Dasein gives itself beforehand its being-in-the-world as something to be understood. The relational totality of this [work or practice of] signifying we call '*significance*'. This is what makes up the structure of the world – the structure of that wherein Dasein as such already is. (Heidegger [1927] 1962: 120)

If the world is a meaningful, significant, relational totality of involvements it is so as no more or less than the expressive realization and manifestation of our concernful being in it. The definition of what it is to be human, in *Being and Time*, is being-in-concern. We find this out, not by contemplating the roomy contents of our minds, but by (for instance) considering the contents of our rooms – not contemplatively as objects-to-be-looked-at (ontology A), but practically as things-for-use (ontology B).

Turning on the television set

Let us then, with these two distinct ontologies in mind, consider the TV set as it appears in the room and what happens when I turn it on. Let us notice how it appears in the room, before it is turned on.[2] There it is; an object alongside the other objects in the room. I see it in terms of its objective properties, the materials it is made from and so on. The housing structure of the set is made of glass and moulded plastic which conceals its complex hidden technology. Its screen is of such and such dimensions. It simply stands there in the room and I observe it as an object. It is easy to look at the television set in this way as it stands there, inert and unactivated. It is, in this mode of perception, there to be used but not in use; an object of contemplation. Now I turn it on. Suppose I try to maintain the objective mode of observation. What would I see? The screen lights up and moving images appear in colour on (or inside?) the surface of the screen and sounds come out of the set.

Is it, in fact, possible to maintain this *objec*tive mode of perception when I turn the set on? Only, I suggest, in a very particular set of circumstances. I want to buy a new set. I go to the department store that sells medium-sized dry goods. There in the department selling televisions, radios, music systems, etc., I see whole banks of TV sets, all partly 'on' (vision on, sound off). Here, I do not watch (attend to) what's on, though. I see the quality of the image on the screen: the sharpness or fuzziness of image resolution, the quality (the balance) of the colour-image, the size and shape of the screen. Here (and only here) I am indeed concerned with the objective properties of the television image and the dimensions of the set. But when I unpack the thing at home and set it up and turn it on, what happens? I find that there's something on: the news, a game show, a movie, a soccer match, whatever. I no longer see the television set. It has vanished.[3] I now am watching and am absorbed by it.[4]

What absorbs me, whenever I turn on, is an on-going something (the news, say) to which I adjust and recompose myself, to which I attune myself, with which I engage. And even if what shows up is something that I instantly judge to be 'not for me', so that I switch off or to another channel, it is still the case that this negative response is an act of disengagement. However slight it may seem, 'turning on' is, indeed, an act with an intentionality structure, indicative of some minimal predisposition to 'being turned on', to engaging with the thing. If I turn on for a particular program which I know is on 'now', I am predisposed to engage with it (however casually), to attune myself to the program and its world and its mood. And even if I am not after anything in particular – if I am just browsing, or channel zapping – it is still the case that turning on is indicative of a predisposition, however casual, to attentiveness of some kind. I am 'in the mood' for watching or listening. I am in the mood for a bit of entertainment, or relaxation or for finding out about what's going on in the world, or even just for having the TV on to alleviate boredom a bit.

Thus far I have considered the act of turning on the television set in two respects: in terms of the transformation of the 'object' – the television set – from an inert 'thing' to an activated appliance and, intimately linked to this, a change in perception from objective observation to concernful engagement. The thing changes and I change with it. This double transformation is evidently a move from the objective world of ontology A to the concernful world of ontology B. A question still to be considered, in these preliminary observations, is what happens to me (or anyone) when I turn on the television set. If turning on the TV set is a very ordinary, everyday act that 'I' perform, then we must ask who is this 'me' and what happens to 'me' when I turn on? Television sets, like all appliances, are designed in such a way that anyone can use them. As such they are for anyone. On the other hand, when I turn on the set, my own personality comes into play and is in play, immediately. There is a change in focus, a shift from one aspect of the self to another. I am anyone as I turn on the television. I am someone as I watch it. *My* preferences determine what I watch.

I have advanced a little way into the enigmatic character of television. I have considered what happens when the television is turned on and noted that a number of transformations simultaneously take place: an inert object comes to life as it is activated. I no longer perceive it objectively but engage with it concernfully. I am *anyone* as I turn on the television set and *someone* as I watch it. In so doing I have imperceptibly readjusted myself – in turning on the TV set I turn on *my* self. But there are further unresolved questions: where am I *before* I turn on the television? And where am I *after* I have turned it on? What of my when and whereabouts before and after I turn on the television?

Before I turn on the television I am in the room; I am in *my place* and *my time*. After turning on, I am in *the time and place of television*. Heidegger saw that, but he did not consider what it meant to say this. He treated the time and place of television as an alien intrusion upon 'my' place and time. He assumed that television takes me out of my time and place and into its world. But evidently this is not so. The astonishing thing about radio and television is that I am in two worlds at one and the same time: my world *and* the world of broadcast television. Rather than signifying the end of 'homeliness', television signals the beginning of our being at home in the world. In turning on the television, I enter a doubled spatiality and a doubled temporality: the 'here' of where I am (in the room) and the 'there' of television wherever it may be (Afghanistan, the moon, the football stadium). The room does not disappear when I turn on the television as it does when I watch a movie in the cinema or a play at the theatre. I have my cup of tea at home in the living room *and* I watch the match taking place in Hamburg. I am *now* (at one and the same time) in a here-and-there; a doubled spatiality. I am *now* in two times at one and the same time: the now of my time (in the room, watching television) and the now of the time of television (as it tells me the news, shows me the match, etc). Broadcasting (radio and television together) creates a *spanned* spatiality and temporality that is historically unprecedented. Any radio listener or television viewer can and does move back and forth between two worlds and times – their own time and the time of the world; their own world and the broadcast world wherever that may be. That is the unique *communicative affordance* of radio and television that has come to define our world and to disclose it as such in the last half century.

The appliance of science

It is time to be more exact about what kind of thing television is. What we see, when we look at the TV set there in the room, is the outer surface of the thing. We do not see the complex scientific-technical ensemble that is hidden inside the moulded, manufactured casing. The TV set – like any car, any computer, any mobile phone – deliberately conceals its complex inner workings, in the same way and for the same reasons (we must suppose) as the human body's outer casing of skin conceals its complex inner workings.[5] Why? Suppose the TV set did not conceal its inner workings? A historical precedent is ready to hand in the early history of radio. In the aftermath of the First World War, 'radio' began as a popular 'scientific' hobby in North America, Britain and elsewhere in Europe before the establishment of regular broadcast program services. In garden sheds and basements everywhere men and boys (it was very much a male thing) were building two-way radio transmitter-receivers or one-way receiving sets to scour the ether for sound signals. In either case, the results were a naked display of valves, knobs, wires and amplifiers. The scientific innards had yet to be encased and its operation required endless fiddling and twiddling. Listening to the signals required headphones. It was not yet a domestic object fit for family living rooms.[6] The mediating stage in the transition from technology to domestic appliance is *design*.[7] It is a basic mistake to think of design as style and aesthetics applied to mass-produced goods, as if it were some kind of value-added. Design is essential to the transformation of user-unfriendly technologies that only trained experts can use into simple user-friendly things that anyone can use. The famous Ekco set, on the British market in 1934, was designed by a leading architect of the time. Its scientific innards were concealed in a circular moulded plastic case made of Bakelite, and just three knobs for volume, wavelength and tuning. It was not a piece of furniture, but a thoroughly new and modern piece of equipment suitable for any household with electricity, and any child could use it.

In the transition from techno-scientific equipment that only experts or dedicated hobbyists can use to everyday equipment that everyone can use, the technical-scientific 'innards' are concealed or 'black-boxed'. This transformation produces what I will call, as a generic term for domestic utilities, an *appliance*. We, the users of appliances, neither understand the science on which they depend nor their equally complex technological application. If something goes wrong, we must call upon the services of the electrician or the gas man to fix it. The 'science' is concealed within a lightweight metal-alloy or plastic casing that is usually white. The outward appearance of the appliance has a functional 'modern' look.[8] It will fit in with other similar appliances in the kitchen or wherever. The appliance is safe. I won't get an electric shock when I touch it. It is easy to use. A small number of switches and knobs are required to turn the appliance on and to adjust its operation for the task in hand: a particular wash-cycle, a temperature and cooking time. It is reliable and durable. It 'works' every time: not now and again or only on Tuesdays, or when it's in the mood. It works like this because it is made to be reliable as is the power source on which it depends. Moreover, it is durable. It comes with time guarantees (for a year or more at least). It will go on working. I expect it to last.

That the appliance is all these things – safe, easy to use, reliable and durable – is not happenstance. It is the realized, achieved and accomplished, practical outcome, through the years, of continuing thought and effort, trial and error; research, development and innovation. It is the result of a complex hidden politics; of consumer activism, lobbying and regulation to make things safer, simpler, more lasting and reliable. And there is one final thing that is built into any and every appliance. It is designed (meant and intended) to be attractive. It may be safe, simple, reliable and durable – but if it is not, at the same time, somehow pleasing and presentable, it will not be purchased. Utilities are above all useful and useable. But they are not only that. They must be, in ways that are hard to specify precisely but nevertheless essentially, desirable. All of this is built into the appliance but invisible. It is the appliance's hidden, historical *care-structure*. It is what 'gives' the thing as attractively 'user-friendly' so that anyone might want it and could use it. It is, in the end, as simple and handy as Heidegger's hammer, but its simplicity conceals a deliberately hidden, enormous, overlooked complexity.

An electrical appliance then – a TV set, washing machine, fridge, lap-top, mobile phone – for it to be such (a handy, available utility that anyone can use) must have the following characteristics. It is:

- affordable
- attractive
- useable
- reliable
- durable
- safe

It must be *all* these things. Take away any one and the thing is no longer an everyday thing for everyday use by anyone. The relational totality of these necessary attributes of an appliance is its technological care-structure. The affordability, utility, reliability, durability and safety of everyday appliances are the by now taken-for-granted pragmatic pre-conditions of what we think of and refer to as consumer *durables* or domestic appliances. These 'indexes of utility' combine to give the efficient (effective) pragmatic conditions of useful useable everyday power appliances. But why should we think of the sum of these characteristics as a *care*-structure. What warrants or justifies such a designation? Because it points to what is hidden in the appliance; namely all the invisible thought, effort, work, intention and attention – in short, the creational, creative care – that has gone into the realization of the appliance *as* the everyday utility that it manifestly *is*. We only realize the importance of the components of an appliance's care-structure as and when any one of them fails. It's too expensive (can't afford it). It's ugly (don't like it: won't buy it). It's too complicated (can't use it). It's unreliable (works sometimes but not all the time). It doesn't last (works fine for a week and then packs up). It's unsafe or only intermittently safe (I get an electric shock when I turn it on sometimes).[9]

The care structure then does not obtrude, doesn't draw attention to itself. Its 'seen but unnoticed' character is its gift; is indicative of *how* it gives itself, of how it is taken *as* given by any and every user. And the consequence of this (of how it 'gives' itself and is taken as given) is that we all do indeed take everyday things for granted because that is what they grant us. Insofar as the things that make up the everyday world are, to all practical intents and purposes, reliable, durable, useable, affordable, attractive and safe, so far too, it follows, is the everyday world itself. The care-structures of everyday appliances are world-disclosing. They disclose a world that anyone and everyone can take at face value, on trust. We can take the world on trust insofar as we can trust the material things of this world. Would *anyone* commit their body and soul to something as mind-bogglingly dangerous (or plain crazy) as air travel if we didn't all trust absolutely that it wouldn't kill us?

Trust in things is not a wager, a pious hope. Still less is it arbitrary or conventional. It is the pragmatic consequence of the labour that is hidden in things, the invisible care structure that gives the conditions of things we can trust and a world we can take for granted. The truth of a thing is no more or less than what it is. And humanly made things disclose (reveal) what they are, as things-for-use, in and by their manifest 'what' and 'how'. But we have seen how any thing, as soon as it is put to use, disappears. I no longer see the TV set when I turn it on. I am absorbed by it as I watch what's 'on' when I turn it on and also my self. Likewise, the hammer, when I use it, recedes from sight. I no longer 'see' it. I use it. Things both disclose and conceal what in fact and as a matter of fact they are. The enigma (the riddle) of everyday things is what they both show and conceal about themselves. The aim of phenomenological analysis is to make explicit what is implicit in the manifest utility of everyday things – namely, the invisible care-structures that 'give' them *as* such; as the manifestly useful, useable, desirable things that we take them to be.

Turning on the TV set (again)

I have so far considered the utility of television as an everyday appliance, which I have taken as the universal index of what in fact it is. Television is television anywhere and everywhere because the technology in its applied social form – the mass-produced TV set – is everywhere the same. I have tried to establish what it means to think of this thing, television, as a technology and have shown how its technological care-structure gives it *as* an everyday utility. I have accounted for its usability but have not yet begun to consider its uses, and to open up that question we must return to the moment of turning on the TV set. *Why* would I (or anyone) do this? What do I want of the TV set? What do I expect? What do I find?

Turning on the TV set is an intentional act (not a convulsive spasm or reflexive tic). Like any everyday act, it is an act of faith and hope. I turn on the TV set (my laptop or mobile phone) with faith in the technology (it will do what I expect it to do) and with hope that it will meet my expectations of it. Faith and hope are underpinned by my trust in the TV set as a reliable utility that will hopefully fulfil my expectations of it.[10] What then do I (or anyone) expect when I turn on the television set? I expect to find the usual things: the usual programs in the usual places at the usual times. I expect this naturally and of course. I expect that the whole regime of television (the system of distribution, the networks, the cable services, the program content that all this delivers) exists in such a way as to be there for me (or anyone) whenever I want it. What converges in the act of turning on the TV set is, on the one hand the totality of practices that make up the services that are delivered and supplied as 'television', and the totality of expectations invested in it by any and every viewer anytime anywhere. *That* these two things meet and mesh, that the expectations are met not now and again but every time (i.e., that the world of broadcasting is delivered in such a way as to be available *whenever* I-or-anyone turn on) – that is the entirely unremarkable and yet astonishing fact. It begins to indicate the expectations that each and every one of us has invested in the kind of world that each and all of us take for granted as the utterly normal everyday world that we do in fact inhabit. It is a world in which everyday expectations are routinely and unremarkably met by reliable worldly care-structures in place to meet them. An *every* day world has such structures always already there in advance for anyone and everyone as the very condition of its everyday possibility.

In turning on the TV, I turn on to, I enter into, the world of television. But what does that mean? What is the worldliness of television? In the first place it means that 'television' is the same for anyone and everyone no matter where they are in the world, both in the form of the technology and in what the technology delivers. It is evidently the case that TV sets everywhere work in the same way and are managed (handled, used) by us in the same way. This, of course, is true of all everyday technological appliances. A Japanese, French or German car or TV set turns out to be the same thing. When I am in these countries, I don't understand (can't use) their languages but I do understand and I can use their cars and TV sets. They are the same there as in any part of the world I may be in.[11] That they are so is the necessary pre-condition of a common world, if by that is meant a world in which any individual can act and interact anywhere any time with the environment because everything in it is familiar, makes sense and is useable. The common world of today depends on the common world-technological infrastructure. Nowhere do you find everyday technologies with a logic peculiar to a particular society or human group that is impenetrable to outsiders. The universal usability of technologies is underpinned by a common logic and a common human understanding that are constitutive of our common humanity and our capacity to 'give' ourselves a historical world. We do, in fact, speak of 'television' as if it were a universal – as if in mentioning it anyone anywhere would know what we meant by it – and that is an effect in the first place of the universal form of the technology. But is it true of the content of television? Does it have a similar universality?

Let us take it as given that a TV set, a car, a fridge, is the same wherever I am. The conditions of its availability for use, the human competences needed to use it, are unchanged whether it is a Japanese, Brazilian or Norwegian TV set. Does this argument apply equally to the contents of Japanese, Brazilian or Norwegian television? Of course, these televisions and their outputs are accessible to most Japanese, Brazilian or Norwegian native speakers – but what about me, a monoglot Brit? There is the unavoidable issue of the Babel of language which is not gainsaid by remarking on the rise of English as today's lingua franca. Does not language difference immediately undercut any claim for the universality of TV output? In the early days of the European

Union, there was much optimistic talk in Brussels and elsewhere about a new European audio-visual cultural sphere or, in common language, European-wide TV services to provide, say, Euro-news for all countries of the union. But the only bit of television Euro-culture that the Europeans have ever been able to come up with is the *Eurovision Song Contest*, a by-now legendary annual occasion for general hilarity (in Britain at least) at the awfulness of the songs, speculation about which one will win and even more about which will come last, perhaps achieving immortal fame by scoring '*nul points*'. Televisions everywhere remain pretty well stuck within national and especially linguistic boundaries. Can they, do they surmount these barriers? What does it mean to speak of global television today in terms of the content delivered by the TV appliance rather than the appliance itself?

Let us set aside the language barrier. Suppose I have an audio machine that I plug into my ears and which gives a simultaneous translation into my language of what I am watching and listening to on Japanese or Norwegian TV, for instance. Suppose, that is, we allow for the translatability of languages. The question then becomes whether Japanese and Norwegian televisions are radically different, perhaps mutually incomprehensible. Are Japanese programs so Japanese that only the Japanese can understand them? I take Japan as an instance for it seems to be (for Anglo-Americans, at least) a kind of limit case of 'foreignness'. I think of my encounter with the WC in my hotel bathroom, or of Bill Murray and Scarlett Johansson in *Lost in Translation*, hopelessly adrift in Tokyo and its amazing, swirling and apparently incomprehensible way of life. British TV went through a phase of showing clips of Japanese 'reality TV' shows (presented by Clive James, an Australian) or Japanese TV ads (Chris Tarrant, a Brit) as hilarious evidence of the weirdness of the Japanese (I'd like to think that Japanese TV had similar shows showing how weird the Brits and Aussies are, as seen on TV – it wouldn't be difficult).

Some years ago I visited Japan to meet up with a friend and colleague, Kazue Sakamoto, to work with her on our joint study of English and Japanese live television coverage of international soccer in the run-up to the 2002 World Cup that was being hosted by Japan and South Korea. Technically and structurally, the coverage was the same: camera work and match commentary were almost indistinguishable. The differences showed up in presentation. Soccer is not a major national sport in Japan, and Japanese audiences are not as familiar with the game as British audiences are. The pre- and post-match studio analysis of the game that Kazue and I were working on was provided by Arsene Wenger (the French-born manager of Arsenal, a leading London soccer team in the English Premier League), who happened to be in Tokyo checking out the talent in the Japanese national team.[12] There were a number of small variations in the presentation and style of the coverage that were subtly revealing of, for instance, gender differences in contemporary Japanese and British culture and society. But the general point that came out of our small comparative study of live coverage of a global sport was that the overall format, the technical resources deployed, the structure of coverage, were to all practical intents and purposes the same. Soccer, in British and Japanese television coverage, was instantly recognizable on television *as* soccer, for the production care-structures that delivered it as such were the same. I watched a lot of Japanese television in my hotel room during my visit, and although I couldn't understand a word of what was being said, I was seldom in doubt about what I was watching: I could instantly recognize Japanese TV programs for what they were. News was obviously news and studio talk shows, reality game shows, drama series were all, and equally evidently, what they were too. And there was a lot of *animé*.

The production care-structure

We nowadays take for granted the range of TV output. There's news of course and news related 'current affairs' programs (*Panorama* in the UK: *Sixty Minutes* in the USA); drama series and serials; situation comedies and stand-up live comedy shows; a wide variety of 'reality' or 'people' programs from *Oprah* to *Big Brother* and beyond; sport; quizzes and game shows; documentaries about history, the natural world, science . . . and so on and so forth. There are a recognizable limited number of different genres of TV output – I mean genres as developed and defined by the industry, not academics. These genres are understood worldwide because they everywhere formed the staple mixed program content of early classic broadcast television. This range of output was formative and remains definitive of the scope of television worldwide today, even though the mixed program services of the early decades have, in the post network era, disaggregated into generic (single-genre) channels – all sport, all news, all music, all comedy, etc. It is also the case that certain new, and thus far peripheral, genres of live or 'open' channel services have developed that exploit new digital technologies and direct interactivity with viewers. There in the outer reaches of BSkyB, for instance, is the *Bang Babes* network of channels in which almost naked young women wriggle about and touch themselves on screen while inviting you to phone in for a chat about what they might do next. Hypertext scrolling across the top of the screen provides phone numbers, while across the bottom of the screen scrolling text-messages sent in by viewers indicate what they would like the babes to do for them.

The form and content of television everywhere, now as in the past, is recognizably the same and is reducible to a small set of industry-generated genres. This does not mean, of course, that television is forever unchanging; that its content is now what it was 60 years ago. Each genre has a history of continuing development, of change and continuity. And an important driver of change across all television output from the beginning to the present has been technological innovation: innovation in the design of the TV set itself and the audio-visual experience it offers (the introduction of colour; increasing sharpness of image resolution; the development of flat, wide screens); technological innovation in the production process (crucially the development of recording technologies and mobile lightweight TV cameras); new technologies external to television but with significant impact on its audience relationship (VCR, DVD, the internet). In the case studies that follow, I consider some historical instances of the role of technologies in the production of certain genres of live television output. Here I am less concerned with particular historical aspects of the production process, and more with the production process as such – as a relational totality of commitments, a care structure.

At any time the available totality of output appears as familiar and taken for granted. If it seems that television has always been there as part of daily life it is because the appliance is simple, safe and reliable and so too what we watch whenever we turn on. As a leisure resource, as something turned to in our free time, our engagement with what we watch had better not be too taxing. It had better not be boring or hard (like work, art or an academic text). It had better be easy, like the ordinary talk that it generates (a theme to be explored in part two); easily and immediately understandable. That it is such things is not a matter of chance. To note that television programs are designed for ready recognition and easy engagement is to reiterate what I have tried to establish about the design of television sets. TV programs give themselves as things to be listened to and watched (to be engaged with) in much the same way as the TV set gives itself as a thing for use. The communicative logic of any program is the same as that of any TV set.[13] And the labour of the production process that gives the programs we care to watch is every bit as invisible as the labour that gives the appliance that enables us to do this. Programs reveal and conceal what they are in the same ways (and for the same reasons – reasons not yet considered) that appliances reveal and conceal what they are as we engage with and put them to use. Ease of use conceals the complexity of the TV set. Ease of access and easy familiarity with TV content conceal its complexity. In neither case do we notice how 'television' is given as an everyday available thing for use. The care structures that 'give' the content that we find when we turn on the TV are just as invisible as the care structures that give the TV set as the useful usable thing that it is. Just as we never see the hidden labour processes that produce the TV set as safe, reliable, durable etc., so likewise we never see the hidden labour processes that 'give' the news *as* news, the drama series or the reality show we may be watching *as* those things, as what they manifestly are and as what we evidently find them to be.

Formats and schedules

What, then, determines the form and content of television output? The answers to this question were worked out first in respect of radio, the parent medium of twentieth-century broadcasting worldwide. All essential issues in the supply of content for television were posed and resolved by radio in the inter-war period. The television industry in Europe and North America was born of the radio industry and is its offspring. The BBC in Britain and the networks in America learnt their business first in radio before the Second World War and transferred what they learnt from it after the war to the new, more complex and costly business of television as it took off in the 1950s. We can understand what determined the content of television by looking at how radio solved the problem, when it went into business, of filling time on air with something for radio owners to listen to. For the radio or TV set to have any practical use, there must always be something there to be listened to or watched whenever anyone turns them on. The supply side task is to meet this elementary expectation. Not only must there always be something available to listen to or watch, it must always be immediately recognizable and intelligible. It's no use turning on and finding something that I can make neither head nor tail of. Why should I waste time figuring out something incomprehensible in my free time? I'll just change channels or switch off. The normalization of output was the task that confronted the early radio industry and their solutions were carried over into the post-war television industry.

The initial problem was firstly, and most fundamentally, what constitutes a thing-to-be-listened-to (a thing-to-be-watched)? And how do you make it? How do you make enough of it to provide a continuous supply of this something, day in day out into an indefinite future? And how do you sequence output? At what times (and why) do you transmit this or that thing-to-be-listened-to? What determines the sequence? The double problem of production was firstly the supply of a content

and secondly its sequencing or scheduling. Both were integrally connected as the fundamental concerns of the broadcast industries, and
finding workable, working solutions to both took time. It took years,
as I have noted, for the radio set to evolve into a standardized, mass-
produced everyday appliance that anyone could use. The revolutionary
Ekco set came on the market in 1934; 12 years after the BBC began
broadcasting a regular radio service. It is hardly a coincidence that the
form and content of radio programs on both sides of the Atlantic began
to settle at around the same time as the listening apparatus became a
mass-produced domestic appliance: ease of use and ease of listening
began to dovetail in the mid 1930s.

An absolutely basic problem that broadcasters faced from the start
was 'the voracious appetite of the microphone' as one British entertainer
put it. The wireless must be fed with a continuous, unceasing supply of
material providing home entertainment for listeners, and this quickly
gave rise to a dilemma for radio producers and performers. Before
radio, all professional entertainment was supplied in public venues
outside the home, and entertainers made a living either by touring the
country doing one night stands or weekly gigs. If they were lucky, they
might obtain seasonal contracts in the larger theatres or music halls. In
any case they relied on one or two routines that they had worked up
to entertain an audience that changed nightly and from place to place.
But after they had appeared on radio once or twice, they had used up,
in two performances, most of the repertoire upon which their liveli-
hood depended. They had performed on radio to audiences of millions,
whereas hitherto they had performed, nightly, to audiences of at most
several hundred. In one or two broadcast transmissions, heard throughout the country, they had used up their entire stock of gags and routines
and had nothing to fall back on. The comedian's dilemma exemplifies
the most basic of issues posed by continuous daily broadcasting – how
to supply something new, not now and again for changing audiences,
but again and again, daily, weekly, indefinitely for the same unchanging
general listening public.

The solution to this problem in Britain was discovered and worked
out in a landmark program of the late 1930s called *Bandwagon*. The
model for the show was taken from American radio: a half-hour blend
of music and entertainment to run weekly for a season (three months or
so) provided by a band and (great novelty) a 'resident comedian'. Arthur
Askey, a well-liked performer on the 'concert party' circuit between the
wars, was the first British entertainer to be given an annual contract by
the BBC. As the BBC's 'resident' comedian, the conceit was developed
that he must reside somewhere in the BBC – in an imaginary flat at the
top of Broadcasting House. Gradually a comic situation was created in

weekly sketches of Arthur living in the BBC as its comedian-in-residence with his side-kick, Richard Murdoch and a bizarre collection of animals, including a goat. Recurring animal sounds, catch-phrases (Aye then-kyew!), routine gags (milking the goat), strange sound effects (gurgling water-pipes) and the knockabout relationship between 'Big hearted Arthur' (Askey was tiny) and 'Stinker' Murdoch (six foot two) began to coalesce into a bedrock entertainment format of radio and television, the situation comedy or sit-com. *Bandwagon* was an enormous hit – the BBC's first real national success in producing entertainment that played to the characteristics of the medium of radio and at the same time resolved the riddle of production that it posed. The sit-com is a format that serves to generate an indefinite number of variations on a single theme: a given situation with one or more characters who are fated, week after week, to re-enact their trapped relationship that always ends in the same way. It is one key instance of the serial mode of production upon which radio and television broadcasting depends for the delivery of an endless daily service of programs.[14]

The principle of formatting was worked out and applied in all areas of production. Drama on radio had at first relied on adaptations of novels, plays for the theatre and authored 'one-off' radio dramas specially written for the new medium. But soon the same problem of limited supply from such sources became apparent, and the same solution was found in two key genres of fiction on radio and television; the never-ending *serial* drama (dubbed soap-operas in the USA in the late 1930s) or episodic drama *series* that operated on the same principle as the situation comedy. Well-established fictional genres from the early years of radio broadcasting include the police series or crime thriller. Another crucial discovery was the broadcasting studio as a production site. We are nowadays completely familiar with the TV news studio, or the studio as a public forum for some kind of talk-as-entertainment in which a well-known host interacts with studio guests before an invited studio audience. Nevertheless, the use and management of the studio as the institutional place of broadcasting, where it was perceived as coming from by listeners and viewers, had once to be worked out and established.

I have traced the British origins of the basic broadcasting studio-based program format – host, participants, audience – back to a little series on the pre-war North Region service called *Harry Hopeful* (Scannell and Cardiff 1991: 340–2). This show established a basic resource of broadcasting that has been worked and re-worked ever since; namely the incorporation of the audiences for radio and television into the programmes themselves. Everyday radio and television is not only for an everyday audience; it is about everyday life, everyday pleasures and enjoyments. It is part of everyday life itself whose meaningful character is in part established as such by day-to-day broadcasting. *Harry Hopeful* was a show in which the entertainment was provided by ordinary people – not professional entertainers – performing as themselves. It was the original template of all later TV quiz and game shows, 'people programmes' and today's Reality TV genres, all of which, one way or another, feature ordinary people drawn from the vast available pool of viewers as the source of the show's entertainment values. Everyday broadcasting is 'ordinary' in manifold ways, and one basic way is its endless use of ordinary people in its programme output (Bonner 2003).

The conditions of the possibility of broadcasting as an everyday service available for anyone and everyone depend upon a particular mode of production capable of delivering a never-ending supply of programs, new every day and through the weeks, months and years. Formatting and serial production is the key to this basic requirement. A program format provides the template for endless variations on the same theme. Just as the layout and design of newspapers remains fixed, with its contents changing from day to day while always showing up in the same places, so too the content of radio and television is delivered through a small number of production genres, each with a few formats that yield difference in sameness every day. The unchanging spatial layout of daily newspapers is matched by the fixed and unchanging temporal order of the daily radio and television schedule whose full significance only becomes apparent when we consider the fundamental question of time and the ways in which it is articulated through each day by the schedules. It would be a basic error to think of broadcasting primarily or only in terms of content. The key to broadcasting is the question of time. Radio and television are both time-based media and the orders of time on which they depend and the temporalities that they themselves create are key themes in what follows.

Turning on the television set (one more time)

I have twice raised the question of what happens when I turn on the TV set. Thus far the emphasis has been on the user of the technology, on how it is available for use by anyone and what anyone finds when they turn on the television. What has yet to be considered is what happens to the thing that is used. What happens to the TV set when I turn it on? How does *it* turn on? How does it change from being inert and inactive to being activated and – and what exactly? I want to say 'to being activated and alive'. When it is turned on, the TV set comes to life. We say this ordinarily. But what could it possibly mean? Do we say this figuratively – as a metaphor or some kind of figure of speech? Do we mean that it is 'as if' the TV set comes to life? Do I just 'think' or 'imagine' this? Surely not. The TV set does in fact come to life when I turn it on, in the same way as my car or the radio when I turn them on. This book is about the meaning of 'live', in relation to television. In common daily usage, we speak of 'live' broadcasting. It is not an academic, analytic term. It is used by the industry to describe live-to-air transmission of certain kinds of program (news, sport, special events) and is so understood in ordinary usage. That certainly is one way in which I understand it in the various case studies that follow. But still there is the question of what gives the possibility of live and in-real-time broadcasting, and the answer to that pushes us back to our initial concerns here with the technologies of broadcasting and its transmission and reception. All depend on the same energy source, electricity which, in the course of the last century, became the fundamental power source of the advanced industrial and post-industrial world.

The domestic appliances I have considered along with the TV set as part of the wired home of the 1950s came into existence at this precise historical moment only because by then nationwide electrical power grids were in place throughout North America and Northern Europe. The long complex process whereby electricity was understood scientifically, generated, stored and distributed by national grids for industrial and domestic use is a classic instance of an utterly taken-for-granted, massive and invisible technological care structure that underpins the conditions of the possibility of everyday life everywhere in the advanced economies of the world today. Electrical power is a natural energy source and we think of it as *live*. Danger: live overhead cables. A live wire is one charged with an electric current and, figuratively, a highly energetic, active individual. The liveness of television and radio has its essence in the electrical power, supplied by national electricity grids, that activates the TV set and distributes the broadcast signals it receives. Live television is an effect of the energizing natural power of electricity, but the meaning of *live* is nothing technological. Our daily life is inseparable from the new technologies of the twentieth century upon which all our lives and our common human world depend. The aim of what follows is an effort at clarifying the experience of being alive in the world today through the electronic technologies of radio and television broadcasting. It is through these and related technologies of communication as much as anything that we have access to, and experience of, the common public world in which we live.

I began by taking seriously an utterly trivial everyday worldly action, something that anyone and everyone does every day, namely turning on the television set. This is, for all of us, a simple unthinking action. And yet, if my attempt at a careful analysis of what happens when I (or anyone) turn on the TV set was at all adequate, it should be evident that small everyday acts conceal enormous issues. I have shown

- The phenomenal complexity of the act itself – the range of transformations that take place when I turn on the TV set.
- The fore-given conditions that 'give' the TV set as a useful, usable everyday utility that enable me unthinkingly to turn it on and use it.
- The taken-for-granted expectations invested in the act – that the whole content of 'television' is presumed as there for me whenever I turn on.
- That the content of radio and television has a formatted, serial structure by virtue of which it is available and recognizable for me or anyone any time, now.
- That the TV set undergoes a radical change of state and comes to life (whatever it means to say this) whenever I turn 'it' on.
- That none of this is visible, yet all of it is immanent in the everyday act of turning on the appliance that opens up access, for anyone and everyone, to the everyday output of radio and television.

Phenomenological analysis operates at two levels. It begins with the *phainomena*, the visible, hearable, palpable things, the world of appearances, the TV set *as* it is there in the room. The second level of analysis, which follows on from the first, concerns how it is that things appear to each and all *as* that which they manifestly and in fact are. The manifest and the hermeneutic 'as' together constitute two fundamental dimensions of enquiry that starts with things *as* they are in everyday life; the manifest 'as'. The hermeneutic 'as' attends to what constitutes things-as-they-are *as such*: the TV set *as such*, the TV program *as such* – news as news, drama as drama, entertainment as entertainment.[15] These two modes of enquiry stand in a dialectical relationship to each other, moving back and forth between what things at one and the same time disclose and conceal about themselves. It is the crucial methodology that uncovers the *care structures* concealed by the world of appearances. The hermeneutics of things as such reveals the care-structures of radio and television – the technological care-structures that 'give' the apparatuses for listening and watching, and the distribution and production care-structures that 'give' what anyone finds to listen to or watch whenever they turn on the radio or TV set. The creative labour hidden in the care structures is a recurring theme in all that follows.

6

Television and technology

What kind of world has TV sets in it?

I have shown that prior to our engagement with the *contents* of television (the programs we choose to watch), there is the small matter of our engagement with the TV set; with the technology that (a) we must be able to afford and possess, (b) have time for, and (c) know how to use *before* we begin to enjoy what it offers (whose promise was the reason we bought it). The question of technology is the necessary entry point into thinking about what television is, and it is a historical question. What kind of a world do you have to have for it to have such things as TV sets in it?

The everyday world of experience (the world as we each encounter and deal with it) is embedded in the enduring historical human world, the final theme of this enquiry into television.[1] What, then, were the world historical conditions that gave the possibility of an everyday world with TV in it? Our first clue, of course, is the moment in which TV enters into the everyday world and becomes an ordinary part of it, and that moment (in the USA and Britain) was the 1950s. Why then, and why there in the USA and Britain? In the concluding chapter of *Media and Communication* I argued that the Second World War was the historical hinge of the last century – the world going into it and the world coming out of it was different.[2] And this was due, I suggested, to a long-term shift in the world economy, in train well before the war but only decisively established in its aftermath, as it moved from an economy of poverty to an economy of plenty. The life-circumstances of individuals were changing from pre-war work-defined patterns of existence to new post-war leisure-defined ways of living. The coercive time of work and the workplace no longer dominated individual life and experience, which now were oriented towards free time. The pendulum was swinging from production to consumption. It was a decisive change of gear in the long, still continuing, world-historical process of societal modernization in which subsistence economies and the forms of life developed in adjustment to them gave way to unprecedented surplus economies of abundance and new ways of life defined by economic choice and freedom.

This structural transformation of the world economy, taking place in the mid twentieth century, marked the passing of the time of the masses and the emergence of the time of everyday life in North America and the northern half of Europe. The time of the masses was defined by the politics of poverty which erupted into historical life in the course of the French Revolution, when the Parisian masses rose in the name of bread and freedom. Poverty at that moment ceased to be a natural fact and became a social fact and a central, unavoidable political issue. In the course of the nineteenth century, the question of the masses became the defining economic and political issue in North America and Europe: mass production, mass politics, mass society, mass culture and, in the end, mass slaughter through weapons of mass destruction. This was the era of Modernity, the era in which the secular politics of European enlightenment were worked through in continuous response to the new mode of production, factory capitalism and its mass-produced commodities, themselves the products of the appliance of science and new power-technologies. It began in the American and French revolutions of the eighteenth century and ended in a global war of the mid-twentieth century. Throughout its length and breadth, the era of Modernity was driven by conflict. Factory capitalism pitted men against each other: class war, the war of all against all. Modernity's self-understanding was articulated as the survival of the fittest in the human and natural world (a nature red in tooth and claw) and its rule for survival was summed up in Jonas Chuzzlewit's grim parody of utilitarianism – Do other men for they would do you. This era ended in the catastrophe towards which it had long been heading: the first fully scientific, technologized, truly global war that killed sixty million people and reduced towns and cities all over the world to rubble.

What came out of the rubble and ruin of that war was a different world that began to show up in the 1950s. In America and Britain, the decisive transition to an economy of abundance made its impact felt in all aspects of contemporary life. The fifties is the pivotal decade of the last 60 years, the historical key to an understanding of the world we inhabit today. In those years, for the first time, the majority of people in North America and northern Europe began to enjoy a life of modest affluence: in Britain the Tories won an election in 1959 with the slogan 'You've never had it so good!', and in the United States its most distinguished economist, J.K. Galbraith wrote a bestselling book in 1958 called *The Affluent Society*. Most people now had a marginal surplus of disposable time and money. The hungry thirties, as they were known in both countries, became a vanishing memory as people, no longer governed by necessity, began to enjoy a measure of freedom and control in the disposition of their lives. This is the world in which something called 'television' appears. What kind of a world is it?

It is a world that has begun to escape from the tyranny of necessity. Why is it a tyranny? Because you *have* to do the necessary things. If you don't you perish. You have no choice. You *must* do what is necessary, hourly and daily. You must provide food, shelter and clothing to subsist. To be poor is to be dominated and defined by necessity, to be driven by its wearying compulsion. Freedom is, in the first place, freedom *from* necessity. The poor are unfree. None of us, who live in a world of television and suchlike things, is poor in that inescapable, primary sense. Who *needs* television? No one. Not in any elemental basic sense; not in the sense that Marx had in mind when he wrote that hourly and daily men must struggle to meet their daily needs. Do they *need* television in large parts of Africa today? The poor of Africa have far more immediate needs than that. So from the start we must think through the implications of television as an *unnecessary* thing and, as such, a formal indication of a world no longer driven and defined by necessity. This world, long in the making, emerges in the 1950s and defines the unprecedented conditions of life that we (the peoples of North America and northern Europe in the first place) enjoy today. To understand it we need, of course, to remember what gives its possibility.

By definition, the revolutionary mode of mass production that is factory capitalism produces more than is necessary. It produces a continuous, unending surplus of material goods. It creates, in principle and in fact, the world conditions, for the very first time, for the overcoming of scarcity, the elimination of poverty, the gift of material abundance, as Marx so presciently foresaw. The modern era experienced the unleashing of the tremendous power of the new mode of production. Marx's analysis of the relations of production in factory capitalism was and remains entirely correct: they give rise to intrinsic conflict over the distribution of the surplus value that the human labour of commodity production creates. The politics of emerging modern democracies, as they began to take shape in the nineteenth and early twentieth centuries, were increasingly focused on the regulation of the conflicted relations of production and on the distribution of the social surplus that the modern economy creates. The distribution of the wealth created by mass production (as Marx foresaw) was and remains the crux of modern politics. We should never forget the exploitative character of labour under capitalism, its destructiveness, the yawning inequalities it creates, the immense suffering to which it gives rise. But, equally, we should not be so overwhelmed by this as to deny what, in the long run, it begins to deliver; what began to shine through in the decades after the war – a world no longer dominated and defined by necessity.

The question of technology

When it appeared in American and British households in the 1950s, television took its natural place along with a range of quite new technologies with which we are all now familiar as 'white goods' or 'domestic appliances'. It makes no sense to think of television except in relation to all the things with which it co-exists, the things whose existence give its own possibility. The wired home of today, with its host of electrical appliances, began to be decisively established through *all* sectors of North American societies and some parts of Europe only 60 or so years ago. Electric carpet cleaners, fridges and washing machines (and a little later, freezers and dish washers) now took the toil out of domestic labour and saved time. In Britain in the 1930s the working-class family wash took a woman four days: on Mondays clothes were hand-washed with soap, water, tin tub, scrubbing brush and board, rinsed and wrung dry by hand. On Tuesdays and Wednesdays they hung out to dry inside (there was nowhere to hang them outside and clothes often took two days to dry through in a cold, damp climate in houses without central heating). On Thursdays they were ironed. Before fridges and freezers, shopping was a daily necessity and involved trips on foot to different shops for different things: to fetch and carry from the dairy, the grocer, the baker, the butcher, the greengrocer, the fishmonger. Today the family shop is done by car once a week in one large convenience store or supermarket. The new domestic appliances that came into general use in the 1950s were labour- and time-saving innovations that freed people from hitherto unavoidable and necessary domestic toil and from time-consuming daily tasks. That was the negative freedom they offered. And what did people do with their newfound free time? They continued to enjoy the services of the pre-war culture industries (radio, cinema and the record industry). And they now began, in millions, to watch television.

More than its precursor, radio, television is pre-eminently a technology whose purchase and use presupposes societies in which the majority of people have marginal surpluses of disposable money and time for its enjoyment. Television was, from the start and has remained to this day, an everyday social medium enjoyed by its viewers in their free time as a leisure activity, primarily as a source of entertainment and (to a lesser extent) as a source of information, a 'window on the world'. The ownership of TV sets presupposed a world oriented to domesticity; a way of life centred on households, the sphere of privacy, home-and-family, whose members are free from domestic necessity, from such time-consuming, dirty and onerous chores as daily fire-lighting, shopping for food, cooking, sweeping, scrubbing and so forth.[3] The new domestic technologies of the 1950s gave the conditions of domestic leisure which television fulfilled so spectacularly: freedom *from* toil and necessity, freedom *for* relaxation and leisure.[4] Ever since then, in European and North American households, watching television has remained the preferred daily leisure activity of whole populations across all classes, for women and men, young and old. I will come to the *activity* of watching television in a moment. But first we need to reflect on what kind of worldly thing it is; the technology of television, television *as* technology.

The question of technology has been a matter of abiding concern throughout the modern era for technological innovation is one of its defining characteristics. What was the industrial revolution if not a revolution in the means of production, a transformation in the relationship between human beings and machines? Older technologies depended on human input and energy; they were hand-powered. The new technologies that brought in the era of mass production had energy inputs from non-human sources (coal, fire, steam; later, gas and electricity) that far surpassed the labour power of human hands and had the effect of inverting the relationship between human beings and their creations. Hitherto, human beings controlled the machines they made. From the nineteenth century onwards, it seemed to be the other way around. It was as if the awesome power of modern technologies produced human beings as their servo-mechanisms, mere cogs in their complex industrial machinery. In the popular imagination of the early twentieth century, human beings were themselves transmogrifying into machines in a machine civilization.

Modern power-technologies right through the nineteenth and the first half of the twentieth century were a constant source of anxiety in literature and the arts, in academia and the popular culture of the so-called advanced industrial societies of Europe and North America. It is not necessary here to sketch in the details. I will simply note, by way of illustration, how the question of technology was thought in the early part of the century by some of the intellectual ancestors of late twentieth-century cultural and media studies. It was a central concern of Critical Theory. Technical efficiency, scientific management in the workplace, was developed in America by the industrial psychologist, Frederick Taylor in the early years of the twentieth century and applied to the automobile industry by Henry Ford. A critique of Taylorism was at the heart of Georg Lukacs's essay, written in 1922 and widely read at the time, on 'History and class-consciousness'.[5] For Lukacs, the application of scientific methods to the achievement of technical efficiency in the workplace was the mark of the definitive reification of modern consciousness. It confirmed Max Weber's melancholy conclusion that instrumental (means-oriented) rationality prevailed over substantive (ends-oriented) rationality in the iron cage of modernity. It was proof of the rationality of the parts and the irrationality of the whole. The world as a whole was no longer accessible to modern thought.[6]

The critique of the culture industries developed by Max Horkheimer and Theodor Adorno, exiles from Germany in America from the mid 1930s to the late 1940s, was premised on the penetration of culture by industrial methods. The technological process itself was at the heart of their critique – mass production was an anonymous, machine-dominated process whose uniform, standardized products eliminated individuality and difference. The inhuman technologies of mass production dehumanized the workers, their products and their consumers. This, though elegantly put, was a commonplace argument. In England at exactly the same time, F.R. Leavis (the perhaps unlikely 'grandfather' of British Cultural Studies) was developing a critique of what he variously called machine- or mass-civilization along the same lines but without the theoretical sophistication (cf. Leavis and Thompson 1932). And both cases were part of a much wider general societal concern with technology as part of an overall logic of domination which threatened to overwhelm vulnerable, isolated individuals. If this now seems somewhat apocalyptic, it should not be forgotten that the Apocalypse was indeed nigh. The destructive powers of modern technologies were unleashed on land, sea and air in a six-year global war whose hideous apotheosis was the instant annihilation of the cities of Hiroshima and Nagasaki by the atom bomb in August 1945.

This brief historical sketch of the technological question in the era of high modernity, from the early nineteenth to the mid twentieth century, though hopelessly condensed, is not, I hope, inaccurate. The dominant perception of technology, for more than a century, throughout the industrial world and in all sectors of society, was fraught with anxiety and for good reasons. Technological innovation drove the economy on all fronts and, in the emerging industrial-military-political complexes of the conflict-ridden countries of the world, weapons of mass destruction were stockpiled and at last put to their destructive use in a war which was, for Horkheimer, the end of reason. It was the end of reason in a double sense: the final end or outcome, the *terminus ad quem* of modern secular rationality and, at the same time, its annihilation.

'The dictators were rational enough to build tanks – others should be rational enough to submit to them' (Horkheimer [1941] 1978: 28).

Heidegger's view of technology was in tune with all this. In a lecture he gave in the late 1940s on 'the question of technology', he argued that the essence of technology was nothing technological.[7] In his lecture he spoke of radar, jet planes, a hydroelectric plant on the Rhine – big 'heavy' industrial things. This was what he thought of as 'technology', and he contrasted these very new high powered things with much older small hand-crafted objects. He reverently discussed the making of a silver chalice, but not the making of a jet plane, for that he could not imagine. Heidegger is distressed by technology, as Albert Borgmann aptly puts it (Borgmann 2003: 420–32). It represents the objectivist, scientific world view in which nature is simply a 'standing reserve', a natural resource to be exploited for instrumental purposes, a mere means to human ends. Technology, the apotheosis of modernity, is the violation of the natural, living world. Heidegger ends by contrasting technology with art. Both, he reflects, were once thought of as *techne*, the products of human skill and craft. Poesy (poetry) comes from *poiesis* – making, creating, bringing forth. The original understanding of humanly made things as a creative act in which our human essence shines forth, gradually splits in two. In modern times technology is the negation of poetry and poetry in turn has dwindled to an aesthetic, cultural activity. Heidegger ends with the hope that, confronted by the frenzied domination of technology, art may recover something of what it once had, in that brief magnificent moment in the life of the Greeks, when it brought forth and illuminated the presence of the gods and the dialogue between divine and human destinies. In poiesis, in poetic making, the essence of truth shines forth. Poiesis once was akin to techne, but now the two are fundamentally different. The more we ponder the danger of technology, the more we must be struck by the saving power of art. Such questioning is the piety of thinking (Heidegger [1954] 1978).

The question reconsidered

It is inimitably put, but we should not fail to see that this was the commonplace thinking of Heidegger's generation for whom art was a consolation and retreat from the wasteland of modern life. Leavis and Adorno both thought in essentially the same way as Heidegger. For Leavis, literature (the great tradition) was life affirming against the deadening stupefaction of mass civilization. Autonomous art for Adorno (art that obeyed its own laws, that was true to itself) stood in lonely defiance of politicized art (art as propaganda: Brecht, Benjamin, Lukacs) and heteronymous mass culture that obeyed the external laws of the market in the pursuit of profit. I grew up with this thinking, but it will no longer do. We need a more adequate understanding of technology if we are to make sense of 'television'. Let me make a number of summary points:

- It is now pure fantasy to think we might live without modern power-technologies by reverting to a pre-technological handicraft world of self-sufficiency. The world we live in is utterly, totally dependent on the new technologies that began to define the post-modern post-war era, and none of us would for a moment choose to live without them. We live in a fully technologized world. We cannot begin to understand our world unless we understand what underpins it: the question of technology.
- The post-modern technologies of the post-war era differ fundamentally from pre-war technologies in terms of their overall *telos* – their human intentionality or purpose.
- Modernity's world-defining technology, its ultimate achievement, was the atomic bomb along with all the other weapons of mass destruction that preceded it – bombers and fighter planes, battleships and u-boats, tanks and artillery; weapons of mass destruction on land, sea and air. Modernity's technological sublime killed 30,000 people in a flash.[8]
- Post-modernity's world-defining technologies do not evoke shock and awe. They are thankfully less than sublime. The TV set, along with computers, the internet, mobile phones and a whole cluster of connected developments represent one key overarching trajectory of continuing post-war technological innovation at this point in time. Its ultimate achievement is the World Wide Web, the Internet, as the bomb represented the culmination of modernist scientific research and innovation over a similar 50-year time-span.
- The technologies of post-modernity represent an intentional turning away from high modernity's technologies of mass destruction. 'It is better to jaw jaw than to war war', that great old warrior Winston Churchill reportedly remarked at a White House luncheon in his honour on 26 June 1954. The post-war technological 'turn' is precisely from technologies of war to technologies of talk (an early definition of television was 'talking heads'). A thing made for killing indicates a world oriented to killing. A thing made for communication indicates a world oriented to communication.
- Technology in the modern era was dirty and dangerous, as was its major power source, coal. Its products were characteristically

big and for collective use. Post-modern electronic technologies are small, clean and safe, and largely for individual use.

- Technology in the modern era was experienced as outside over and above everyday life; as part of the 'logic of domination' that seemed to overwhelm and threaten the vulnerable silent majorities of mass society. In the post-modern era, technology is intrinsic to everyday life; it is its life support system. The domestic technologies of the 1950s defined and continue to define the moment at which everyday life was finally established as an unobtrusive good in itself for the majority of people.

- The domestic electrical appliances that came into common use in the 1950s constituted the material basis of a culture of everyday life for everyone. I have tried to show what it means to speak of something as an *everyday* thing: an affordable available thing for use made in such ways that *anyone* can use it, *anytime, anywhere*.

- The technological care-structure of everyday things gives them as things-for-use by anyone, while concealing the enormous complexity of the hidden human labour that produces them as such. That is their gift, what they grant us – that we can take them for granted, as we do.

- The power appliances of everyday life are empowering. The word 'power', so often used negatively in academic discourse to mean domination or imposed control from above, also means to enable, to empower, to bestow the capacity to act and thereby to control one's life. Everyday technologies are individually empowering and as such are small objects of desire and personal empowerment. We are not in their thrall. They do not control us. We are in control of them as we put them to use. That they are so is their sought-for, achieved and accomplished effect. They were made to be so.

- In modernist thought, human beings were becoming automatons, robots, machines living in a machine-dominated world. Technology was thus the defining mark of human alienation from self and others in a reified world. Post-modern technologies reconcile us to our worldly selves and the everyday world in which we live with others. That, in essence, is what it means to speak of them as user *friendly*.

- Technologies have their life histories of continuing development and change. Today's TVs are, in fact, better all round than they were 60 years ago. The history of the TV set is one of continuing improvement: from black and white to colour > better sound and colour quality > sharper and more defined image resolution > bigger, flatter and wider, less bulky screens. In all this what is improved is the viewing experience, the pleasure of watching television.

- Everyday technologies are world constituting in a double sense: they make up the immediate world of everyday experience (the *umwelt*: *my* world). At the same time, they establish the world-historical character of life today; not just my world but the whole world as an available (*zuhanden*) whole for anyone, anytime, anywhere.

- Everyday things, as such, are universals. They are not like local languages, cultures, customs. They are the same everywhere. No matter where I am, a car or a TV set is a car or a TV set and usable as such. It makes no difference where it is made: Japanese cars and TV sets are purchased and used in the USA and Europe and everywhere, though any stranger visiting Japan for the first time will likely find its local language, culture and customs foreign and strange.
- The common world we inhabit has no common language, politics or culture. It is (and always has been) a common world of material things that are everywhere essentially the same, the products of the world economy.
- The material things of the world have a common, universal pragmatic logic-of-use that is implicated in their manufacture and design. The study of their care-structures discovers this implicit communicative logic as the common ground of the universal usability of everyday things. The logic-of-use that constitutes the usability of things grounds the intelligibility and availability of the world as a whole for anyone and everyone anytime, anywhere. It is indicative of the structure of that understanding which constitutes our common humanity.
- Today's communication and transport infrastructure give the unprecedented life conditions in which we find ourselves today. We live in a common world continuously made visible as such to anyone, anywhere, by the new communications technologies that developed in the second half of the last century. The world-historical character of life today is disclosed by television routinely in day-by-day output and in exceptional world-historical moments. But prior to the visible world disclosed by television is the form of the technology and its universal pragmatics of use that gives entry and access to the visible common world of today as routinely disclosed in its output.

This kind of thinking reverses the modernist thinking sketched above. Instead of seeing mass manufactured things as against the interests of the masses, it sees them as in the universal general interest. The defining characteristics of mass-produced things – the endless supply of exactly the same thing – was taken by a pre-war generation of intellectuals as indicative of the liquidation of difference, standardization, levelling down, homogenization, etc. OK. You *could* see it like that. But we might just see this sameness as the priceless gift of mass-made goods. And that equally it is no bad thing that I am just like everyone else in some fundamental respects, *pace* Heidegger, Adorno and co. The sameness of things reflects *our* fundamental sameness. If we and our things were essentially quirky, we would not know how to use anything or how to talk to anyone or do anything together. The gift of mass production is the limitless supply of the *same* things *every* day. As these things spread round the world, they constitute a common material world in its everyday availability for anyone and everyone, anywhere.

I have called this the post-modern world in order to indicate its difference from the modern era that self-destructed in the global catastrophe of the first (and hopefully the last) truly modern scientific technological global war. 1945 was an end and a beginning. The post-modern world appears in the 1950s and television is perhaps *the* new and defining post-modern technology of that decade and since. Academic thinking discovered and named 'the post-modern' 20 years or so later than this at the end of the 1970s – theory comes *post festum*, as Marx observed.[9] In Britain, Cultural Studies read the 1980s as *New Times* (Hall and Jacques 1989). These new times were understood as characterized by a transformation in the mode of production from Fordism to post-Fordism, accompanied by the disappearance of the masses (Hebdige 1989: 76–93). But the end of the masses became apparent in the 1950s. Two key books of that decade (*Personal Influence* in the USA and *Culture and Society* in Britain) both proclaimed the fading of mass society, mass politics and culture and the emergence of a sociable, peopled world of ordinary, everyday life. This then new phenomenon was the original object of nascent cultural studies in Britain and a new sociology of everyday life in the USA. The thinking of the 1950s broke decisively with the modernist thinking of the thirties in sociology, literature, history and philosophy, and came up with new ways of engaging with the transformed post-war world. It was genuinely *post*-modern thinking. It is ironic that the thinking of the seventies, even as it discovered the 'post-modern', was often last-gasp modernism, especially in the desperate search for the lost totality; the totalizing Theory of the whole social formation that would explain everything (Anderson 1969). 1980s postmodernism rejected that – incredulity towards grand narratives was its motto, supplied by Lyotard. But the thinking of the 1950s had made this break 30 years earlier.

Conclusion

The world as it is encountered is nothing more or less than the relational totality of things that make up the immediate environment in which each of us live. The crucial point is how we think of *things*: as mere Things (inert objects to be looked at objectively: ontology A) or as humanly made things-for-use by people living in a peopled world (ontology B). Under this second aspect, things are part of the life of the world, which is to say they are part of *our* lives.[10] These 'things' are not some inert backdrop to a life that goes in front of them, as it were, but untouched by them. They are not just 'stuff' or clutter in our lives. The world as we encounter it is always, in every situation, the relational totality of material things that allow us to do what we are doing there, wherever we might be. This world, our world today, is a totally human world whose conditions of existence are given by human technologies. As such technology (for us) constitutes the conditions of existence. Take away the infrastructure and our world (the world as *we* know it) collapses. Any technology is world disclosing. Television shows us this in its technological form *and* in what it opens up when we turn it on – the life of the world, life-as-lived by the generations of the present as shown *live* on television.[11]

To understand our fully technologized world of today, we must grasp where it has come from. We need to remember the world before television and the necessary preconditions that made possible a world with things like TV sets in it. To grasp this we must go back to the world of the thirties, forties and fifties, the decades whose convulsive transformations yielded the essential lineaments of the world we inhabit today. 'We' here means, as I have been at pains to insist, the privileged postmodern beneficiaries of the conflicted era of industrial modernization. The working through of that long revolution is now spreading from where it first took off in Europe centuries ago throughout the whole world at a rapidly accelerating pace. The cutting-edge work on television today is about its impact in Africa, India, Brazil, China, Japan, Korea and the Middle East. It is here in these parts of the world that the engagement with the experience of modernity is now most intensely joined and television is central to that engagement and experience. Everywhere the transition is in response to the same thing: the working-through of the world-historical process of societal modernization driven by the transition from economies of scarcity to abundance. The study of television today in these and other countries illuminates the world-historical character of life today: a common world, a common humanity at different stages of historical evolution – pre-modern (as in many parts of Africa), modernizing (as in India and China) and post-modern (as in some parts of Europe and North America). It is *this* world, I hope, that is illuminated by enquiring into the meaning of broadcast tele-technologies whose essence is their liveness.

Part two

Television and the meaning of *live*

7

The meaning of *live*

The liveness of television is the *leitmotif* of this book. It is not to be thought of as if it were a technological effect, a peculiar technical property of the medium itself. The essence of technology is nothing technological. If we are to understand what it is to be what in fact we are, we discover this, I have argued, in what we have made of things. The enduring world of humanly created things, reveals and conceals the truth of what it is from those who made and make it what it is. It seemed, in the era of modernity, as if human beings were becoming machine-like: monstrous, alien and inhuman. Technology appeared as something external to humanity; part of those impersonal forces of domination, imposed from above, that threatened the liquidation of the individual. But post-modern technologies – of which television and all related tele-technologies are but one formal indication – are not life threatening, but life supporting. They tell us – in their user-friendly ways – about who and what we are.

For each and every one of us the life that is mine is a fore-given temporal structure whose constitutive moments are birth and death. What stretches out in between our beginning and our end is the span of life, the time of my being in the world. This time (life time) is universal and particular. It has a for-anyone temporal structure that every particular someone encounters, undergoes and lives through as their ownmost existence. This life-as-lived is situated in what Heidegger calls both the *umwelt* and *mitwelt*: the round about me world of everyday life in which I live with others. I encounter my being in the world as a particular temporality – the time of my presence in the world; the time of my being alive; the time of my being with others. These are the times of all the generations of the living. These times are, at one and the same time utterly impersonal (for anyone and everyone), and in each case uniquely particular. They stand in a dialectical relationship to each other: the *longue durée* of the historical human world in play with the life-times of those who dwell in it at any given time.

The unfolding time of human history and the unfolding times of the living intersect (at any time) in the immediate now of the present: not the inhuman punctual (intelligible but meaningless) now of ontology A, but the human experiential, phenomenal now, the meaningful now-of-concern (ontology B). It is being-as-becoming the past and the future in and through the living moment, the here and now in which we speak and act. This order of time is not some external temporality imposed upon us by the non-human world. It is essentially and uniquely human though we never experience it as such. It is our own most intimate order of time because we create it; we uniquely bring it into being through the immediacy of our concerns in the living moment of the speech-act-event. It is this moment that is reflexively disclosed by tele-technologies of communication whose essence is their liveness.[1]

Being in concern is not some state of mind. It must be realized and brought to life as such. Concern is realized in two basic human ways: in speech and action, words and deeds. Both are intimately connected with one another. We may think of them as fused together, as flowing into each other in the speech>act>event. In either case, words and deeds are brought forth (as Heidegger would say) in the immediacy of concern: they are expressively realized *as* speech and action in the moment of their being enunciated and enacted. This moment, the moment of the coming into being of an utterance/event is the *living* moment in which human concerns come expressively to life, in which they are realized: in which they are made *real*.

The living moment lives and dies, comes and goes in the phenomenal now of concern. The words, even as I speak them, fade and give way to the what-comes-next of utterance. The event, as it unfolds, has being-towards-its-end as its defining forward momentum in time. How fragile, transient and perishable they seem. Words and deeds fade instantly as they vanish into the night of the unrecorded past. How shall it be known what was spoken? How shall it be known what was done? Were it not for technologies of record there would be no history. Neither words nor deeds are in themselves historical. They become so only as witnessed, narrated and recorded (these three necessary things and in that order). The wondrous technologies of writing mark the beginnings of historical time. We would not know of Socrates and Jesus were it not for their followers who wrote down their words and deeds, the stories of their life and death. But the written record is only a trace of what they said and did. I read the words of Jesus as he speaks to the crowds on a hillside overlooking the lake of Galilee. I read the words of Socrates in animated conversation with his young friend Phaedrus, in a grove outside the city of Athens. I read of the circumstances that brought them both to public trial and death. But I cannot ever see them, nor ever hear their words.

For thousands of years writing, in its many transformations, has been the sovereign way in which the past has been preserved and the words and deeds of the dead generations have been renewed in the life and times of the present. In the last century, two revolutionary technologies of record – the audio- and videotape and then digital recorders – have transformed the relationship between the living and the dead, past and present, as they put on record (for the record), words and deeds – speech-act-events – in their living enunciatory moment. Both technologies were developed in response to the exigencies of live broadcasting; first on radio and then, a generation later, on television. Through these technologies history is transformed. Technologies of writing produce history in the present *as* the past – the past as moving away from the present. The new audio-visual technologies record history in the making: the future as it comes to presence; history in the making of the immediate unfolding now of concern, realized as such in the enunciatory speech-act-event. The past is no longer preserved indirectly in the trace of the written. It is preserved directly (*en direct*, as the French say) in its own living immediacy in audio-visual recordings.

It has become customary, in media studies, to think of recording as the opposite of 'live' (Bourdon 2000). This antinomy has always been noted as *the* difference between the spoken and the written; the breath of life in living speech in contrast with the dead letters of the written/ printed text. Writing preserves what was spoken but at a loss. It *cannot* preserve the immediacy of living speech. It is at best no more than a silent trace of what was said but with the crucial loss of the living voice. This was the forceful objection to writing famously made by Socrates and ironically preserved by his follower, Plato, in a famous written text, *The Phaedrus*:

> You know, Phaedrus, writing shares a strange feature with painting. The offspring of painting stand there as if they are alive, but if anyone asks them anything, they remain most solemnly silent. The same is true of written words. You'd think they were speaking as if they had some under-standing, but if you question anything that has been said because you want to learn more, it continues to signify the same things forever. When it has once been written down, every discourse rolls about everywhere, reaching indiscriminately those with understanding no less than those who have no business with it, and it doesn't know to whom it should speak and to whom it should not. And when it is faulted and attacked unfairly, it always needs its father's support; alone it can neither defend itself nor come to its own support. (As quoted in Peters 1999: 47)

John Durham Peters takes this passage as exemplifying one fundamental kind of communication – *conversation*; live and direct talk,
normally and normatively between two people. Dialogue was Socrates'
preferred method for the pursuit of truth which can only emerge, as he
argues here, in questioning, interactive talk between people who are
present to one another. Only in this kind of discourse can distortions
and misunderstandings be untangled in the back and forth of question
and answer, a progressive clarification of meaning and understanding.
Communication, for it to be real-and-true (genuine and authentic)
must be immediate: it must be 'soul-to-soul, among embodied living
people, in an intimate interaction that is uniquely fit for each participant
. . . Distortions in communication for Socrates arise from the disappearance of a personal nexus' (Peters 1999: 47).

It is precisely this that is redeemed by technologies of *live recording*
for both radio and television. Audio (for radio) and audio-visual recordings (for television) capture and preserve live speech-act-events as they
unfold in the immediate now of their coming into being. Without these
technologies, radio and television would be strictly unhistorical – there
would be neither record of, nor testimony to, their output. Their study
would be so severely restricted that it is hard to conceive how academic
disciplines might develop to engage with them. There would be no
'texts' (programs) to discuss and analyse without readily available
recordings of them. One would have to rely on memory; or on detailed
notes taken as one listened and watched. At best one might be able to
reconstruct them indirectly from written traces. I have done this myself
in early work, for instance, on radio news in the UK. There are no
sound recordings of any news programs until 1938 and the Munich
crisis. There are no preserved scripts of complete news broadcasts until
the Second World War (with the fascinating exception of BBC news
bulletins during the General Strike of 1926). What news was like, for
the first 20 years of broadcasting in Britain, can only be conjectured
from fragmentary traces in the written record (Scannell and Cardiff
1991: 105–33). Early radio news remains strictly pre-historic.

Talk is as old as humanity, but it only entered fully into history with
the development of sound recordings. Events, too, are as old as history
but only very recently have they been covered live as they happen by
television cameras and simultaneously recorded. Hitherto, historians
have depended on eyewitness reports (as written down), written documents, photographs, paintings and film. But none of these captures
the unfolding event as it comes into being, live and in real time – as
live-and-recorded television does, by now routinely, as we shall see.
This study of live broadcasting presupposes technologies of record that
make it available for that purpose. 'Recorded live' is not an oxymo-

ron. Audio-visual recording redeems the living moment from death. Whenever I hit the replay button, the living moment comes to life once more. Resurrection – time and time again – is the unconditional promise and guarantee of audio-visual recording technologies. The past comes to life and lives again. I can stop it at any moment. I can rewind and replay. I can fast forward. In the living moment itself we cannot do this (though we all have wished at times that we could). In the recorded living moment, I can play with time, with the past-present-future of the immediate now at any now point. I can stop time (how impossibly strange that is . . . how really unreal!). I can work it back and forth. The dialectics of immediacy become available to scrutiny and analysis. I can begin to figure out the workings of time. It can be analysed in fine detail – as we shall see in due course when I come to consider what happens on television when goals are scored in soccer matches.

My concern in what follows is with two fundamental aspects of live broadcasting: speech and events. In both cases I try to show what is at stake in their management by the hidden production care-structures that work to produce them as to-be-heard-and-seen. This will, I hope, tell us something essential about how radio and television is produced *for* listeners and viewers; in what ways and with what effects. But more than this, I assume that studying the management of liveness on radio and television casts light on the human situation as such, if it is the case (as I suppose) that the management of liveness is what confronts us all at every moment of existence: from individual lives, to the historical life of nation-states and beyond. For it is not just those working in radio and TV who confront liveness as something to be managed and dealt with as best they can. What they confront, we confront in every moment of our waking lives. The problems they face in managing 'liveness' are the problems we confront in the management of our lives in the course of a lifetime. What are those problems? Most basically they concern what it is to speak and act without guarantees in the immediacy of the phenomenal now of concern. We must commit to speech and action. In so doing we realize our existence. We make it real. We do so always without knowing for sure their consequences. We do so aware of the fallibility of what we say and do: that our words and actions may fail. They may be misunderstood, they may not succeed, they might have unforeseen and undesired outcomes. This is the *politics* of the present. It is an *existential* politics that discloses the human situation and the unavoidable dilemmas and uncertainties that we confront as we live our lives caught up in the immediate now-of-concern. There is a danger in everything we say and do: a possibility, every time, of performative failure and unanticipated and unwelcome consequences. At the same time, everything we say and do presupposes some felicity, some good and happy outcome, however small and fleeting. Anxiety and desire (one to be hopefully overcome; the other hopefully to be realized) are twin underlying concerns in the management of liveness, the situations in which we speak and act, from the level of individual lives and their affairs to the affairs of the nations of the world. It is this that is disclosed when we examine what is at stake in the management of speech and action, live and in real time, on radio and television.

The management of liveness

Two topics, then: speech and events and their enactments on radio and television. I will deal with each separately, trying to get to the essence of what they are as fundamental human acts. Each is to be understood as an aspect of the other. To speak is to act; to act is to articulate. Each is to be managed and both give rise to two basic management problems; one negative, the other positive. The demonic problem of live speech-act-events on radio and television is the ever present possibility of their breakdown, either through technical error or human performance failure. Damage limitation is a cardinal consideration in the management care-structures of live-to-air talk and events on radio and television. But this concern is inseparable from the problem of bringing speech and actions 'to life'. What does this mean? It is maybe not so obvious as the negative problem of technical and/or performative breakdown. But it is every bit as crucial.

Consider the difference between what the surveillance camera records and what the television camera shows. The surveillance camera in a public space (an airport, a shopping mall) is fixed in place and is either static, or rotates on a preset sweep of the environment that never changes. It has no human operator. It automatically records what it 'sees', what is in range of its lens. What it records has the quality of immediacy, but not of liveness. It produces a visual record, but not one that is watchable. The point was made rather brilliantly by Andy Warhol whose (in)famous videos of sleep and the Empire State Building reveal, via a perspective of incongruity, what needs to be done in order to make something watchable. That means to bring what is visible 'to life'. How is this effect, the effect of liveness, there in television production but not in the surveillance camera (or Warhol's)? What is the difference?

What is it that the surveillance camera lacks? The moving image that it displays is of poor visual quality; it is static and soundless. It manifests no human agency. It is no more than a mechanical device of record. There is no motive, no intentionality, no concern in what it 'blindly' and 'unthinkingly' records. It is not watchable because it is not meant to be watched. It is only watched with great care when its surveillance function is called upon. Who, in Britain, can forget the blurry and indistinct image (as shown on television) taken from a CCTV system in a shopping mall of a boy holding the hand of a little child. It records the moment that the two-year-old Jamie Bulger, momentarily separated from his by-now distraught mother, is picked up by two ten-year-old boys who will lead him out of the mall, to a nearby railway line where they will torture and kill him. It is but one image from the random record of the mall's CCTV system, found by the police as they painstakingly sought to reconstruct what happened to Jamie Bulger when he became separated from his mother. It is an ocular proof, no more than that, of what in fact happened. It is the product of a technology whose function is impassively and mechanically to record what immediately passes before it – this being no more or less than its purely technical capacity in play.

The recording function of radio and television equipment works in support of and in tandem with the work of live transmission. This is *never* just a matter of sticking a microphone or a camera somewhere, turning it on and, as it were, hoping that something of interest might result. The liveness of radio and television broadcast is not some inherent technical property of technologies of production, transmission and record. It is the worked at, achieved and accomplished effect of the human application and use of technologies whose ontological characteristic is immediate connectivity. The surveillance camera captures a soundless visual immediacy. But liveness is something that has to be brought to life precisely in and by the motivations, intentions, care-and-attention that is implicit in everything we get to see and hear on radio and television, and none of which is visible as we watch and listen. It is there in the grain of the voice (as heard), in 'being there' (as seen and witnessed). It is that which is experienced: the 'content' if you like of so-called 'lived experience'. And this experience is always the effect (the upshot) of the situation and its situational characteristics. The most basic work that broadcasting does is that of creating and producing both listening and viewing *as* a situation, as something to be experienced, as an *available* experience for anyone and everyone. The unmotivated and strictly inhuman surveillance camera produces the visible as a natural fact (ontology A). The motivated humanly directed TV camera produces the visible and hearable as an available experience (ontology B) for anyone.

Availability is never just a natural occurrent fact. It is, as Heidegger painstakingly argues, the outcome of human labour that produces the human world as ready-to-hand and thereby available within range of human concerns. And this he thinks of as a very basic human accomplishment that he calls 'making the remoteness of something disappear, bringing it close . . . *In Dasein there lies an essential tendency towards closeness*' (Heidegger [1927] 1962: 139, 140; original emphasis). 'With the "radio", for example [and remember this is written in the early 1920s when radio was in its infancy], Dasein has so expanded its everyday environment that it has accomplished a de-severance[2] of the "world" – a de-severance which, in its meaning for Dasein, cannot yet be visualized' (Heidegger [1927] 1962: 140). And what this points to is an existential pragmatics of spatiality as situationally defined in terms of near and far from a situated someone some where (experiential space: ontology B), rather than abstract distance as measured in metres or centimetres (geometric space: ontology A). The remarkable achievement of radio and television is to bring the whole world within the range of in each case my concern and in doing so to make it part of in each case my everyday life – day by day and every day. This 'de-severance' is the globalizing effect of tele-technologies. How is it done?

The pragmatics of space, foreseen by Heidegger, was explored in the pioneering work of the anthropologist Edward Hall who wanted to understand the *proxemics* of human interactions. How close or distant (near or far) are people to each other in social situations? How does closeness or distance affect the nature of the social situation in which participants find themselves and the ways in which they interact with each other? How do you figure it out? Hall's solution was as brilliantly simple as it was practical. He used *voice* as the measure of the spaces of human interaction:

> One common source of information about the distance separating two people is the loudness of the voice. Working with the linguistic scientist George Trager, I began by observing shifts in the voice associated with changes in distance. Since the whisper is used when people are very close, and the shout is used to span great distance, the question Trager and I posed was, How many vocal shifts are sandwiched between these two extremes? Our procedure for discovering these patterns was for Trager to stand still while I talked to him at different distances. If both of us agreed a vocal shift had occurred, we would then measure the distance and note down a general description. (Hall 1966: 109–10)

Hall found four distinct spaces-of-interaction: intimate, personal, social and public. Each has a 'near' and 'far' aspect and, of course, they shade into each other. In intimate space people's bodies are intertwined or touching. Personal space (between two and four feet) defines what Goffman calls 'the territories of the self' whose boundaries can only be crossed with express permission. Social space (4–12 feet) is the space of everyday interpersonal interactions. Beyond this lies public space:

12–25 feet in its near aspect; 25 feet and beyond as it becomes increasingly distant. Voice defines the boundaries of these spaces: the whispers of intimacy, the quiet murmur of close personal talk; the ordinary conversational voice of interpersonal interaction and the loud, impersonal voice of someone addressing an audience of some sort in some public space. These voices implicate what Hall calls different 'situational personalities': the wholly personal and private at one end of the scale, the wholly public and impersonal at the other end. And in between, the inter-personal: the social spaces of everyday life in which people encounter and deal with each other as 'persons'. It is this situational space that is created by the voices of radio and the look of television as the public communicative space of interaction between broadcasters and audiences. The communicative ethos of radio and television is oriented towards the norms of ordinary everyday talk between people. It endlessly produces the situational space between broadcasters and their listeners and viewers as that of conversation. The proxemics of broadcasting are fundamentally oriented to interactions between people as persons; not the domain of the purely personal at one extreme, nor the purely impersonal at the other, but the intermediate zone of inter-personal interaction whose communicative medium is *talk*.

In the chapters that follow I will explore in a little detail the spatial and temporal proxemics of radio and television as communicative and experiential effects produced by microphones and cameras. But first I would like to draw attention in advance to the general implications of the utterly familiar communicative and experiential situation of listening and viewing that we all now take for granted. It has radically transformed available ways of being in the world throughout the world. It is the most important world-historical *effect* of radio and television. It has produced (in play with other tele-technologies) a *communicative* world in which people everywhere talk to each other more and more. Just how remarkable this is forever escapes our attention in the viewing and listening situations of everyday life as created by radio and television broadcasting. It escapes notice precisely because the circumstances of viewing and listening are very quickly taken as natural and given, and this is the naturalizing effect of the hidden care-structures (the invisible human labour) that produce it as such. The de-severance that is accomplished by the creation of the communicative and experiential spaces of listening and viewing is the abolition of distance between the public world as a whole and the everyday life-world of personal experience. From the beginnings of radio and television through to the present, the public world has entered into the hitherto private world of domestic existence which in turn has crossed over into the common public world of radio and television. The transformation of the conditions of public and private life is the most fundamental effect of radio and television everywhere. It has been from the beginning and continues to be, an evolving world-transforming historical process.

In the classic 'broadcast era', the de-severance effect of radio and television was largely within the proximal boundaries of nation-states. It then seemed natural to experience radio and television as 'British', 'American' or French' or whatever. In the last 30 years or so, continuing innovation in telecommunications on many inter-connected fronts has created our contemporary post-modern experience of living-in-the-world as truly global. This astounding de-severance has created the unprecedented world-historical conditions of life today, with profound and far-reaching political, cultural and social implications for human peoples worldwide that we the living are engaged with and working through right now. We are, for the first time in history, confronted by our common humanity as a matter-of-fact everyday historical reality through the interplay of the cluster of tele-technologies that produce it as such and bring it within the communicative and experiential reach of anyone, anywhere, anytime. Being-in-the-world now means not the immediate, situated 'my-world' that Heidegger opened up for thinking in Division One of *Being and Time*, but that world as situated in the globalized common world that tele-technologies severally and together have everywhere brought within the proximal space of a conversation for everyone.

Methodological matters

But how to explore this? It is the most difficult methodological question that has confronted me in working out and working through the concerns of this book. I do not have access to and knowledge of all the television and radio services in the world today. No one has. So how can I possibly think and write of global broadcasting as if I knew what it was? I can do so only if the claims that I have made for the universal logic-of-use implicated in all human technologies are valid: if it is the case, as I suppose, that radio and television (like cars and fridges) have the same logic-of-use everywhere. This universal pragmatics is disclosive of a shared and common historical humanity. I have allowed for 'local' language and cultural variations country by country. There are different 'televisions' and 'radios' around the world when it comes to what is seen and heard in any concrete situation of listening and watching. But I assume that the common ground everywhere is the viewing and listening situation that the care structures deliver *as such*. I assume that the relational proxemics created by radio and television are everywhere more or less the same. *My* experience of television is the common human experience of television – not, of course, my 'subjective' response, but the dialectical play of the common experience as given by television (for anyone and everyone watching the soccer match the world over) in play with the particular experience of it that is in each case mine. *That* is the viewing situation as such. That is what warrants me taking what is called television as a common worldly phenomenon grounded in common human experience.

These are huge assumptions, but they are precisely the assumptions that we all in fact take for granted in all our everyday dealings with the world of experience as we encounter it in our daily lives. The crux in these assumptions is their dependence on the category of 'experience' and its dependence, in turn, on a hermeneutics of trust. Both those terms – 'experience' and 'trust' – were explicitly marginalized in academic thinking as it (and I as part of it) began to engage with the question of television in the 1970s.[3] In what follows I explicitly wish to redeem them from the academic pawn-shop while putting in pawn (for present purposes) the terms 'critical' and 'theory' that displaced them. The experience of television (not a theory of it) and an implicit trust in that experience (rather than an explicit suspicion of it) – these are key themes in what follows. The stories of Heidegger and television that I began with exemplify the tensions and contradictions between academic thinking and everyday experience. When he 'thought' of technology and television, Professor Heidegger (renowned sage and deep thinker) deplored them both. When he experienced television in a friend's house, Heidegger-as-ordinary-person was ecstatic. He had seen the German soccer team led by the legendary Franz Beckenbauer. He had witnessed the return of the heroes and the gods, not in mortal and immortal combat before the walls of Troy, but in triumphant battle for the World Cup of 1974! My task is to show how it is indeed possible for anyone (including Heidegger and critical theorists) to have an experience watching television; and that this experience is meaningful, genuine, authentic, real and true to the extent that the hidden production care-structures of television produce it as such.

But how to do it? – that is the methodological question. I offer four little case studies: two that explore broadcast talk and its spatial proxemics, two that explore television events and their temporal proxemics. Separately and together I take them as exemplifying what is at stake in the management and production by broadcasting of speech-act-events as to be experienced live by listeners and viewers situated in their own time and place. Some justification of this is called for. First, I take it that the proper object of study is *broadcasting* and by this I mean two things. That radio and television are always to be thought of and studied together as fundamentally complementary media whose differences supplement each other in common everyday usage. Secondly, that the *broadcast* effect of central broadcasting institutions (NHK, BBC, CBS, etc.) remains a central object of enquiry in the study of radio and television (Scannell 2013).

In the next two chapters I give accounts of developments in the management and production of live talk on early radio and television. The production methods and techniques of radio and television all once had to be worked out. As the problems they encounter are resolved, these techniques become routine and taken for granted. They are quickly picked up and adopted elsewhere, though I know of no detailed study of the migrations of equipment and production techniques from one country to another. If we are to understand how radio and television 'work' it is always illuminating to look at moments when what works gets worked out. Discussion on radio and television today is a commonplace daily experience. *The Brains Trust* (BBC 1942) was the first radio programme in Britain to produce live unscripted talk-as-discussion for listeners. How to produce unscripted talk between four discussants that would be interesting and entertaining for listeners was the underlying concern of the program – its invisible care structure. I show how this was worked out and with what effects for wartime British audiences. The focal concern was with the move from scripted to unscripted talk, a move which, as we shall see, raised basic questions about the liveness of broadcast talk. Scripted and unscripted talk on radio and television is a motif that runs through all the following chapters.

Examples of programs that somehow do not work are rare but revealing. *Person to Person* (CBS 1953) broke new ground for television. The program had two basic ideas: that it might be possible to revive the lost art of conversation – in spite of television – and secondly, that this conversation should take place with people in their homes. Almost all early television was broadcast live from the studio, but there was a strong impulse, from the start, to get out of the artificial space in which television produced itself at first and into the world, into people's lives, into the places where they lived. This crossover – out of the studio and into the world – was a transformative moment for television that began to establish it as an integral aspect of everyday life today. It was the moment that television began its essential work of doing 'being-in-the-world' on behalf of viewers. It is in this 'doing' that television's worldliness resides: that basic way in which it is in, of and for the everyday world; in which it mediates between the life of the world as a whole and the lives of individuals around the world today. It is in this that the interaction between the public and the private/the private and the public resides.

It is not a big step from speech to action. J.L. Austin's performatives are speech-act-events. 'I name this ship'; 'I hereby sentence you to death'; 'I now pronounce you man and wife': his well-known examples of 'doing things with words', of words as speech-acts, all presuppose a real-world situation in which the utterance of certain words have real and consequential effects by virtue of the circumstances in which they are said. Austin calls these circumstances 'the felicity conditions' of performatives. But what produces the felicity effect, if not the care structures that combine to 'give' the nature of the occasion in which these things can felicitously (that is, meaningfully and effectively) be said? Performatives – whether words or deeds – do not 'work' except in the appropriate situations of their utterance and enactment, and these must be always already in place before and after any particular speech-act-event. Austin's examples point to unusual situations with a ceremonial, public ritual character: the launch of a ship, the moment of sentencing in a law court, the marriage service. Such occasions are the topic of Daniel Dayan and Elihu Katz's study of what they call 'media events': a key work in the study of television which I discuss in chapter 11.

Dayan and Katz have produced a sociology of televised occasions, focusing on their ceremonial, ritual character. Here I am concerned with an ontology of televised occasions that attends to their temporal proxemics. I move from a study of being-in-place (the spatial proxemics of talk on radio and television) to a study of our situated being-in-time; the time of our being *in* the event as it unfolds live and in real time. I offer first an exemplary case study of the things we make to happen and then of the things that happen to us and their live coverage by television. I take the topic of sport (international soccer) as a key instance of the meant and intended occasion, and catastrophe (the attack on the World Trade Center) as a defining instance of the utterly unexpected event. In each case, I explore how television engages with the event as it unfolds live and in real time. Each has a particular focus on the temporality of the living moment, our situated being in time.

This book is an engaged debate with Heidegger about what it is to be alive and living in the world; the human situation as each and all of us encounter it *en direct* and live; the experience of being in the world in time and place. I take this to be a meaningful question and television to be a meaningful way of trying to explore it. We know what Heidegger thought of television – not a lot! And we know what happened when he watched it – he was carried away in rapture. The older he became, the more Heidegger assumed a lofty detachment from the mundane world; the more he saw himself as a thinker who, in his hill-side hut high above the valley, looked down on the world below as under the sway and dominion of technology.[4] But now and then he came down from the mountains and returned to ordinary existence. This ordinary Heidegger and his occasional experience of soccer on television is an underlying inspiration for the second half of this book as it engages with the meaning of *live* through the liveness of broadcast radio and television.

8

How to talk – on radio

The Brains Trust

The Brains Trust was the first unscripted live discussion programme on British national radio in which the speakers responded spontaneously and without foreknowledge of them, to questions sent in by listeners.[1] It began in response to a request by the BBC planners of the Forces Programme, in the autumn of 1939, for something that would alleviate the boredom of the British Expeditionary Force[2] and at the same time respond to an identified felt need for information and discussion in the most general sense. This particular programme request could have been passed for development to any one of three production departments in the BBC: Talks, Features or Variety. Each had a quite different internal culture, with a different ethos in relation to their common task of making programmes. In short, if the programme went to Talks its defining communicative characteristic would be 'intellectual'; if it went to Features, it would be 'artistic'; and if it went to Variety it would be 'entertaining'.[3] It was therefore a crucial decision to send it to Variety, thereby prefiguring the decisive communicative form the programme would take. But even then, within any production centre there are different producers with different attitudes and styles towards the common task of producing, in the case of Variety, entertainment. Thus, it was significant (it made a difference to the subsequent history of the programme) that the Head of Variety, John Watt, chose to delegate its development to the good genius of Howard Thomas. Individuals can and do make a difference within the corporate culture of production in the BBC, which Thomas had joined in 1940, from a career until then in advertising and commercial radio.[4]

The brief Thomas received from Watt was succinct: to create an informational programme that was 'serious in intention, light in character'.

The form that the programme eventually took was 'no sudden inspiration. Like most good and simple ideas it was hammered out during weeks of hard thinking' (Thomas 1944: 13). Thomas wanted a programme with 'mass appeal', to bring listeners into 'personal' contact with some of the best brains of the day in the most friendly and informal way. They had of course been heard on radio before. Indeed the mission of the Talks Department, before the war had been precisely that. Yet if the idea had been developed by Talks, so Thomas argued, it would have put enlightenment before entertainment whereas he put a premium on the latter. The kind of talk that Thomas wanted to capture was something like table-talk, the lively after dinner conversation of the educated intelligentsia. 'Spontaneous answers by interesting people – that was it'. The key to securing the effect of liveliness and spontaneity was to have a panel of speakers and a Question Master (Howard coined the term) to introduce the speakers, to set them the questions and to control and manage the talk that went out over the air.

Thomas put up his ideas for a programme he originally thought of calling *Any Questions* in a seven-page memorandum to the Head of Variety.[5] It was accepted, and he now began the task of transforming ideas into reality. Questions were invited, on air, and they came in, at first in a trickle then a torrent. By the time its fame was established, the programme received two and a half thousand questions a week, rising to a peak of just under four thousand. It took two staff two full days each week to deal with such a volume of mail. Many letter writers wanted further information on topics discussed the previous week, and they were supplied, where appropriate, with suggestions for further reading. Questions suitable for the programme were classified into broad topic areas and then selected both for variety of subject and in relation to the interests and personalities of the speakers. Thomas would then go home with a bundle of about a hundred possible candidate questions and whittle them down to a dozen or so. Then, as the questions began to come in, his main concern was to pick the right speakers and find the right way to bring out the best in them at the microphone.

He found a perfect mix in the balance between the characters and performances of the three regular panellists. There was Julian Huxley, the scientist: knowledgeable and factual, perhaps rather dry and occasionally irritable, but whose solidity and seriousness was the backbone of the programme. Then there was Cyril Joad, a philosopher – never short of an opinion, widely read, a fluent and occasionally brilliant speaker who, even if he didn't know what he was talking about, was never dull. He and Huxley were perfect foils; their disrespect for each other's views and their willingness to 'mix it' brought a clash that attracted millions.

These two, though very different, were clearly 'brains'. The last in the original triumvirate was not, but Thomas insisted on him, overriding objections to his inclusion and arguing that it was essential to have a link between the professors and the listeners who had never heard a professor. Archibald Bruce Campbell, an ex-navy man, was widely travelled with a colourful turn of speech and an attractive broadcasting manner. His no-nonsense common sense views could bring the talk down to earth again after the lofty flights of Joad. Campbell was relished by listeners for his curious bits of information and odd facts. He once declared on the programme, in all seriousness, that he knew a man so allergic to marmalade that whenever he ate it for breakfast, steam came out of his head. Like the other two, he was a natural performer. Thomas did not create, or even develop their radio characters, but he did carefully choose them *as* a combination. What they stood for seemed, to him, the right blend; the cool brain, the ready tongue, the voice of experience (Thomas 1977: 74).

The programme was recorded each week on Friday afternoon, either on film or tape, in the BBC's Maida Vale studios. It was recorded 'live', in one continuous take, as the discussion unfolded in the studio.[6] Although there was sporadic behind the scenes discussion about whether the programme should be transmitted live-to-air, recording was preferred for a number of reasons. In the early years of the war, all programmes were scripted for security reasons, and it was to overcome this considerable handicap to its spontaneity that Thomas decided to record it each week (Thomas 1944: 82). There were further advantages. It gave time-flexibility to broadcasters and performers, allowing the programme to be recorded at a time convenient for the panellists and freeing them from the obligation to be in a BBC studio each week at the time of the programme's transmission. Moreover, it gave the possibilities of repeats (the programme was broadcast twice weekly) and for transmission in the BBC's rapidly expanding wartime overseas services.

Before the weekly recording session Thomas first took the weekly panellists out to lunch at the BBC's expense. A drink or two – no more – lest excess should dull their subsequent performance, was allowed to the participants. Both food and drink, as legitimate programme costs, had to be wrung from an unwilling BBC administration, but Thomas defended the expense as a necessary preliminary to getting the best out of the speakers. It helped them to relax, it introduced guests to the regulars, it created familiarity, it got them talking to each other. Once in the studio they were seated at a table with a microphone in the middle. Every session began with a ten-minute warm-up with a couple of unrecorded questions put to the panel by McCullough. This preliminary was essential in a number of ways. It was indispensable for newcomers, allowing Howard Thomas to spot their idiosyncrasies and, where possible, correct them. Some, when speaking, would turn to the person next to them, thus deflecting their voice from the microphone. Others would talk at the table, holding their heads down as they spoke. Others covered their mouths. There was the occasional over-emphatic table-thumper. Some could not keep still, leaning forwards then stretching backwards, twisting and turning their heads – the result, as heard by listeners, was an unpleasant series of gushes and fades as their voices came and went. While Thomas attended to such matters, the sound-engineers attended to the properties of the speakers' voices in relation to the microphone and its properties. Pitch and volume had to be adjusted and balanced to produce an even-sounding pro-gramme for absent ears. Shouters could be softened, whisperers coaxed to increase their volume. Naturally loud voices were placed at the corners of the table, at an angle to the microphone. Quiet voices were placed full on to it. As a rule this was where women were positioned to stop them raising their voices and sounding shrill. Joad and Huxley were always placed opposite each other to allow them to spar more easily.

After the warm-up the programme quickly slipped into the real thing. The green light came on. The programme was now live-to-air and 'on record' as McCullough deftly introduced each participant before sailing into the first question. Thomas himself always sat in on the sessions. Positioned slightly behind McCullough and away from the table, he tried, from moment to moment, to hear the talk with an ear for the listener. When he felt a discussion was getting too wordy he would pass a note to the question master telling him to wrap it up. Thomas was always keenly sensitive to the programme's pace, tempo and balance. To maintain tempo he would, if necessary, switch the order of ques-tions. If, for instance, Joad had discoursed at length on a philosophical question, he would tell McCullough to bring forward a question on snakes for Huxley.

It was extraordinarily hard to convince listeners that the talk was completely unrehearsed. The BBC publicly guaranteed the questions were not known in advance by any of the panel. Thomas would point out how it was virtually impossible to read (or, for that matter, write) a prepared script in the completely natural manner that characterized *The Brains Trust*. It was the spontaneity, the slips, the verbal clutchings in mid-air and the occasional flooring of the speakers that listeners enjoyed. Such spontaneity, as an achieved effect-in-public, as an effect-for-others, never simply happens. It must be planned and worked for. If it is to be achieved, it must be so effortlessly. Here is Joad, in full flight, on the question, 'What is happiness?'

In Aristotle's famous metaphor
it's like the bloom on a young man's cheek in perfect health.
It's not a part of health, but it's something added.
Its a its a si:gn that the organism is functioning appropriately
on an appropriate subject matter.
Well now I should think I should like to put that
by saying that happiness is something
that doesn't yield itself to direct pursuit
but comes incidentally.
It's not a house that can be built with men's hands.
It's like the kingdom of heaven.
it can't be taken by storm.
It's like a flower that surprises you.
a sort of song that you hear as you pass a hedge
rising suddenly into the night.
I'd I'd like to say that er really
the best recipe for happiness that I know
is not to have leisure enough to wonder
whether you're being miserable or not.
In other words, it's a by-product of activity
(.)
McCullough.
Well I'm sure that uh.
all over the country uh.
at the end of that . answer to that question
there was a burst of applause.
I would just like to say that ah
Professor Joad answered that without any notes
and without knowing what the question was.
.hhh you may find it difficult to believe
I do very much so sitting here watching him
and I congratulate him

Talk in public

The immediate impact of *The Brains Trust* in wartime Britain was in large part due to a felt need for spontaneous, open public discussion in a time of grave national crisis. The three regular speakers, Huxley, Joad and Campbell became household names, and their idioms of speech quickly became catch-phrases: 'It all depends what you mean' (Joad), 'When I was in Patagonia' (Campbell). At the height of the programme's popularity, *Life* magazine sent over its star photographer from the USA for a three-page photo-spread, and special filmed versions were recorded and shown in the Odeon cinema chain.[7] In London, political meetings were arranged according to *The Brains Trust* format, complete with question master.[8] They were, in Thomas's account, very successful, helping to dissolve the barrier between platform and audience, and displacing the solo performer, the drab speaker 'who trudged through his notes and unloaded his clichés on an unhappy audience' (Thomas 1944: 9). When millions of people had become accustomed to ready speech, ready wit and cogent arguments, Thomas predicted, they would have neither time nor patience for the old-style public speaker. *The Brains Trust* had two kinds of listener: those who attended to the substance of what was said – the 'earnest seekers after knowledge' – and those who were entertained by the personalities of the speakers, the crackle of opposing opinion, by the play of wit and the occasional sheer brilliance of the talk. The programme's format was a device for producing such effects; talk-in-public as an art, the art of conversation.

The recently developed history of conversation reveals something of the anxieties experienced, over the centuries, by people when, in social gatherings, they know they will be called upon to enter into conversation with strangers. Conversation, of course, leaves no historical trace, but since the beginning of book publishing, there has been a continuing flow of guides and manuals to conversation throughout Europe, offering advice to the anxious about how to succeed in this social art (Burke 1993: 89–122). Much of the advice, in the many European manuals and guides from the seventeenth century onwards, amounts to the kinds of common-sense considerations attended to by both the producer of, and the listeners to, *The Brains Trust*. Don't talk about yourself all the time; don't monopolize the talk; don't talk for too long; don't interrupt – such commonplace rules of conversation have, as Peter Burke notes, been passed on down through the centuries (Burke 1993: 94). The last point was particularly keenly felt by listeners to Joad and company. Howard Thomas notes that on one occasion a lady MP, who was particularly prone to jump in while others were talking, received over 800 letters of complaint. Equally listeners disliked too many ers and ums – guest speakers and McCullough were frequently taken to task for this failing. All listeners admired the felicity of fluent, extempore speech.

If we ask where, in England, such an art was supposedly cultivated, we return to the dinner table, or more exactly the high tables of nineteenth-century Oxford and Cambridge. At those tables, Matthew Arnold noted, there were 'professional conversationalists, as at the present time there are professional beauties' (St George 1993: 50). Those with a reputation as 'conversationalists' were, in the nineteenth century, frequently invited to dinner in the expectation that they would sparkle at the table while others would listen. They would go primed with a supply of information, anecdotes and witty epigrams that they had already prepared and committed to heart, and they arrived determined to get through their fund of talk no matter what (Benson 1906: 66). Joad granted that he, as a university professor, was quite at home with the idea of saying publicly what he thought about all manner of things because that, so to speak, went with the job. Pierre Bourdieu, in his monumental study of cultural distinctions as markers of social difference, discusses what he calls 'the entitlement effect' in relation to the academic elite in particular. By virtue of his status *as* a professor, someone like Claude Lévi-Strauss was, he argued, entitled to speak outside his own particular sphere of knowledge (anthropology), and indeed derived additional prestige from so doing (Bourdieu 1984: 22–5). It was thus entirely apt for someone who was, as the French say, an accredited *maître penseur*, to appear on radio or television talk-shows and hold forth on art, politics and the state of the world in general. Such publicly performed fluency is part of the job of being a public person.

Such persons were invariably men. In mixed social gatherings, women rarely spoke other than to admire, flatter or encourage males holding forth.[9] As for public speaking, women were invisible since there were virtually no openings for them in public life. Thus, finding good women speakers for *The Brains Trust* was one of Thomas's hardest tasks. Women, he declared, had never inspired affection on radio. They did not seem to radiate the warmth, geniality and friendliness a man could engender. They were more conscious of their radio audience, more inclined to think in terms of how they sounded to listeners and thus tended to become too self-aware and unnatural. It was hard to find a 'human' woman. They were over-careful and over-cultured in their speech and it was no easy matter to find women who could mix, 'in something of an after-dinner fashion with a company of men'.[10] In spite of all this, Thomas did discover some excellent regular women participants for the programme, most notably Agnes Hamilton, Jennie Lee, Dr Edith Summerskill and, above all, Barbara Ward, whose lucid answers and attractive style made her a favourite with listeners. These, along with Sir Malcom Sargent, Kenneth Clarke, Gilbert Murray, Sir William Beveridge and an unnamed 'eminent physician' (Lord Moran, Churchill's doctor) made up the roll-call of the best-liked regular guests on the programme in its first few years.

Today we assume that we are all entitled to our opinions; not merely to 'think' them, but to express them publicly and have them respected (or, at least, allowed) by others. At the start of the twenty-first century, the notion of discussing things in public and in private, as something that anyone and everyone does, is entirely unremarkable. But it was not always so. Broadcasting, in the last century, transformed our ideas about who was entitled to have opinions and on what. In the early twentieth century, in British society at least, there was a great deal that could not be talked about in private or in public. It was a conversational rule that sex, religion and politics were not suitable topics for discussion – or at least not in the presence of women, children or servants. The loosening of 'the universe of discourse' (of what can be talked about and by whom) is a feature of the second half of the twentieth century. It is intimately linked with the ubiquitous presence of radio and television broadcasting in the daily lives of whole populations whose combined effect has been the transformation of the social and political public sphere.[11]

From scripted to unscripted talk

The most basic characteristic of radio and television, as time-based media, is that they are potentially live-to-air and in real time. In live, real-time broadcasting, there is no interval between the production, transmission and reception of programmes, and in the early years of radio and, later, television, *all* broadcasting was live and in real time. In such circumstances, what is effective talk on air? The pre-war BBC Talks Department came gradually to see that the talk it produced for transmission should try to be like ordinary conversation. Listening to radio was a leisure activity, a pastime located in the contexts of ordinary, daily, domestic life. Radio talk, for it to become effective, had to learn to move from existing forms of public talk towards the usual forms of ordinary plain talk, the talk that goes on at home, at work or on the buses between families, friends or work colleagues. But the key difference between such talk and radio talk for the first 20 years or so of the BBC's activities is that all talk on radio was scripted in advance and read to air in live transmission.

Not the least of the benefits of scripted talk, from the BBC's point of view, was that it allowed complete institutional control over what could be said at the microphone. In other words it was, potentially, a form of censorship. Offensive, libellous or politically dangerous remarks could be (and were) pencilled out of the scripts submitted in advance to the Talks Department by those invited to speak at the microphone. So long as speakers stuck to the script, and they invariably did, there was no danger of them saying the wrong thing. There is no doubt that the control of live talk on radio through the requirement that it be scripted served, in part, as a useful way of eliminating in advance the possibility of something untoward or unacceptable being said on air. But this does not begin to explain why the production of live talk at the microphone should be such a desirable thing, nor why, when done well, it should meet with such instant acclaim as *The Brains Trust* did. For all its advantages in terms of control, the basic problem with scripted talk is that it is hearably so. Everyone can immediately hear the difference between scripted and unscripted talk. To our ears scripted talk sounds staged, artificial, flat, lacking in spontaneity and immediacy in comparison with what we take to be the *real* thing: spontaneous, natural, unscripted and, essentially, *live* talk. Pre-war talk on radio almost always meant *a* talk written and presented by an authority or expert of some sort; talk as monologue. Talk as discussion – a group of people freely holding forth on a range of given topics in the studio – did not exist.

The programme's immediate impact testifies to the pleasure of hearing real live talk between people, live on radio. Let us see how it was managed, bearing in mind that the key design consideration is that this talk should be something that listeners would, in fact, want to listen to. This means that it must somehow show, in the design of the talk, that it is managed with listeners in mind; that listeners can recognize that the talk produced on radio is, in the first place, for them. The talk in the studio is *between* those present but not, in the first place, *for* those present – it is for listeners who are not there. The radio audience is not an overhearing audience. To overhear means to listen to something not meant or intended for overhearing ears. If you tap into a telephone conversation, accidentally or not, you are eavesdropping on talk between two people producing talk with and for each other, but not for you, the lurking third party. Is radio talk like that? And if not, must it not be the case that talk-on-radio should somehow be evidently and hearably meant to be listened to by listeners?

In an essay on 'Conversation' written a decade or so before broadcasting began in Britain, A.C. Benson suggested that what was most needed in social gatherings was 'a kind of moderator of the talk, an informal president':

> The perfect moderator should have a large stock of subjects of general interest. He should, so to speak, kick off. And then he should either feel, or at least artfully simulate, an interest in other people's point of view. He should ask questions, reply to arguments, encourage, elicit expressions of opinions. He should not desire to steer his own course, but follow the line that the talk happens to take. (Benson 1906: 67)[12]

Such was the role of *The Brains Trust*'s question master, Donald McCullough, whose assigned task was to moderate the talk produced in the studio in the interests of absent listeners. McCullough, at all points in the broadcast, acted as the intermediary between the live interaction in the studio and the absent radio audience. He acted as the on-stage (on-air) manager of the talk in the studio. He introduced the programme and the speakers and brought it to a close. He read out the questions sent in by listeners, nominated the first speaker in response to them and monitored the ensuing discussion. The rules of engagement were few but vital. When McCullough read out the question, anyone who wished to speak could raise their hand but not speak until he had identified them by name. This served two purposes: it made it clear, for listeners, who was speaking and, at the same time, it prevented overlapping talk. In test trials of the programme, a laissez-faire speak-as-you-like policy was adopted. Such 'high involvement' talk may be exciting for participants but off-putting for audiences since it becomes hard to follow who is saying what or what is being said. The simple system of one-at-a-time was adopted in the interests of listeners, though at the possible expense, Thomas noted, of lively debate and discussion. It was a delicate task to find the right balance between encouraging spontaneity while, at the same time, ensuring that it did not become *too* spontaneous, with the speakers becoming so involved in the discussion that they forgot the primary consideration of absent listeners for whom, they were, first and last, performing.

If McCullough was the on-stage manager of the occasion, Thomas was its off-stage manager, and they worked in tandem. In attending to the voices of speakers, to how they sat at the table, to whether they spoke too quickly, or gesticulated too much, or talked at too much length; in considering the tempo of the talk as it unfolded, in occasionally changing the sequence of questions for greater balance and variety – in all these ways, Thomas dealt with the production of live-to-air discussion on radio as something whose communicative intention was that it should be found to be entertaining by its designated absent audience. If audiences did indeed find that it *was* an entertaining programme then, as I have tried to show, it was no accident. It was rather the meant and intended outcome of a wide-ranging set of considerations and stratagems which, separately and together, combined to produce talk-on-radio as something with enjoyably listenable properties for absent listeners. For audiences, and indeed for most academic analysts of broadcast output, radio and television programmes have a largely taken-for-granted character. The work that goes into their making is unnoticed by audiences and unconsidered by academics in their respective assessments and evaluations of what they have seen and heard. The virtue of making explicit the underlying significance of practical considerations and decisions in the production process is that it begins to account for how programmes do, as a matter of fact, work as that which they are found to be by broadcast audiences.

The administration of discussion on radio

In this account of *The Brains Trust*, I have tried to show a number of things: first that the transmission of the programme was a complex, thoughtful, pre-planned process, involving creative effort, care and attention to such technical matters as seating, microphone position, sound balance and so on, and such performative con-siderations as the speakers' voices, how they sounded, when they should speak, for how long – and more besides. And since the pro-gramme was recorded 'live-to-air' (i.e., without the luxury of retakes to redress technical problems or performative failures), it required careful preparation and planning to bring it off without glitches in its moment-by-moment recording for later transmission. None of this was visible; all of it was hidden from listeners. What should we make of this?

> Today conversation itself is administered. Professional dialogues from the podium, panel discussions, and round table shows – the rational debate of private people becomes one of the production numbers of the stars in radio and television, a saleable package ready for the box office; it assumes commodity form even at 'conferences' where anyone can 'participate'. Discussion, now a 'business', becomes formalized; the presentation of positions and counter-positions is bound to certain prearranged rules of the game; consensus about the subject matter is made largely superfluous by that concerning form. (Habermas [1962] 1989: 164)

This is the nub of Habermas's argument about the structural transfor-mation of the public sphere – the collapse of an early nineteenth-century bourgeois culture of active critical discussion in private life and its supersession by 'a public sphere that the mass media have transmog-rified into a sphere of culture consumption' (p. 162).[13] Talk in *The Brains Trust* was formalized and, yes, there were pre-arranged rules of turn-taking for this particular conversational game. It was, indeed, administered. But what, exactly, is the objection to this? Talk in public is not the same as talk in private. In the latter case, we speak amongst ourselves and how we speak is our concern and no-one else's. But talk-in-public is another matter. The speakers at the microphone are talking between themselves but not *for* themselves. Their talk is, at all points, produced for absent others and thus how it shall be heard is a public, not a private matter and an unavoidable, cardinal concern of the programme's production. This talk, it is true to say, was managed and administered, but *in the interests of listeners and for their sake*. On the basis of the available evidence, it seems safe to say that it was heard as such.

Listeners *were* interested in and engaged by unscripted discussion at the studio microphone.

Embedded in all aspects of the programme was a *care* for the listening experience that the programme was deliberately meant and intended to produce. What was the effect it aimed at, if not what Andrew Tolson calls the *liveliness* of live, unscripted talk-as-discussion at the microphone as an engaging experience for listeners (Tolson 2006: 12–13 and *passim*)? The administrative care of the programme had one aim – to produce talk that sounded as if it was not administered, not managed, not controlled, but seemingly impromptu, unrehearsed and spontaneous.

How to be sincere – on radio

Is that a trick and a deception? Academics might think so, but listeners did not. Ordinary talk at the microphone was, at the time, a novel and perplexing public phenomenon, not only in wartime Britain, but also in the USA. There was no contemporary academic research into the impact of radio in Britain at this time. In the USA, however, it was the sustained focus of attention in the emerging sociology of mass communication at Columbia University, pioneered by Paul Lazarsfeld and his colleagues. The picture we get of American society, from their work, is of an urban world characterized by chronic economic insecurity, exploitation at work, loneliness and distrust; a world inhabited by isolated vulnerable city dwellers who do not talk to each other. It is a world drained of meaningful experience. That is how Herta Herzog pictures her women interviewees in her pioneering study of what listening to radio means for them (Herzog 1941). Her subjects are mainly lower income women from New York who listen regularly to 15-minute episodes of daily serialized dramas on the radio. Her study of them is tellingly called 'On borrowed experience': radio soaps, as Herzog interprets them, are a compensation for lives shorn of meaning. They provide company for lonely individuals, an ersatz daily substitute for actual experience. Bernard Berelson's (1949) study of what the daily morning newspaper means for people (and how they felt without it during a six-week strike of New York journalists in 1945) concurs with Herzog's study of radio. For many readers, their daily paper is a comfort blanket, a source of security 'with which to counter the feelings of insecurity and anomie pervasive in modern society'. 'Anomie' was a key concept in the work of Robert Merton, one of the most influential sociologists of his generation. In his elegant study of *Mass Persuasion*, Merton glosses anomie as a sociological term to describe 'a social disorder [. . .] in which common values have been submerged in a welter of private interests'. It indicates 'a background of skepticism and distrust stemming from a prevalently manipulative society' (Merton [1946] 2004: 10). In the book's key chapter, on the social and cultural context of the study, America of the early 1940s is grimly described as existing in 'a climate of reciprocal distrust' and experienced by those who live in it 'as an arena of rival frauds' (Merton [1946] 2004: 143).[14]

And yet something else is peeping through in all this. There is a tension between the data and the academic interpretations of them. All the studies are liberally illustrated with quotes from the interviewees and (if we read with our ears) we hear the voices of ordinary men and women saying what the media mean to them. One woman, Herzog tells us, rings up her friend several times a week just to talk over what's going on in their favourite soap. A newspaper reader declares that 'you have to read in order to keep up a conversation with other people'. The newspaper, as Berelson comments, 'has conversational value', like the radio. There is a real discrepancy between Merton's interpretation of the radio broadcast that is the object of enquiry in *Mass Persuasion* and the responses to it of radio listeners. It is an investigation of what must rank as one of the earliest 'media events' – a newsworthy phenomenon created by radio, a radio event; in this case an all-day 'talkathon' in which the then famous radio singer, Kate Smith, urged listeners every 15 minutes for 18 hours to contribute to the latest government war bond drive. Forty million dollars worth of bonds were sold as a result of her efforts (see Scannell 2007: 64–70 for a fuller discussion of this classic study in the effects tradition).

Merton thinks of this as mass persuasion. The many voices of his text think of it quite differently: they hear Smith as a friend, as someone who speaks as a person and to them *personally*. Although Smith was one of the highest paid entertainers on radio with weekly earnings from her two shows alone of a staggering $17,000, she was still heard by listeners as an ordinary person, like you and me and everyone. And this was an effect of her projected 'self' on radio. She came across as a case of the genuine article, the real Kate Smith and she did so through the way she spoke to listeners:

- She was speaking *straight to me*.
- You'd think she was a personal friend. *I feel she's talking to me.*
- It seems that she's sitting in your kitchen and talking to you. *The way it would be with a friend.*
- She's spontaneous; her speech isn't forced. It's natural, *makes me feel I'm talking to my neighbor over the wash-line.* (Merton [1946] 2004: 61; original emphases)

This is how listeners hear her, and it is the effect, in part, as Merton notes, of a deliberately personalized discourse of you-and-me:

- *You* can help *me* send this war drive over the top.
- *You and I* might send this way over the top. (ibid.: 60)

The deictic markers ('you', 'me' and 'I') indicate an assumed and taken-for-granted relationship between speaker and listener(s), a relationship that is implicated in the use of such *personal* pronouns. If Smith is heard to speak as 'a person' and if listeners hear themselves addressed as 'persons' (and that is what they report), then this implicates an *inter-personal* relationship as an effect of the words that are used and the ways they are used. But it is not just the cosy use of 'you' and 'me' that produces this effect. Listeners hear themselves addressed as if they were in conversation with Smith – as if she was 'sitting in your kitchen and talking to you' or as if 'you were talking to [her as your] neighbor over the wash-line'. Merton notes and accounts for this conversational effect as cumulative. Through the day 'there was *reciprocal interplay*, for the audience was not only responding to Smith, but she was also responding to her audience and modifying her subsequent comments as a result' (p. 39; original emphasis). Thus 'the usual radio monologue became something of a conversation' (ibid.) in spite of the fact that this was scripted talk. Listeners know this and yet hear Smith speaking as if in her own voice, and not as the mouthpiece of others: 'When others say something, you know it's what their agent has written down' but 'with Kate Smith, she just talks what she thinks'. It is not what was written down, nor a matter of 'just talking words. It was she herself actually meaning it, *meaning it*, and wanting to have it strike home' (p. 84; original emphasis).

The key word that captures how Smith was heard by most listeners was *sincerity* and this, in the end, is an effect not of what she says, nor whether it is scripted or not, but of *how* she says it. Listeners to her believe in the sincerity of what Smith says, because she *sounds* to them as if she believes what she says in spite of her words being scripted for her by others. As Merton puts it: 'Groping for a distinctive and specific "cause" of their belief in Smith's genuine patriotism, *informants refer to her voice as manifestly sincere*' (p. 104; emphasis added):

- I know she was in earnest because of the way she talks. That can't just come from the mouth, it comes from the heart.
- It's in her speech. When she asks for anything, she gives it everything she's got. *It's in her tone. There's something in it that begs and asks; it's hard to explain.*

- She's so sincere. *It's her tone, no matter what she says, you sit there and listen.* (p. 104)
- She talks as *if she herself is going through all that. What she said she really felt herself*; you knew she wasn't just reading a script. (p. 105; all emphases as in the original)

The upshot of this – what the data disclose – is that listeners believed in Smith, because they *heard* her as sincere, and so they got on the phone and did what she asked them to do to the tune of 40 million dollars worth of war bonds. They did this because they heard her as friend, as someone like themselves, as someone they felt they knew personally. In short, they trusted her. And yet Merton thinks of American society as defined by mutual distrust, an arena for rival frauds; a society in which everyone is on the make and looking out for number one at the expense of everyone else. Commercial media are in the business of mass persuasion and, as such, epitomize the prevalently manipulative character of contemporary American society. Why, if this is so, do listener's not 'see through' Smith's performance? Are they cultural dopes? Lazarsfeld, who had persuaded Merton to study the Kate Smith broadcast, thought it was 'bizarre' – the whole affair was so obviously staged, in his retrospective opinion (Merton [1946] 2004: xlii–xliii). For both of them, what the data disclose – namely the novel phenomenon of sincerity as a valued aspect of talk on radio – is inexplicable.

I had not read *Mass Persuasion* when I was working, some years ago, on a preliminary study of the communicative ethos of radio and television in Britain that included a chapter on sincerity as an effect of the singing voice on radio (Scannell 1996). It was a case study of a famous wartime radio programme called *Sincerely yours, Vera Lynn*, the brainchild of the man responsible for *The Brains Trust*, Howard Thomas. I was amazed by Merton's study for I had looked at *exactly* the same thing in Britain at exactly the same time. Vera Lynn, I learnt from Smith's biographer, was regarded in the USA as the English Kate Smith, while she, in turn, was regarded in Britain as the American Vera Lynn (Hayes 1995: 57). Two famous radio entertainers of the day, then: each an extremely popular (and highly paid) singer with a weekly programme in which they not only sing but talk to their radio listeners. Their performative style, on either side of the Atlantic, is caught in a single word: sincerity. There was no equivalent sociological study of Vera Lynn at the time in Britain, for sociology as an academic discipline did not yet exist, so we do not know how she was heard by ordinary listeners. But the popular press of the day was unanimous in its verdict on her show, when it first aired in early 1942 (the year before Kate Smith's war bond broadcast):

- It's not only her fresh young voice, but – well, there's no other word for it – it's her sincerity. (*Woman's Illustrated*, 21 February 1942)
- Partly it's that low, caressing quality of her voice. But also in that voice you catch the simple sincerity of a humble girl unspoilt. (*Sunday Pictorial*, 1 February 1942)
- [It's] not only the completely natural, unstudied quality of her singing that reaches out to people's hearts: there's no other word for it – it's sincerity. (*Empire News*, 31 March 1942)

I too, like Merton, was struck by the discrepancy between the perception of the performer as ordinary and 'just like us' while she was, in fact, one of the highest paid entertainers of the day. I also noted how controversial Lynn's performative style was – much liked and admired by its audience, but regarded with disdain in the higher management circles of the BBC and elsewhere in the upper reaches of class-bound British society. She became, to her intense irritation, the butt of female satirists in smart metropolitan cabaret and revue on the London stage.

Thus the question of sincerity as a performance in public achieves social and cultural visibility in two very different places at exactly the same time and quite independently of each other. In each case it is widely liked and admired by the audiences for popular music and radio, but regarded with suspicion in the more educated upper reaches of society. How might we account for this historical phenomenon? It is surely more than a felicitous coincidence, this outbreak of sincerity in war-time America and Britain in the early years of the 1940s. We will not account for what is going on, however, if we simply attribute it to commercialism and consumerism – which is how Riesman, explicitly following Merton (p. 194n.3), understands what he calls, in a section header, 'the cult of sincerity':

> In a study of attitudes towards popular music we find again and again such statements as 'I like Dinah Shore because she's sincere,' or 'that's a very sincere record,' or, 'you can just feel he [Frank Sinatra] is sincere'. While it is clear that people want to personalize their relationships to their heroes of consumption and that their yearning for sincerity is a grim reminder of how little they can trust themselves or others in daily life, it is less clear just what it is that they find 'sincere' in a singer or other performer. (Riesman [1950] 2001: 194)

Is 'sincerity' no more than a projection by listeners of their subjective longings onto an object that objectively is the opposite of what they yearn for – a manipulative faking of sincerity for commercial (profit) motives? So how is sincerity to be accounted for as experienced by listeners in the voices of Smith and Lynn as they speak and sing? It is, as much as anything, the effect of technology. Sincerity, both in speech and singing, on radio and in gramophone recordings, is an effect of the microphone.

All technologies have pragmatic functions that shape and structure the scope and scale of their use. The microphone is a device for the amplification of sound and as such has implications for the social proxemics of the human voice in action. All radio output is reducible to two basic categories: music and talk. The radio microphone had profound consequences for the ways in which the human voice is deployed as it sings or speaks in front of it. Music is the easiest way of filling time on radio, and from the start to the present has always constituted the bulk of what is transmitted, everywhere. When singers came into radio studios in the early years of broadcasting to perform at the microphone, it was immediately found that they had to stand about six feet away from it otherwise they would shatter windows and the eardrums of listeners. Singing in public at the time required voices capable of filling a large auditorium, whether an opera house or a music hall, without the use of any technology to amplify the sound produced by the singer. Hence all performers in public learned to pitch their voices loud and strong for a large audience in a large public space and, in the case of opera, over the sound of a large orchestra. The microphone transformed the proxemics (the social space and hence the social relations) of singing. In the thirties, singers at the microphone discovered that they could stand close to the microphone and lower their voice instead of standing back and bawling at it. A new technique of 'close-mike' singing was developed in the USA and Britain, labelled 'crooning' at the time. This was not exactly a term of endearment and the new style was controversial on both sides of the Atlantic, but it did change how singers could use their voices and the experience of listening to singing. Kate Smith in the USA and Vera Lynn in Britain both used the microphone to sing and speak to their radio audiences.

The microphone transforms the spatial dynamics between the singer, the song and the listener, bringing all three closer to each other and thus into a more intimate, personal relationship in which the singing voice 'speaks' to an individual person rather than bellows at a large collective gathering in a large public space. Singing is personalized. The singer now performs in his or her own 'natural' voice, instead of the pervasively 'unnatural', artificial operatic voice that characterized the dominant style of singing in public before the coming of the radio. In the 1940s you heard the voice of Frank Sinatra as the voice *of* Frank Sinatra; that is you heard him singing in his own voice (not an artificial, 'operatic' voice) and as the person that he was and you heard his song as if it spoke to you, personally. That is why he was heard as sincere – as

Riesman noted. Close-mike singing is conversational in style (it implicates a you-and-me relationship). The words (what the song is saying) become more important. The voice, as it is lowered, as it comes closer to speaking or even murmuring, is heard as less artificial and more natural. It also is more expressive. It lacks the remarkable aesthetic range of operatic voices – nearly all close-mike singers are baritone or contralto – but what it lacks in vocal range it makes up for in a quite new range of expressiveness. More pathos, humour, sensuality and sexiness – in short, more personality and mood – can be projected by the singer crooning into the mike than the stage performer projecting out into the auditorium.[15]

What is true of the social relations of public singing is equally true of the social relations of public speaking. What was talk-in-public before radio and television? It largely consisted of a speaker and an audience in a defined public space. The lecture, the sermon and the political rally – these were the most familiar forms of public discourse in the early decades of the twentieth century.[16] In all of them, a public speaker addressed a crowd. Each had a distinctive performative rhetoric, a style of speaking, that marked it *as* the lecture, the sermon, the political harangue and underlined the status of the lecturer, the preacher, the politician as distinct from his (and public speakers were invariably male) massed audience of indistinguishable individuals. Again, as in styles of public singing before radio, public speakers must make themselves heard at the back of the assembly they addressed and they spoke as public persons, not as themselves, to an undifferentiated massed audience and not a constellation of individuals.

In Britain, it took the BBC Talks Department some time to learn how to talk to its absent audience of listeners. None of the existing models of public speaking was found to work and this for one overwhelming reason: the circumstance of listening to the radio did not correspond with the circumstances of listening to a lecture, a sermon or a political harangue. People listened to radio in their homes as part of domestic daily life. In that situation and those circumstances, listeners did not want to be lectured, preached at, harangued or generally 'got at'.[17] They wanted to be addressed by the radio in ways that were appropriate to the situations and circumstances in which they were listening. Broadcasters soon learnt to adapt a conversational style of address, to talk to the listeners 'out there' as if they were an audience of one, to draw them into a conversation. Conversation is a distinctive kind of talk. Perhaps its defining characteristic is best understood negatively. It is not institutional talk which pre-allocates speaker roles and the distribution of who says what. In the classroom, the surgery or the law court, one class of speakers controls and defines the interaction: teachers, doctors and lawyers ask questions and pupils, patients and plaintiffs answer them. Conversation in non-institutional situations and settings is a jointly managed interaction in which speaker-listener roles are evenly distributed and participants are equally involved in the business of starting it, keeping it going and closing it down. It presupposes a shared responsibility for the management of the interaction. Something of this is implicated in the new style of talk developed on radio and television and made possible by the communicative affordances of the microphone (what it allows for and facilitates).[18] To be sure, all talk on radio and television is institutional. Responsibility for what is said, first and last, resides always with the broadcasters who control the management of talk on radio and television. But it is oriented towards the norms of ordinary conversation in non-institutional settings, in everyday situations and circumstances, because that is where it is heard and responded to.

Whenever we turn on the radio or television today, we most likely will encounter, in any non-fictional programme, people in various situations producing unscripted, spontaneous talk of some kind or other. We are seldom aware, ordinarily, that this talk is something that has to be managed in ways that are specific to radio and television, because broadcast programmes do not, on the whole, reveal the conditions of their production. We are even less aware that there was once a time (now long gone) when broadcast talk was scripted. Practices have their histories too. Their recovery helps us understand that how broadcasting works is the outcome of accumulated knowledge and know-how, worked out as practical solutions to immediate issues at the time, and subsequently routinized as taken-for-granted institutional practice.

The ontology of voice

The programmes I have discussed are all indicative of the impact of talk as an interpersonal interaction in public. It was something quite novel – to hear spontaneous unscripted discussion at the microphone, or neighbourly, friendly sounding talk (though scripted) that was heard as sincere by many of Kate Smith's listeners. It is the microphone that produces these effects by virtue of the new social proxemics that it creates, bringing speakers and their listeners within the inter-personal space of a conversation. This de-severance transformed talk-in-public, hitherto the loud impersonal voice of a speaker in a one-to-many setting, into the voice of a person speaking 'as a person' (i.e., personally) to others as individual and particular persons. But what is it that we hear in the human voice as it speaks? We hear many things, all at once. Voice reveals the age and sex of the speaker. It may tell us where the speaker comes from and perhaps their social class. But above all what we hear in voice is the anima (the soul) of another living human being. In the animation of the human voice as it speaks, we hear the being of the speaker animated and brought to life. It is not an effect of what is being said, but the way it is said. The sound of our voice reveals how it is with us in our very being as we speak and perhaps against the grain of what we are saying. Our voice may sound heavy, flat, tired, edgy, happy, angry, bored, sad, frightened and much much more. Our ears are attuned to the mood of speakers as disclosed by what their voice expresses. We hear how it is with speaker right here and now: their living being (their soul) disclosed in the phenomenal now of utterance.

Sight has a primary evidential character: seeing is believing. Hearsay offers no such testamentary guarantee. But what we always hear in the human voice is the sound of life. The silence of the grave: the sounds of life. 'I am always overwhelmed' Derrida tells us, 'when I hear the voice of someone who is dead, as I am not when I see a photograph or an image of the dead person [. . .] I can be touched, *presently*, by the recorded speech of someone who is dead. I can, *here and now*, be affected by a voice beyond the grave' (Derrida 2001: 71). And why? Because recording technologies capture and preserve the living human voice that comes to life again each time in every replay. For Derrida (and for me) 'the recording of the voice is one of the most important phenomena of the 20th century for it gives to living presence a possibility of "being there" anew that is without equal and without precedent' (Naas 2012: 142). The defining ontological characteristic of the human voice is liveness. The liveness of radio and television is not an effect of visual immediacy but of the sounds of life that the invisible production care-structures of both media *animate* for listeners and viewers in live-and-recorded transmission.

Try watching television without sound . . . a soccer match, say. It is lifeless. To experience the game, you must *hear* it. Seeing it is not enough. Television is not *just* or even primarily 'a visual medium'. It is the combination of all the sounds – the crowd, the commentary and all the ambient background noise – that brings the occasion to life. 'The power of television', Derrida rightly observes, 'is vocal' (Derrida 2001: 71). Glossing this observation, Michael Naas notes that 'whereas the image can always be questioned in its purity and presence, the voice presents itself to experience as much more natural, much more alive, and so much less suspect' (Naas 2012: 142). Radio and television problematize what it is that we see in seeing and hear in hearing. Real or not, genuine or not, sincere or not, in short, true or not – such questions are unavoidably posed in respect of everything that we hear and see via broadcast tele-technologies. The unscripted sounds more spontaneous (more genuine, more natural: less planned and controlled, less staged and artificial). It seems to guarantee the authenticity of what is being said and thereby the authenticity of the speaker. It contributes to an effect of sincerity; the speaker as a case of the real and genuine thing, the one-and-only truly authentic 'me'. But sincerity involves a performative paradox when it passes out of the domain of everyday life and onto radio and television. We all know that everything on radio and television is a performance (we know this because that is what both media have taught us). But can sincerity be performed? And if it can be performed, then it can be faked. Sincerity which depends on naturalness, spontaneity and genuineness, secures its effect by its apparent effortless artlessness. It is harder to secure this effect on television when you are acutely aware of being looked at. On radio, looks do not matter, but on television they are unavoidably crucial: the look of those *on* television in relation to the look *of* television – a look that is produced always with the absent on-looking viewer in mind. How to be on television, while subject to its unblinking gaze, is no natural thing, as we shall see when we turn to examples of early live television programmes that tried to produce unscripted, spontaneous conversation for absent on-looking viewers in America and Britain.

9

How to talk – on television

Person to Person (CBS 1953–9)

Person to Person began on 2 October 1953. The concept was simple: 15 minutes or less of talk between Ed Murrow, in a New York CBS studio, and famous Americans in conversation with him from their own home. Prospective participants in the show received a letter of invitation in which Murrow professed to

> an old-fashioned belief that all of us are curious to see how others live – particularly those we've read or heard about but seldom, if ever, had an opportunity to meet ... What we hope to do is ask our guests to show us about the house and then sit down for a little informal talking. Who knows, in spite of television, it may still be possible to revive the art of conversation. (Persico 1988: 344)

The problem was that Murrow was not very good at chit-chat, the technology was new and cumbersome and the guests often uncomfortable (Sperber 1986: 424). Reviews at the time were mixed at best. *Time* magazine, commenting on the first broadcast thought it was 'substandard Murrow, marked by aimlessness and silliness'. Gilbert Seldes, perhaps the most influential American cultural critic of the time, deplored the show as a betrayal of Murrow's talents – a view shared at the time by many of his friends and co-workers in radio and television.

Murrow was one of the most famous broadcasters of his day. He was a pioneer of radio journalism in the run-up to the Second World War, and his legendary broadcasts to America from London during the blitz made him a household name. After the war he switched to television and led the way in the development of television news and investigative journalism. He and Fred Friendly co-produced *See it Now*, a weekly news and current affairs program that courted controversy. Its greatest moment came in 1954 when the show took on Senator Joe McCarthy, exposing him as a bully and a liar. The program won public approval and critical plaudits, but its ratings were never high and it struggled to maintain sponsorship. After a few years it was broadcast only occasionally, not in a prime time slot and without advertising sponsorship to sustain it. *Person to Person*, on the other hand, did well in the ratings, never lacked sponsorship and millions of Americans who never tuned in to *See it Now*, watched it week after week – 8.3 million of them by 1958. In CBS the two shows came to be seen as epitomizing a split between a 'high' and 'low' Murrow and, by extension, between highbrow (good) and lowbrow (bad) television. Murrow was more at home in the former than the latter, but while *See it Now* brought him elite peer approval and critical esteem, *Person to Person* made him moderately rich and widely known to ordinary Americans. It also eventually embroiled him in the great television quiz show scandal of the late 1950s.

In 1958 it became publicly known that one of the most popular shows on television, *Twenty One*, was rigged from beginning to end. Viewers had believed that contestants – drawn from the general public – genuinely struggled to come up with answers to questions of which they had no foreknowledge. As they mopped their brows and muttered to themselves, the tension in the studio increased as the rewards grew. It was hugely popular – and completely fixed. Contestants were given the answers in advance and were coached in how to perform on television for a live studio audience and the vast viewing public. Winners were chosen for their audience appeal, losers given a small pay-off for taking a dive. When the story of game-fixing broke (it was not strictly speaking illegal, since there were no regulations in place), it created uproar and a huge sense of betrayal. President Eisenhower called it 'a terrible thing to do to the American people' who had, in all good faith, taken at face-value what was, in fact, a deception. The networks scrambled to protect themselves from further revelations. In March 1959, Frank Stanton, president of CBS, publicly promised transparency in all the network's programs, including *Person to Person* whose participants knew the questions they would be asked. Conversation, he seemed to imply, like game shows, was rigged in advance. Murrow was outraged and responded through the *New York Times* who ran a front-page story headlined 'MURROW SAYS STANTON CRITICISM SHOWS IGNORANCE OF TV METHOD'. 'Surely', he was quoted as saying, 'Stanton must know that cameras, lights and microphones do not just wander round a home. Producers must know who is going where and when and for how long . . . the alternative would be chaos' (Sperber 1986: 579).

The issues at stake in this controversy go to the heart of the management of live broadcasting on radio and television. Any live-to-air transmission involves pre-planning and rehearsal. The alternative, as Murrow points out, would be chaos. And yet the problem with *Person to Person*, as we shall see in a moment, was that it was too obviously rehearsed. The planning and preparation was visible in live transmission, generating a sense of 'staginess' in the viewing experience. The crux of all live broadcasting is that it must, on the one hand, be pre-planned and prepared in manifold ways. And yet all this (the program's care structure) must be invisible, must vanish into the immediacy of the transmission itself and the immediacy of its experience. If the efforts of production and transmission of the live speech-act-event begins to show, it punctures the effect of live immediacy for audiences. The immediate now is the base, the bedrock, of live broadcasting upon and with which broadcasters work in order to create programs with 'program values'. Program values are most fundamentally to do with their listenability and watchability. Broadcasting takes live connectivity (immediacy) as its starting point. Working with the extraordinary constraints that this imposes (the ever present possibility of technical failure and human error), broadcasters work to produce the immediacy of the living moment as an experience for any listener or viewer. This transformation calls for a sustained, focused attentiveness to what they see and hear. And, of course, it requires a great deal of pre-meditated care and preparation (any program's fore-structure) in order to produce an effect of unpremeditated live immediacy.

The awkward effect

Person to Person was broadcast live-to-air and recorded on tele-cine. The earliest television cameras were designed for studio use and were similar in some respects to the film studio camera. There were equally important differences, however, in the quality of the image that each produced, but especially in the circumstances of their use in the production process. Like the film camera, the TV studio camera was large and heavy and hard to move about quickly in any direction. Neither camera could respond rapidly (spontaneously) to what is going on around it and hence things had to be arranged to happen in front of it (what film studies calls the 'pro-filmic' – the carefully pre-planned shot designed and framed 'for' the camera to record). *Person to Person* had a stagey look and feel to it as we shall see in a brief discussion of a very early program (31 October 1953) in which Murrow conversed with the newly married John F. Kennedy and also his wife, Jacqueline.

We start in the New York studio of CBS with Ed Murrow speaking direct to camera.

EM: I'm told that all little boys have dreams.
Some of them want to be policemen.
Others would like to be a football star.
Others would like to be the skipper of a navy ship
Or perhaps a United States Senator.
Or married to a most attractive bride.
Senator John Kennedy of Massachusetts has
accomplished all these things
In his thirty six years except being a policeman
(0.5)
The Kennedys were married last month
They're still looking
(cut to profile shot of Murrow)
for a place to live in Washington
On weekdays
(cut to exterior of apartment block)
they stay in Boston
(Slow zoom in on Kennedy apartment)
at what used to be the bachelor establishment of the
senator.
It's on the third floor of this building that you're looking
at now
Over a barber shop just on the edge of Beacon Hill **(end
of zoom)**
Five blocks away is North Church where the lanterns
were hung
on the night of Paul Revere's famous ride.
The Boston massacre took place not far from here.
But so much for history . **(repeat of profile shot)**
Let's go and meet the newly weds
Are you there Senator? **(cut to Murrow looking at the
Kennedys in their apartment)**
JFK: Yes right here Mr Murrow

The first change of shot – to Murrow in profile
looking at the 'magic' studio window through which
the Kennedys' apartment block can be seen – matches
the discursive change from the introductory topic
(Senator John Kennedy and his achievements) to
his marriage and where he and his bride are now living. The magic
window shot gives way to a slow zoom (in focus) in on a window of the
Kennedy apartment as Murrow reads aloud from his notes on where
they live. The next shot, which returns to the studio with Murrow in
profile, shows him now looking at Senator and Mrs Kennedy in their
apartment. Persons and place – the two key deictic components of
the program – have been established for the viewer who is, from the

start, implicated both visually and discursively as a participant in a live three-way interaction, courtesy of 'television', between Murrow in a New York CBS studio, the Kennedys in their Boston home, and millions of viewers in their homes.

After a brief opening conversation with Mrs Kennedy about the wedding, Murrow asks the Senator if he would 'show us around your uh uh apartment for a bit'. Both of them rise from the couch they have been sitting on and Mrs Kennedy leaves the room as her husband moves towards a small table with a photograph on it: the next conversational topic. A close-up shows it to be a photograph of the whole Kennedy family taken in England, as Kennedy tells us, in 1939 – just before the start of the war. The last time they were all together. 'Well, Senator', Murrow says, 'you had some anxious moments during the war – you were in PT boats,[1] weren't you?' This cues Kennedy to move to a table against the wall in another part of the room. On the table is a model boat and beside it a round object and these turn out to be the next two topics of conversation. The boat is a replica of the one that Kennedy commanded in the war and which was almost sliced in half (with Kennedy on board) by a Japanese naval destroyer. The crippled boat made it to shore a week later on the remote and tiny Pacific island of Nauru, and Kennedy tells a rather obscure story of how he gave a coconut with a message written on it to a native islander. It turns out that the round thing beside the model boat is that same coconut, preserved and mounted as a memento. Kennedy picks it up as he talks of it and when he's finished Murrow asks; 'Senator, what's that picture just above the coconut there on the wall?' Cut to a close-up of an American naval battle ship which, as it happens, is named after Kennedy's eldest brother Joseph ('Joe Jnr') killed in action during the Normandy landings in the European theatre of the war. There's one other thing on the table which Kennedy picks up as he finishes explaining the painting. It's a letter he tells us that he received a year ago, from the commander of the Japanese destroyer that sliced into his boat, wishing him well – and he proceeds to read it aloud for viewers.

That exhausts the topic of the war and the strategically placed conversational objects related to it. Kennedy now returns to the sofa in the middle of the room and sits down as Murrow asks him a couple of political questions (one about the Cold War; the other about the Taft-Hartley law),[2] which Kennedy answers at some length. Mrs Kennedy returns and sits down beside him holding an American football: the next conversational cue.[3] It's from Harvard and its Jack's favourite wedding present, she tells us. Another question on domestic affairs elicits another lengthy reply from her husband as Mrs Kennedy sits gamely beside him staring into the middle distance. And then there's an abrupt topic change:

> **EM**: Um do you do you uh have a chance to do much reading?
> **JFK**: Yes uh well (.) I used to very much
> 'nd I uh try to do as much as I can now
> **EM**: Have you found anything that uh
> has been particularly useful for uh
> perhaps I could use the word 'inspirational' to you?
> **JFK**: Well I uh do have something here (*reaches for book behind the sofa*)
> written by Alan Seeger who as you'll remember
> was uh born in New York
> 'nd uh fought in the Foreign legion
> 'nd uh was killed in the First World War in 1916 (.)
> he wrote that famous poem 'I have a Rendezvous with Death'
> 'nd uh just before he died he wrote a letter home to his mother
> which I think has good advice for all of us.
> He said (*reads letter*) . . .

And that's it. After Alan Seeger's uplifting words, Murrow briefly thanks Senator Kennedy and the program ends. It has lasted exactly 11 minutes and 43 seconds.

The program limps along with a leaden predictability, heavily semaphored by Murrow's questions and Kennedy's movements from one darn thing to another – the photograph, the model boat, the coconut, the painting, the football that Mrs Kennedy just happens to return with and the all too conveniently placed book on the back of the sofa. The staginess of it all is compounded by the peculiarly awkward dynamics of the interaction set-up between Murrow in New York, and the Kennedys in their Boston apartment. Why didn't Murrow just go to Boston and talk to them in their apartment? He couldn't. Each half hour program consisted of two live interviews with different people in different places. The resulting dynamics, however, of the remote two-way interaction

between Murrow and his guests produced some strikingly odd visual moments as framed by the immobile television cameras.

The first glimpse of the Kennedys at home comes as Murrow, having invited viewers to meet the newlyweds, inquires 'Are you there, Senator?' A cut from the exterior apartment block to the interior of the Kennedy apartment displayed on the studio 'magic window' produces a curious visual composition. Kennedy is in fact replying to Murrow – 'Yes right here Mr Murrow', he is saying in his flat Bostonian drawl – but that is not apparent from the image that frames his reply. There was no TV monitor in the apartment displaying Murrow to the Kennedys, but only a speaker at which their gaze is directed in this opening shot. They are speaking to where they hear Murrow coming from, but the studio shot produces Murrow as an observer of an interaction in the apartment in which the Kennedys appear to be talking with an invisible someone other than himself. When Murrow switches to Mrs Kennedy, she too continues gazing in the same direction as she replies to his question. The overall effect is of a strange visual disconnect between the distant parties to the conversation.

Movement is tricky for the bulky cameras in the small Bostonian apartment. When Murrow closes the opening conversation on the wedding with a request to the Senator to 'show us around the apartment', Kennedy moves away from the camera and Mrs Kennedy appears to walk into it as she makes her departure. On her return, with the football, she momentarily swamps the screen and distracts her momentarily startled husband from his conversation with Murrow. Later, when Kennedy, by invitation from Murrow, is reading from Alan Seeger's inspirational text, a cutaway studio shot shows Murrow busy lighting up yet another cigarette. Mrs Kennedy, sitting beside her husband, appears to be listening with all due attention to the inspiring words of the poet to his mother. Murrow in the studio is apparently more interested in his cigarette.

The awkward staginess of the program as it unfolds and its visual solecisms along the way are compounded by its conversational infelicities. It had set itself an awkward task, for a three-way conversation is more difficult to bring off effectively on television than a two-way, since the third person, at any moment, will appear to be excluded from the inter-action – two's company, three's a crowd. It is a delicate task to maintain a balance between the participants in a three-way so that none seems left out or marginalized. Talk on television is not some simple one-size-fits-all kind of thing. There are different kinds of talk for different kinds of broadcast occasions and all had to be discovered and worked at to produce forms of talk appropriate to the situations in which and for which they were intended. The elements of the political interview had already been worked out, by Murrow no less, on early network televi-sion. But how to produce 'conversation' was at that exact moment a journey into the discursive unknown for *Person to Person*. It was the first venture, by the then new medium of television, into the home. What kind of talk is appropriate to that particular situation – what is the talk that takes place in homes everywhere? The answer is of course chat or conversation. The stated aim of *Person to Person* was to revive the *art* of conversation – on, but in spite of, television. What, however, is that art?

How (not) to talk on television

Conversation-as-art was formalized and cultivated as such by a privi-leged leisured class, the French nobility of the seventeenth century and reached full flower in the pre-revolutionary salon culture of the eighteenth century (Craveri 2005). The aim of this novel salon culture, hosted by aristocratic women, was to bring the sexes together for the sake of agreeable, witty, entertaining conversation. In this remarkable, utterly artificial milieu, men and women came together on equal terms and momentarily enjoyed the purely sociable pleasure of each other's company expressed and experienced through the sparkle of freely flowing talk between them. It was quite pointless and unnecessary and that was the mark of its freedom. Conversation acquires this distinctive meaning in the period of early modernity. It meant a social gathering, an 'at-home'; a meaning shared with the Italian *conversazione* – an evening gathering for informal conversation and recreation or, more formally, an educational *soirée* or social gathering for discussion of the arts, literature and science. Such talk, while it aspired to be a free and spontaneous pleasurable thing in itself, was never without its artificial side. It always required careful management – the preoccupation of any good society hostess – and was seldom without anxieties for its participants; hence the ceaseless flow of conversational manuals with advice on what to do and what not to do in order to 'make' agreeable and 'good' conversa-tion (Burke 1993). British society hostesses of the nineteenth century would invite 'professional' male conversationalists (most famously, Oscar Wilde) to their dinner tables. They went already primed with the anecdotes and witty throw-away remarks that they would work into the table talk which it was their task to enliven – for their talk was their meal ticket, as it was for prized conversational wits of lowly rank (such as Diderot and Voltaire) in the aristocratic French salons of the preceding century (St George 1993).

Murrow was a professional talker – on radio first and then television. But he was not good at making conversation:

> **EM:** Are you there Senator?
> **JFK:** Yes right here Mr Morrow
> **EM:** Good evening sir
> **JFK:** Thank you
> **EM:** Good evening Mrs Kennedy
> **JLK:** Good evening
> **EM:** I er understand that the two of you had a very much publicized courtship
> uh how did the two of you meet?
> **JLK:** We met um at the house of a friend about three years ago
> (.)
> **EM:** And you ah used to be a reporter didn't you?
> **JLK:** Yes I did
> **EM:** And you (.) uh first met the Senator when you interviewed him?
> **JLK:** Well I met – I interviewed him shortly after I met him
> (.)
> **EM:** Well now which requires the most diplomacy
> To interview senators or to be married to one?
> **JLK:** Um (0.7) well (.) eheh (0.5) I gue-
> **JFK:**   [overlapping] being married to one I guess (.)eheh
> **EM:** Well uh 'uv have you opened all your wedding gifts?
> **JLK:** Well I've opened quite a few of them
> 'nd I've sent them all to Washington (.)
> We just have a couple back here
> **EM:** Uhuh
> (0.5)
> uh Senator I wonder if you would show us around your apartment for a bit

This less than sparkling exchange with Mrs Kennedy has several stumbling moments. Murrow has his list of questions and he sticks with it. Mrs Kennedy has said that she and 'the Senator' first met at a friend's house. Yet Murrow persists with his prepared line that 'you first met the senator when you interviewed him' and is gently corrected by Mrs Kennedy in reply. He then comes up with another crafted question that floors Mrs Kennedy who is momentarily lost for words and rescued by her husband with an answer on her behalf. Murrow turns to the topic of 'wedding presents', shows no interest in the reply and abruptly switches to the Senator. At no point here or later is Mrs Kennedy integrated into the program as a participant on an equal footing with her husband. She is seemingly there as yet another conversational object along with the photograph, the model boat, the coconut and the football in a program almost exclusively about Senator Kennedy. At the very end she is conversationally disappeared by Murrow in his closing thanks. 'Well Senator Kennedy thank you very much for letting us come to visit you and will you also express our thanks to Mrs Kennedy'. Mrs Kennedy is in plain sight sitting beside the Senator as Murrow says this, but it is as if she is not there in the room with him.

Asking questions is what interviewers do in an interview – a form of talk invented by radio and television in the first place for dealing with politicians. But asking questions is not the same as 'making' conversation. These two different forms of talk have different objectives and different techniques. The object of the interview is to extract information and to persist in this should the interviewee prove reluctant to part with it. It is a strategic, instrumental form of talk with a particular focused objective. The object of conversation, however, is talk for its own sake – talk-as-entertainment as an end in itself. Murrow knows how to talk to Kennedy. He can elicit information about the Senator's (very famous) family and his wartime experiences. He knows how to ask a politician political questions. But he does not know how to talk to Mrs Kennedy. He has no conversational skills. He has no small talk. Small talk is made of pleasantries which make it pleasant (pleasing). Murrow cannot do this. He can talk man to man but he cannot talk to a woman. He just lobs his pre-planned interview questions at Mrs Kennedy, without modifying them in response to what she says. He does not know how to play the conversational game. Mrs Kennedy is visibly smiling to herself as she exits after her brief exchange with him. She had virtually no purpose on the program except, as Persico points out, 'to play a stylized fifties wife – to be there, a worshipping smile on her face, an attractive ornament' (Persico 1988: 348). The art of conversation had been cultivated by high-born French women of the eighteenth century as a way of bringing the sexes together for the sake of sociability. The stated ambition of *Person to Person*, in its letter of invitation to participants, was to revive it – to bring it back to life. Its resuscitation, however, proved difficult for Murrow.[4] He was ill at ease with glamorous women,[5] and the peculiarities of interaction at a distance (from studio to remote location) compounded his conversational woes.

At Home

Three years later in 1956 the BBC launched *At Home*, a little programme series with exactly the same aim as *Person to Person* and in a
very similar format. The Outside Broadcasting Department took its
cameras into the homes of well-known persons in British public life for
a short, live transmission in which the chosen public person interacted
for their cameras with the BBC's Richard Dimbleby. Dimbleby was the
best known and most respected broadcaster in Britain at that time – a
counterpart in many respects to Murrow in the USA. He had joined the
BBC's then very new radio News Department in 1936 as a reporter,
and had pioneered the eyewitness report, live and into the news, before
the outbreak of the Second World War. During the war he was, for
the first few years, the leading and virtually only BBC newsman actually reporting from the war zones. He and Murrow knew each other as
broadcasters in wartime Britain. Dimbleby's skill as a conversationalist
was developed in a very popular radio programme called *Down Your
Way* (something of a model for *At Home*) in which Dimbleby would
visit an English country town or village to engage some selected locals
in small talk. His reputation as *the* BBC commentator on state occasions was confirmed for life by his coverage of the Coronation of Queen
Elizabeth II in June 1953. His abilities as an interviewer were honed on
Panorama which began in 1954 and remains to this day the BBC's flagship weekly current affairs programme.

Outside broadcasts – known as OBs – were regarded by the BBC in
the 1950s as the jewel in their television crown and the OB Department
was the most prestigious one in which to work in the very early years.
OBs were mainly used for live coverage of sport and special public
occasions (most notably the Coronation) and were regarded as the
main reason why people went out to buy television sets. They provided
direct, immediate live access to the world and what was going on in it.
But now and then OB resources were used to make what were called
'feature' programmes about people and places *in situ*, allowing them
to be seen in their own and proper habitus by the new viewing public.
At Home was an OB feature programme and, in the transmission I will
come to in a moment, its cameras accompanied Richard Dimbleby on a
visit to Lambeth Palace, the home (more exactly, the residence) of the
Archbishop of Canterbury and his wife.

At Home, like *Person to Person*, filled a half-hour slot of television
time, broadcast live and simultaneously recorded on tele-cine. The
visit to Lambeth Palace contained two filmed sequences – one right
at the beginning, the other halfway through – that had been shot and
edited ahead of time by the small BBC Film Unit (then a sub-division

of OBs) for inclusion in the live transmission. They were shot on the then standard 35mm camera used in the film industry. Both sequences were soundless, with a static, photographic quality. The first is mainly of the exterior of Lambeth Palace: the building and its gardens, with a look inside at the library. It is accompanied by a voice-over commentary written and spoken by Dimbleby. The second sequence shows more of the palace's interior: the chapel and the picture gallery of dead archbishops.

The opening sequence starts with a shot of Parliament and then pans slowly right to a view of Lambeth Palace on the opposite bank of the Thames. This establishing shot makes visually explicit the close proximity of Church and State in Britain, a key motif in the ensuing conversation with Dr Geoffrey Francis Fisher. Superimposed on it are the opening credits in copperplate. The use of this font hints at a more specific meaning of *At Home* in the 1950s,  which has since disappeared from English usage. It invokes a social practice in place since the nineteenth century and on the point of extinction at the time of the broadcast. It was customary in Victorian and Edwardian 'polite society' for people (almost always the lady of the house) to be 'at home' at certain times on certain days of the week.[6] This meant that she was available to be visited not just by friends or family but by any member of the same social milieu who chose to call. It was a well-established ritual occasion: callers would present their visiting card to the servant who answered the door bell. The visiting card displayed in copperplate the caller's name and address, hence the use of this font for the opening credits. The servant presented the calling-card to the lady of the house who would then decide whether she was or was not at home to this particular visitor. If not, the snubbed caller would be told that the lady of the house was not 'at home'. If she decided to be at home, the caller would be ushered into the drawing room by the servant, and a very English ritual of tea and small talk would then ensue.

As the introductory film sequence about the Palace of Lambeth ends, there is a smooth cut to the imposing main staircase of the palace and Dimbleby, now live on air, welcomes viewers to the programme:

Dimbleby: And it's here at the top of the main staircase of the palace that you join us at this moment. It's here in fact that the Archbishop usually greets his guests

And if I may say so your Grace
it's very good of you
to let us invade you in Lambeth Palace tonight
Fisher: Well I'm delighted (.)
more or less er (.)
to receive you here.
Now let's go into my study and put me through it
Dimbleby: Thank you (.) we will

What is apparent in this brief exchange is a shared sense of the invasive, intrusive character of television for which acknowledgement and thanks must still be given. A few years earlier the BBC had fought a vigorous campaign to persuade the royal advisers and the same Archbishop of Canterbury to allow its television cameras to broadcast the coronation of Queen Elizabeth live from inside Westminster Abbey. Fisher (who conducted the religious ceremony) at first resisted. He thought television 'too enquiring' and the presence of its cameras would be 'a gross violation of the rightful intimacy of the service' (Wolfe 1984: 498). Gradually, reluctantly, Fisher and the other lay authorities relented as they came to appreciate the value of the young queen being seen to be crowned before all her people and not just the privileged few present at the service itself. Even so, the BBC still had a struggle to get its cameras in position for full coverage of the service in the abbey. At first Fisher was willing to allow the cameras inside the church only at the west door. This was the entrance to the nave where most of the distinguished congregation was to be seated. From there, only a very distant and restricted line of sight to the altar was available, for it and the choir stalls were separated from the nave by a massive rood screen. Further tortuous negotiations at last resulted in the cameras being allowed east of the screen with full visual access to the ceremony. There then followed further protracted debate about what kinds of camera shot were and were not permitted: no close-ups and, at particularly solemn sacred moments, symbolic shots of sacred objects were to be substituted for shots of the personnel most closely involved in the service at that moment (Scannell 1996: 80–3).

Dimbleby had been the BBC's commentator in the Abbey for the coronation ceremony. There was doubtless a hint of that past battle in his courteous thanks to the Archbishop for now allowing Lambeth Palace, just across the river from the Abbey, to be 'invaded' by television. Fisher in turn is less than wholly delighted to receive the BBC[7] and seems to regard the whole thing as a bit of an ordeal as he invites Dimbleby into his study to 'put me through it'.

Maintaining a smooth flow of chatter as he steers Fisher to his prearranged position for the cameras in front of the imposing mantelpiece

in the study, Dimbleby now begins the formalities of
the occasion:

> **Dimbleby**: Now sir you to to identify you.
> are Dr Geoffrey Francis Fisher.
> the ninety ninth Archbishop of Canterbury
> **Fisher**: That is correct

This, on the face of it, is a deeply uninformative conversational gambit, for clearly Dimbleby knows who
he's talking to and presumably Fisher knows who he is as well. It is, of
course an introduction on behalf of that absent third party, the television viewing audience, which is now provided with three facts about
the person addressed: that his name is Dr Geoffrey Francis Fisher, that
he is the Archbishop of Canterbury, and that he is the 99th incumbent
of this office. To which of these three facts about himself does Fisher
respond?

> **Fisher:** That is correct (.)
> you've been doing some mathematics
> **Dimbleby:** (*sotto voce*) I have
> **Fisher:** I've been called everything from the
> ninety seventh to the hundred and third.
> .hhh but I am the ninety ninth(.)
> Saint Augustine being the first

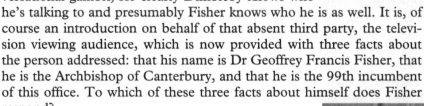

Dimbleby's conversational opener furnishes Fisher with immediate possibilities in terms of developing the topic as to who *exactly* he is. Of the
three facts presented, one is more vulnerable than the others. Fisher's
own name and current status as head of the Anglican church are pretty
unarguable facts about him, but that he is, in fact, the 99th holder of
the office is more contestable, as Fisher himself goes on to make clear.
It is a more questionable and thereby more 'talkable-about' datum
than the other two items of information. Dimbleby's *sotto voce* overlapping acknowledgement that he has, indeed, been doing some maths
implies that he has done his preparatory work before this conversation.
That, of course, is part of his job as a broadcaster and Dimbleby was
famously diligent in his pre-broadcast preparations. While name and
occupational status are the commonplace facts about certain kinds
of broadcast interviewees (those who are being interviewed by virtue
of what they do) that are established immediately by interviewers,
the extra datum is strictly surplus to the situational requirements of
the broadcast interview. So its motivated inclusion may be meant to
serve as a conversational offering. It furnishes a topical resource – it is

remarkable and thereby talkable-about – and is immediately treated as such by the person to whom it is offered. As this conversation unfolds, the preliminary 'fact' that Fisher is the 99th Archbishop serves as a basis upon which to explore the function of the Anglican arch-episcopacy of Canterbury within the long tradition and history of British church and state relations. This tiny speech fragment sets the direction and tone for the whole of what follows.

Dimbleby amiably encourages Fisher to say more about himself and he cheerfully does so. All his life, he tells us, he has been 'in the unhappy situation of telling other people what to do' – first as headmaster of Repton,[8] then as Bishop of Chester, followed by London and, finally, as Archbishop of Canterbury. Dimbleby underlines for viewers his exalted rank and status as head of the Anglican Church and as one of the most senior lay officers of the state: 'For you rank before the prime minister and immediately after the royal family.' Having thus established for his audience the eminence of the person to whom he is speaking, Dimbleby now steers the conversation to a matter that is, he claims, very much in the minds of people at this time; divorce and the feeling many people have that the church is 'a bit em (.) I don't know if "old-fashioned" is the word for its attitude'. Fisher robustly dismisses all criticisms of the church's position:

> We're fighting a great popular wave of stupid emotionalism.
> We are fighting it and winning the battle [. . .]
> We are the only people who are looking to see
> what effect will this matter of divorce have
> upon the well-being and wholesomeness of the nation
> in five years . ten years from now.
> And we are looking forward
> to see that the nation remains stable in its moral basis

Could there be, Dimbleby wonders, a change in the Church's law on divorce (which then excluded divorced men and women from the Anglican Communion)? Good Lord no, exclaims the Archbishop. And even if we wanted to, it would take 15 or 20 years to bring about change. So, says Dimbleby somewhat obscurely, there could be no question of changing the present law in the last few months to suit any particular case? Oh dear no, no chance at all, the Archbishop replies. Now the point of the preceding question – and indeed the drift of the whole discussion of the Church's attitude to divorce – becomes clear at last in Dimbleby's final question, for it is that towards which all that has gone before is carefully leading:

And one other question if I may ask you sir
and one I think that is burning very much in the minds
of many millions of people today
(0.4)
the the case of er Princess Margaret's decision about her
plans.
I imagine that most people in the country
must think that you as Archbishop
was very closely connected with that decision
(1.0)
Could you say something about that?

And one other question,
sir, if I may ask you

Dimbleby's face and body work as he puts this question is a study in itself. Although it's shot in black and
white, one can almost see him turn pink as he stares
at his feet and asks the Archbishop to comment on
Princess Margaret's plans. Those plans – a delicately
evasive phrase – were known and familiar to everyone
in Britain at the time. Indeed, there had been talk of
little else in the press for weeks. But what was, nearly

The case of Princess Margaret's
decision about her plans

60 years ago, a live and burning issue of the day has today shrunk to a
historical footnote. The young princess had fallen in love with one of her
late father's equerries, Group Captain Peter Townsend who was, alas,
a divorcee and worse, a commoner. Church law and state protocol at
the time required of the princess that, if she chose to marry Townsend
(which she could do only in a civil ceremony at the registry office), she
would lose her public, royal status and must retire into private life. In
the end, Princess Margaret released a brief statement to the effect that
she had no plans to marry Peter Townsend who, by this time had done
the decent thing and disappeared to France.

Fisher waffles on in reply. It was the princess's own choice. She
sought to know God's will on the matter and when she had worked that
out she made her decision. Only those who had prayed for her could
really understand what she must have been through. Dimbleby gently
prods him: 'The Prime Minister has made it very clear that there was no
state pressure and you can say –'. Fisher comes in firmly. 'There was no
church pressure either.' So that's all right then. With an almost audible
sigh of relief at getting through the tricky part of the business, Dimbleby
now moves on to safer, surer ground: 'Now, sir, our tour of Lambeth
Palace. Ninety-nine archbishops!' And so much history to go with them.
It is, to begin with, a virtual tour. Fisher puts on his spectacles as the
second pre-recorded film sequence comes up on viewers' television
screens and on a monitor in the study which he watches as Dimbleby
nudges him through a conversation about the long history of the palace

and its previous incumbents. A shot of the ruined chapel – bombed during the war – precedes a montage of it in its restored state, including a lingering shot of the pew where Queen Elizabeth sat during its post-war service of re-dedication.

Dimbleby was notoriously fond of the pomp and ceremony of church and state and was formidably well informed about their histories. He

certainly appears to know as much if not more about the preceding 98 archbishops as the present occupant of the See of Canterbury. As the film sequence ends and we return, live, to the Archbishop's study, Dimbleby picks up the cope that Fisher wore for the Coronation[9] to show to viewers. He places it on Fisher's shoulders and there is a brief discussion of its glorious colours and the precious stones with which it is encrusted. The two now move off into the corridor, pausing to appreciate portraits on the walls of dead archbishops before entering the dining room where yet more portraits (including one of Fisher done by a prisoner) elicit yet more appreciations.

Now it is time to meet Mrs Fisher. Dimbleby heads in the direction of the drawing room while the Archbishop disappears off set for a moment. As Dimbleby enters the room, two women rise to meet him. One is Mrs Fisher wearing what looks suspiciously like a dead fox round her shoulders. She introduces the other as 'my sister, Miss Forman who runs all the domestic side of our life here for us'. In the brief conversation that follows Miss Forman's face is never seen, nor is she at any point drawn in as a participant in the talk. It seems as if she is there for the sake of protocol. It is not proper for Mrs Fisher to be alone in her drawing room with a strange man and so Miss Forman is present as her chaperone.

Dimbleby sits down and affably introduces Mrs Fisher to the television audience: 'You're not really just er the wife of the Archbishop of Canterbury. You are very much Mrs Fisher too aren't you'. Mrs Fisher doesn't know about that but Dimbleby sails smoothly on. 'You write and speak a lot' he tells her (or, rather, viewers), 'and I'm not at all sure

you might not have been called a suffragette.

that some little time ago you might not have been called a suffragette'. At this Mrs Fisher demurs. She won't be called that, but she is 'strongly in favour of women having their proper share of things' and the conversation moves on to the role of women in the Anglican Church. After some discussion of this, Dimbleby observes that he had always thought it remarkable how Mrs Fisher managed to combine all this work with being the mother of such a big family.

'Well, they *are* all now grown up' is the mild response. Dimbleby presses her to tell about her six sons. As Mrs Fisher works her way through each one of them in turn, her husband enters and stands beside her chair, producing an awkwardly composed three-shot of the seated Dimbleby and Mrs Fisher and the standing Archbishop looking down at them both. Dimbleby jovially works him into the conversation:

> **Dimbleby:** I've been hearing about Mrs Fisher as a feminist (.)
> She's she's something in her own right
> Are you ever known sir as the husband of Mrs Fisher?
> **Fisher:** I am whenever I go to meetings of Mothers' Unions
> where I have to make it perfectly plain
> that the Archbishop of Canterbury is more important
> than the ex-president of the Mothers' Union (.)
> And they don't believe it even then

It's time now to wrap things up. Dimbleby gets up and moves round to stand behind Mrs Fisher producing an even more awkwardly tight three-shot of himself and the Archbishop and the head and shoulders of the seated Mrs Fisher who is not sure quite where to look. 'Well, now', he says, laughing, 'in order to keep the er peace I think we'll end the discussion there. But ah seriously your Grace for letting us come to Lambeth Palace and talking to us so freely tonight, our most grateful thanks. And to you, Mrs Fisher for being such a gracious host as well. Good evening.' That last remark is directed, with a bow and an ingratiating smile, at the off-camera and still seated Miss Forman. 'Well, we've enjoyed it immensely', replies the Archbishop. 'Thank you'. 'Thank you.' Fade to an exterior shot of the palace over which the final credits scroll.

Being at home in the world

The art of conversation takes two forms. On the one hand, there is the conversationalist; the raconteur, the wit who amuses and entertains the company with verbal fluency and epigrammatic turn of phrase. Oscar Wilde, Dorothy Parker and Gore Vidal were renowned conversational wits in their day. On the other hand, there is the less showy accomplishment of drawing out the person with whom you are speaking, of encouraging them to talk, of easing the conversational flow. Dimbleby had mastered this skill, Murrow had not. His question to Mrs

Kennedy – 'Which requires more diplomacy; to interview a senator or to be married to one?' – is quite witty, but at the expense of Mrs Kennedy who is flummoxed by it. It creates an awkward moment, rescued by John Kennedy's intervention to fill the hole in the conversation that has opened up. Dimbleby understands and inhabits his role as a conversational host on television and comes across as comfortable with himself and the situation. His skill lies in putting those to whom he is speaking at their ease, as he coaxes them through the novel and discomforting experience of talking on television for invisible millions before an invasive clutter of cameras, arc-lights and production personnel in their own living space. He has the advantage over Murrow, to be sure, of being there with those to whom he is speaking, as he gently nudges the conversation along, maintaining its smooth flow. His interaction with the Archbishop is a skilfully designed journalistic interview disguised as amiable chat or small talk, yet all the while steering towards the final question about Princess Margaret and her plans. This was certainly by prior arrangement with Fisher, but it is laid down with cunning indirectness and the viewer does not see it coming, whereas all the topics in the Murrow-Kennedy interaction come on cue with a thumping inevitability. Fisher's remarks about Princess Margaret made the front page of most of the national press the following day, for it was a journalistic scoop. They were the first public comments on the story from anyone close to the royal family. Large chunks of the interview were printed verbatim and the London *Evening News* thought that the programme had provided 'a supreme example of the impact of television when it goes out into the real world, and with mounting excitement, brings directly to us something that is both unexpected and significant . . . the sense of mounting tension riveted one's interest and made one wonder what on earth was coming next' (Dimbleby 1975: 348–9).

Communicative ease is the crux of this chapter. How might we explain the small awkwardnesses that have been its topic? And why does it matter (if it does)? The labour of the live production of *Person to Person* appears as laboured and it makes for a discomforting viewing experience. We might explain this in social or psychological terms. Our personal sense of ontological security is perhaps momentarily disturbed.[10] Perhaps we feel ill at ease because we sense that others are. If they are, in Goffman's terms, momentarily discountenanced (if their face is at a loss), this generates anxiety which we, as viewers, may share. Such explanations certainly clarify why momentary disruptions to the sociable fabric of an everyday occasion on television may make for a troublesome (or possibly amusing) viewing experience. But there is more to it than this, I think.

Technical failure and performative error, the demons of live television broadcasting, show up in our kind of world as the exception rather than the rule in everyday life. As a rule we wake up each day expecting that the day will be an ordinary day in which we will do what we must, meet and talk with others, get about our affairs and accomplish all this without undue complications. That we can do so is the gift of the hidden care structures that hold the world in place through time; that produce and reproduce it as a working, workable, workaday world and in so doing guarantee our ease of being in it. It is this that is at stake in the small technical and performative failures of *Person to Person*, whose awkwardnesses make visible the work (the care) involved in its making. It troubles our expectation that things will work easily and effortlessly. It is this huge, all pervasive, natural and taken-for-granted trust in them that underpins our everyday world and conversations.[11] Our everyday things and our everyday language work in the same way and both are underpinned by the same (Gricean) logic of use. This logic of use is a communicative logic, the intrinsic structuring logic that is the pre-condition of human interaction – with things, with words – for human purposes. This logic, immanent in the use and usage of words and things, is what makes the world and language *work*: for and not against us. It is this that guarantees our ease of being, our being at home in the world. The workability of language and world is always, only and ever the transcendent impersonal collective accomplishment in time of a single, common humanity, the upshot of human thought, application and labour for anyone as someone any place any time. But both will always appear to us, even as we use them, as if they were natural and given without any effort on our part. When that effort shows, we notice it and are discomforted. Why?

The immense, the truly overwhelming complexity of the everyday world and our everyday language is what we never ever see precisely because it is this that is intentionally concealed from us by the very ways in which both work: they are made and meant for ease of use, for *effortless* use. To be effortless they must render their own effort invisible. That is their gift, what they grant us – that we will take them both for granted – as if they were simple, natural self-evident facts of life. The dialectic of truth (the immanent truth of the human world) lies in what at the one and the same time it reveals and conceals about itself. The hermeneutics of trust that I am at pains to clarify and justify is grounded in a simple recognition that what the world endlessly conceals from us (its fathomless complexity) is its greatest gift. Simplicity and ease of use is the absolute precondition of all everyday things that make up the everyday world and of our everyday medium of communication, talk. Things are meant to work because they were made to work for anyone anywhere anytime. And so too, words. When things go wrong and words go awry (in a TV program, for instance) it matters. We notice. We care. Meaning and intentionality suffuse every humanly made thing and everything we say and do. Care *as such* is the irreducible mark of a being for whom everything (but *everything*) matters, for whom everything is meant and meaningful, no matter how great or small. Care is the meaning of meaning, the foundational characteristic of a being that dwells in a world of its own making in which everything is meaningful because it was made and meant to be so. This was the great discovery towards which Heidegger journeyed in his quest for the truth of what it is to be human, in the first part of *Being and Time*. It is, for me, a gentle irony that what he so wonderfully uncovered I should rediscover in two old television programmes from the 1950s, whose common theme – being (*At Home*) in the world – was his starting point.

The impulse behind *Person to Person* and *At Home* was the same: to engage with real life, to get television out of the studio and into people's homes. Murrow had originally wanted to include ordinary Americans, to show the new viewing public to itself – a mailman, a clerk at Macy's for instance. One early interview was with a Grand Central Station redcap (porter) in his Harlem apartment. 'And what do you do when you get home?' Murrow asked. 'I look out of the window. I watch TV' was the reply. Complaints rolled in. 'If I want to see how the average guy lives, I can visit my relatives' was one response (Persico 1988: 345–6). Ordinary Americans quietly faded from the program. Viewers wanted a glimpse of the homes and lives of the famous. On both sides of the Atlantic the famous were much of a muchness: a mix of celebrities from the entertainment world, the great and the good. On the American side, there were the Hollywood stars. On the British side, there was the grand nobility whose stately homes were perhaps the star attraction. But one of the most sought after couples for *Person to Person* were the Duke and Duchess of Windsor (former King Edward VIII of Britain and his American wife, Wallace Simpson) whom staffers pursued for three years before they consented to be visited by the show.

The programs I have discussed are small, early markers of what John Thompson calls the transformed 'conditions of visibility' brought about by broadcasting (Thompson 1995: 119–48). Today there is nowhere in the world, no person, no event that is beyond the reach of that 'enquiring' medium whose intrusive presence in Westminster Abbey was resisted in 1953 by Dr Geoffrey Fisher. Television's cameras enter the home and lay it open to the public gaze. What had hitherto been hidden from history is now, in one and the same moment, made visible in live transmission and historicized as it is recorded. Both programs give off information about their life and times; how people spoke, the clothes they wore, the character of social relations between the sexes; attitudes to divorce and the emancipation of women. What begins to be captured in both is something now endlessly displayed on television today, namely ordinary, everyday existence that hitherto had been very largely unobserved and unrecorded and thereby unhistorical. Death has overtaken Ed Murrow and both the Kennedys, Richard Dimbleby, Archbishop and Mrs Fisher. Yet all come to life and re-enter the present, at the press of a button or the click of a mouse, for later generations to relive a moment in the life of a generation of the dead, preserved for the historical record in archives of the earliest years of live television broadcasting.

Coda: the look of television

The direct-to-camera look is perhaps the most fundamental way in which television distinguishes itself from the fictional narrative regime of cinema and establishes itself as a real-world interaction between broadcasting and its viewers. In the regime of looks produced in classic fictional cinema, the characters look at, turn away from and avoid looking at each other in a variety of ways. But none ever turns to look directly at the camera still less to address it, for this would destroy the film's fictional effect, the willing suspension of disbelief on which it depends. The look-to-camera on television generates a number of standard implicatures.[12] First, that the looker is a real person whose look has an intended recipient. Second, that that recipient is a real someone somewhere in their own space of viewing in the same real time of the broadcast transmission. Third, that this intended someone turn out to be, in each case, me: the for-anyone-as-someone effect of the direct look-to-camera. It establishes the *Person to Person* effect – the experience of being spoken to directly as a person by someone speaking as a person. This effect is the product not simply of the direction of the look but of its spatial proxemics. Visually the viewer is within the space of a conversation – not an intimate space but the sociable space of an inter-personal interaction. The sound of Murrow's voice (its pitch) secures this effect: not whispering or shouting, but talking directly to camera. The camera functions as a proxy for the viewer securing eye-contact with Murrow in the TV studio. He is sitting, not standing. He is seated in an easy chair not perched on a stool or behind a desk. His line of gaze implicates a recipient similarly seated and at the same eye-level. For each and every viewer, the experience is the same: 'He is speaking to me. I am spoken to': a person-to-person inter-personal interaction.

I want to look more closely, for a moment, at the direction of Murrow's gaze in his opening address to camera (arrows indicate the direction of his eyes. Up indicates to camera):

↑ Senator John Kennedy of Massachusetts has
accomplished a::ll these things
In his thirty six years except ↓ being a policeman ↑
(0.4)
This . seems to be the marrying season ↓
for senators ↑
(.) ↓
The Kennedys were married
last month → ↑
They're still looking ↓
for a place to live (**cut to profile shot of Murrow**)
in Washington

The downwards and sideways glances generate standard Gricean implicatures as motivated departures from the norm of sustained eye-contact in direct address to camera and, by implication, viewer. Each invites a different standard inference: sideways – he's looking at someone/something else (a momentary distraction); downwards – he's looking at something in his lap (his notes). In either case, the loss of direct eye-contact momentarily disturbs the sought-for effect of person-to-person communicative rapport.

The direct look is fundamental to television and its real-time, real-world relationship with viewers, but it gave rise to all sorts of headaches in the first years of the new medium, especially for all those who had to read to camera from a script. This was never a problem for radio. But it was for television news from the start. BBC television news, when it started up in 1954, had no visible studio newsreader. Senior management preferred the anonymous invisible authority of unseen radio news broadcasts and felt that to show the newsreader would somehow personalize the news and undermine its authority. The upshot of this was a news bulletin read by an unseen voice over a sequence of still photographs, occasional silent filmed news clips, maps, diagrams and captions. The results were predictably dire and greeted with derision in the press. It was quickly conceded that it was necessary to have a newsreader in the studio to introduce the news, provide continuity between items and close it down. But how do you read the news to camera? If you just keep your eyes down on the script all the time, this is a visibly peculiar viewing experience. Is he reading aloud to himself? Why doesn't he look at me? So newsreaders were asked to look at the camera as much as they could, but this was equally disconcerting. With eyes that flickered up and down from the script on the desk to the camera in front of him, the newsreaders (all male in those far-off times) appeared to be positively shifty and furtive – as if they could not bring themselves to look the honest viewer directly in the eye. And of course they were prone to lose their place in the script as their eyes moved continually away from and back to it. The *Daily Mirror* (a leading British tabloid) ran a two-page spread with the banner headline 'THESE ARE THE GUILTY MEN' and beneath it photographs of BBC newsreaders with eyes downcast on the script or looking (seemingly nervously) up from it.[13]

As everyone knows, the solution to this problem was the auto-cue or tele-prompter, a technical device developed in the USA in the early 1950s and immediately taken up in Britain and elsewhere precisely to secure the 'sincerity effect' of direct eye-contact with each and every viewer. This 'magical' effect, secured by unseen technology, has given rise to suspicion in some academic quarters. 'What are we to make of the interposition of this text that someone reads', Derrida asks, 'while pretending to look straight into the eye of a viewer who he or she can't see and who, in turn, can't see that the person addressing him may at the same time be in the process of reading from a prompter [. . .]?' Derrida is voicing his suspicion of this pretence while speaking impromptu and *en direct* to camera in an interview with Bernard Stiegler recorded for *l'Institut National de l'Audiovisuel*, the French national sound and television archive. He is responding (at length) to a question from Stiegler about his (Derrida's) concept of 'artifactuality' – a portmanteau coinage that plays on artifact, actuality and artificiality. Derrida had invented the term in an interview earlier in the same year (1993). We philosophers need to acknowledge the artifactuality of tele-technologies, he remarks:

> Hegel was right to remind the philosopher of his time to read the papers daily. Today the same responsibility obliges him to learn how the dailies, the weeklies, the television news programs are *made*, and *by whom*. He must ask to see things from the other side, from the side of the press agencies as well as from that of the teleprompter. We ought never to forget the full import of this index: when a journalist or politician seems to be speaking to us, in our home, while looking us straight in the eye, he (or she) is in the process of reading, on screen, at the dictation of a 'teleprompter', a text composed somewhere else, at some other time, sometimes by others, or even by a whole network of anonymous authors. (Derrida and Stiegler 2002: 4; original emphases)

So what are we to make of this 'actuality effect' in 'the domain of "live" communication', he goes on to ask:

> How [should we] proceed without denying ourselves these new resources of live television while continuing to be critical of their mystifications? And above all, while continuing to remind people and to demonstrate that the 'live' and 'real time' are never pure, that they do not give us intuition or transparency, a perception stripped of interpretation or technical intervention. Any such demonstration already appeals, in and of itself, to philosophy. (ibid.: 5)

Derrida is quite right, I think, to insist that philosophers today have a responsibility to learn and understand how television programs are made. It is a fundamental assumption of this book that the communicative effects of radio and television are the products of an almost wholly invisible production process. But my interpretation of their effects is quite contrary to his. In this and the previous chapter, I have been concerned with broadcast talk and the ways in which broadcasters on radio hearably speak as if to 'me' and on television are seen to do so. The communicative, experiential effect is, in each case, the outcome of a particular technology; the radio microphone, the television camera. The small matter of creating and maintaining eye-contact with the viewer, even while reading what is being said, is indicative of a wider general adjustment of the production culture of television to the communicative norms of inter-personal relations – a key theme of this and the preceding chapter. Eye-contact between participants in talk (or lack of it) carries normative implications of directness (or not), openness (or not), transparency (or not). In sum, it generates inferences as to whether or not participants are being frank, genuine and sincere in their self-presentations and in their demeanour and disposition towards each other. And underpinning this are basic matters concerning trust. This trust depends on, is a result of, performances that generate effects of trust. From this perspective, we might then see the teleprompter not so much as an object of suspicion (as it is for Derrida), but rather as a technology of trust. That was and remains the effect it was designed to secure.

10

The moment of the goal – on television

Formatting liveness

The Singer of Tales by Albert Lord is one of those rare books that transform the existing understanding of a subject.[1] It was well known that Homeric epic was part of an oral tradition and transcribed, anonymously, at some point. But the simple question, first raised by Milman Parry, Lord's teacher at Harvard, was how was the poet able to perform something that, when transcribed, was thousands of lines long? More exactly, in the performance situation, how is the poet able to produce a narrative of great length with a sustained, continuous fluency of expression? Is it learnt by heart? Is it a miraculous feat of memory? But if so, from whom did the poet learn the story? The answers to such questions may appear as difficult to conjecture as the songs of the sirens, but Parry found a brilliant solution. He was aware of a still extant tradition of oral epic poetry in southern Yugoslavia. He therefore went to Macedonia in the 1930s and studied both the poets and their performances, making many recordings of the epic poems which they sang in a sustained recitative style, self-accompanied on the *guslar*, a one-stringed, bowed instrument rather like a lute. From this detailed fieldwork an understanding emerged of how epic poems were composed, learned and transmitted. It was 'a study in the processes of composition' – not another *theory* of composition but derived, rather, from 'the facts of the practice of the poetry' (Lord 1965: foreword, unnumbered).

The key point of the study concerns the relation between composition and performance. In written traditions, the work (a poem, a piece of music, a play) is first composed as a written text, a process which allows for numerous false starts, revisions, rewrites and so on before a final 'clean' text is achieved with which the author is satisfied as worthy of performance. None of this is possible in unwritten, oral traditions of composition. Composition and performance are inextricably laminated together. Each and every time, the performance is the composition; the composition is the performance. How then is this done, as an achieved and accomplished act free from mistakes, false starts, re-starts, memory lapses, etc.?

It is well known that the epic tradition (as it appears transcribed in written texts) is formulaic: the dawn, in Homer, is always 'rosy fingered', the sea is always 'wine dark', Diomedes (one of the Greek heroes) is always 'the breaker of horses'. In Anglo-Saxon poetry there are standard kennings (poetic phrases) for the sea (the swan's way), for the long-boats (the 'foamy necked floater' with its 'ring-necked prow'), for the lord (the ring-giver) that are drawn from the poetic 'word-hoard', the shared stock of common descriptive periphrases. In the Song of Milman Parry, composed in his honour by Milovan Volicic, the Professor becomes a 'grey falcon' who flies over land and sea to Yugoslavia and the ship in which he journeys, the Saturnia, is a grey falcon too (Lord 1965: 272–5). There are longer formulaic set-pieces: descriptions of journeys, battles, horses and weaponry that recur, with small variants, in any particular corpus. Any poem is put together from the common stock of phrases, descriptions, themes and story-lines, which together constitute the epic narrative tradition.

When transcribed onto the page in poetic 'lines', each appears to consist of a half line made up of a discrete single phrase (noun-verb, say) which is repeated or inverted in the second half line (verb-noun). These 'half-line' phrases, the basic building blocks of the narrative, are adjacent to but not linked to each other, the defining characteristic of parataxis: 'the arrangement of clauses or propositions without connectives' (Chambers 2011). Parataxis is the fundamental technique whereby long oral poetic narratives are put together. In transcription it is clear that rhetorical devices of alliteration, assonance and so on – 'lel letteres loken' (loyal letters linked) as the Gawain poet put it – bind together the minimal paratactic building blocks of the story. Lord notes that when the songs are performed, the poet may run through up to 20 lines with great rapidity before pausing, using the *guslar* for continuity, as he reflects on the next part of the story.

How is this relevant to our understanding of radio and television? Suppose we simply refocus, not in terms of oral and written poetry, but in terms of live performance. Then we might see that what is at issue is the *management of liveness*. The problem for the performer is the production *every time*, of an effective performance. The story must be told well. It must be eloquent in its turn of phrase and coherent in its storyline. It must be free of anxiety and error. It must not lose the plot! It must appear in all respects as an artless effortless performance – time and time again. There is no need to suppose that a poem was learnt by heart and committed to memory so that it somehow came out exactly the same time after time – hence the old chestnut about illiterate peoples having amazing memories! What Parry and Lord investigated and discovered were the *necessary* devices for the production of something that is, each and every time, within the frame of the tradition and yet fresh, spontaneous and appropriate to the nature of the occasion that has elicited the particular performance. The simple but fundamental point I wish to derive from the work of Parry and Lord is that *formatting* is the basic device for the effective management of *any* live performance-in-public, where the task involved concerns the production of continuous fresh talk or an extended narrative of some kind. Formatting draws on a lexicon of stock phrases with parataxis as its basic technique for putting them together.

Formatting radio talk

Erving Goffman's lengthy study of radio talk contains a couple of fascinating passing remarks about the relevance of the work of Parry and Lord to the problems of the production of what he calls 'continuing fresh talk' in live-to-air broadcasting by radio presenters and DJs:

> A lay speaker, thrust before a microphone, likely would not have the ability to do this. Yet, when one examines how this editorial elaboration is accomplished, it appears that a relatively small number of formulaic sentences and tag phrases are all that is needed [. . .] A DJ's talk may be heard as unscripted, but it tends to be built up out of a relatively small number of set comments, much as it is said, epic oral poetry was recomposed during each delivery. (Goffman 1981: 324–5)

The study by Graham Brand and myself of a three-hour live-to-air DJ program on British radio in the 1980s, *The Tony Blackburn Show*, elaborated on Goffman's basic insight. The problem facing any DJ in the radio studio is the production over a span of time (three hours in Blackburn's case) of continuous, fluent 'live' talk which gives identity, structure and content to the program from moment to moment across the whole period. At stake in this is not just the formatting of discourse, but the formatting of time. Thus the three-hour span of the programme is broken down into manageable time segments, punctuated on the hour and half hour by boundary markers; news bulletins, weather checks, travel and traffic updates. Certain things recur at the same time each day – the Birthdays and Anniversaries phone-in comes in the last half hour and the final 15 minutes is given over to closing-down routines and promises of renewal on the following day. Certain things recur on the same day each week. If it's Wednesday, it's time for Sex and Sympathy, in which that ever-interesting topic and its attendant problems are discussed. In all this what is at stake is the management of 'empty time' (time-to-be-filled) which is made manageable by its articulation into smaller distinct segments within an overall three-hour continuum. In every three-hour programme, between 30 and 35 records will be played; say 11 three-minute recordings which leaves about another 30 minutes in the hour to be filled by talk. Time and talk are inextricably enfolded in each other.

Tony Blackburn Show
BBC Radio London, 1986
[*music fades*]
1   **TB** Paris and *I Choose You.*
2   It's now seven minutes before eleven o'clock.
3   Your main funking funketeer.
4   Your Boss with all the hot sauce.
5   Your Leader . . . (*pause*) . . . Me.
6   Right . Now Dave in Greenford says 'Drive safely 'n love to you'
7   to wife er Jill who's on her way to Radlett at the moment.
8   Mark in Bermondsey sends all his love to fiancee Sally Ann
9   And also Rachel or – yes it is – Rachel in Barnet says 'Love you'
10   to husband Peter who's working at Shenley Hospital hrrhmmm.
11   oh dear must clear my throat.
12   Right . Now em Gary's in Camden . Hello Gary [phone conversation with Gary continues]
(Brand and Scannell 1991: 217)

This fragment of live-to-air talk is embedded within a larger half-hour formatted time segment called London Love, in which listeners are invited by TB to 'show you care for the one you love' by phoning in if, for instance, they have just become engaged or are getting married or are back from a honeymoon or want to make up after a quarrel. The calls are taken in pairs between suitably romantic numbers, and this bit of talk follows on as the record fades.

A crucial task for live radio talk is to maintain, from moment to moment, the nature of the occasion. More exactly, this means orienting listeners to the programme's what, where, who and when; its fundamental situational components. In relations of presence, the nature of the occasion is a given, visibly available to co-present participants in the interaction. For the broadcaster in the studio talking into the air, it is never apparent who is listening. Radio talk is of necessity designed for an audience that is constantly coming and going. It can never be assumed, at any moment, that any listener who has just tuned in knows or understands what's going on. So as the music ends Blackburn goes into an identity routine: three things are identified: the music just heard, the time and the speaker. The logic of this small sequence is a *chrono-logic*; it is determined by time.

Blackburn's first utterance is in response to what immediately precedes it – the music. It generates standard inferences of the kind identified in Sacks's famous discussion of a child's story: 'The baby cried. The mommy picked it up.' We hear, Sacks points out, the second utterance to mean that the mommy who picks up the baby is, in fact, the mommy *of* the baby, though that is not said. And we further hear that she picks up the baby *because* it is crying, though this is not said either (Sacks 1995, vol. 1: 236–66). It is not *said* that the music just heard is a song called *I Choose You* performed by a singer called Paris. We *hear* this as what is intended by Blackburn's utterance via the Gricean maxim of relation (be relevant). If Blackburn's utterance is meant as relevant in its precise moment of utterance, it is strongly implicated that what he says is connected to what immediately went before. 'Paris and *I Choose You*' is an utterance whose sense is determined by its temporal adjacency to the moment just now past.

Although it is an utterance without a verb, its grammatical tense appears to be the historic present; it speaks of the past in the present. What, then, is the next-most-relevant thing to say? 'It's now seven minutes before eleven o'clock.' The time check attends to the embedded temporality of the preceding utterance and resolves its ambiguity (past or present?). 'That was then. This is *now*.' It re-establishes the temporal footing of the programme in the immediacy of its live-to-air now, and at the same time orients the present towards the future. 'It's now seven minutes *before eleven o'clock*.'[2] The hours are horizonal moments within the programme's time-structure and are anticipated as such. They are boundaries when one time-segment ends and another begins, a transition marked by the news headlines. Thus the time check does not simply attend to the immediate (punctual) now. It attends to and articulates its temporal continuity from moment to moment. What next? Your main funking funketeer (1) . Your boss with all the hot sauce (2) . Your leader (3) . [Who?] . . . pause [for effect] . . . Me. It is, of course, assumed that this irreducible 'me' needs no further identification, since listeners are not treated as strangers, but are addressed familiarly as 'members'; i.e., as ratified participants in the discursive world that is *The Tony Blackburn Show*. Blackburn's self-stylizations as the Boss, the Leader and so on are drawn from the programme's word-hoard as part of the routine that routinely establishes the world of the show as it is talked into being each day. Regular listeners *know* who is the leader of 'the gang' and play along accordingly in the various phone-in routines that are part of every show (Brand and Scannell 1991).

Max Atkinson has discussed in some detail the significance of three-part lists in his study of political oratory, a significant genre of live public speaking (Atkinson 1984: 157–63 and *passim*). We can observe throughout this scrap of transcribed talk the unobtrusive presence of triads. The sequence under discussion consists of three tellings, the third of which is glossed in three ways before the final, terminating revelation of who is speaking here, namely 'Me'. The next sequence (lines 5–10) whose opening and closing boundaries are marked by 'Right', has three greetings which are passed on to listeners. Atkinson argues that, in various ways, a three-part sequence brings something to resolution and closure. Quite often the first two parts set up a contradiction that is resolved by the third part. In political oratory, applause invariably comes on immediate completion of a rhetorical third part (Atkinson 1984: 60–3). We may detect a movement towards closure of the whole opening sequence in the increasing economy of utterance in the three parts of the third telling, before the terminal monosyllabic 'Me'.

This tiny scrap of on-air radio talk highlights a fundamental aspect of the management of liveness, namely the achievement and maintenance of *continuity*. Continuity is about movement *in* time and the movement *of* time. In respect of broadcast talk, it involves segueing from one thing to another without pause (as Blackburn does) while maintaining fluency and coherence. Fluency is more than an uninterrupted flow of one darn thing after another. It presupposes a texture of relevance between them which depends on an implicit logic that connects one thing and another in succession. Underpinning the transitions from moment to moment is the movement of time itself, time-as-such. The phenomenal now – the moment of liveness – is always a past becoming present and a present becoming future.

Blackburn's talk segues from moment to moment, articulating continuity between then, now and next. He unobtrusively attends to these temporalities as structuring the relevance of what he says. Parataxis – the arrangement of clauses, or propositions without connectives – is as much the basis of DJ talk as of epic poetry. What connects Blackburn's three paratactic utterances coming out of the music is a chrono*logic* that links three apparently unconnected statements by their unobtrusive adjacent temporal relevance to each other. That was then. This is now. It is me.

Live multi-camera television sports coverage

If *spoken continuity* is achieved on radio DJ programmes through the formatted talk of its presenter, when we turn to television coverage of live events we find that continuity is achieved in the first place through its visual presentation backed up with spoken commentary. But the underlying issues are the same: to establish a logic of *visual continuity* as a self-explicating phenomenon whose intelligibility is determined by a strict temporal chronologic that generates narrative coherence and continuity. Having shown there to be a temporal texture of relevances implicated in a sequence of DJ talk, I turn now to the chronologic implicated in formatted visual television sequences in live-to-air transmissions of international soccer.[3]

David Bordwell and Kristin Thompson's account of continuity editing in *Film Art* is the classic work on the subject, and provides the best way into the question of visual narrative in television (Bordwell and Thompson 2001: 262–78).[4] Continuity editing's aim is to tell a story coherently and clearly. Its basic purpose is to create a smooth flow from shot to shot (ibid.: 262). The movement from shot A to B, etc. is achieved via the 'cut', probably the most basic editing device in film. Continuity cutting, however, seeks to be seen but unnoticed. It should appear seamless, 'so that nobody knows [notices] there's a cut in there' (ibid.: 289). Cutting, unlike other filmic devices (fades, wipes or super-impositions) implies no necessary connection between shots and, indeed, montage editing trades on this to achieve metaphoric 'third' meanings. It is thus a paratactic device; a system of placing disparate things adjacent to each other in such a way as to implicate a 'logic of continuity' between them. The 'what next' in terms of what we see is determined by temporal adjacency. What motivates the up-coming 'next' shot in each case in any sequence is determined by that which immediately preceded it. The smooth segues of continuity editing render themselves invisible for the viewer who is caught up in the action, in what's going on from moment to moment in the narrative. The effect of a continuous real-time event is built up incrementally shot by shot, with a single camera. The sequence was not necessarily shot in the order in which it is viewed. Not all the shots were necessarily filmed on the same day. To maintain continuity between shots, detailed notes must be kept on studio set-up, lighting, camera and actor positions, costumes, the position of the furniture, etc. And of course there may have been re-takes of each, if not all, the individual shots which exist in the first place as separate 'pieces' to be stitched together at a later stage. The moment of shooting and the moment of editing are quite distinct in fictional film narrative. In other words, film-making is an essentially literary process. It too, works to a script. The process of film-making, like that of writing, allows for, indeed presupposes, re-writes, alterations and all kinds of editing and re-editing before a final 'well-made' version is published or, as they say in film, 'released'.

All this is quite different from multi-camera live television coverage of real-time, real-world events, which has more in common with the live performing arts (music and theatre) than with cinematic or literary production. The essential concern of the live performing arts is a flawless performance 'on the night' of the musical or theatrical event, so that it comes off without a hitch. The commitment to the event by its producers may have many motivations, but these are subsumed by the overriding obligation (that all accept) to bring it off and make it happen as a case of 'the real thing'. This commitment is both awesome and mysterious. It is awesome in that the burden of responsibility for successfully bringing off the event is indeed great and induces anxiety and fear of failure (mingled with excitement and anticipation) that grow as the moment of the event draws closer. It is mysterious in that it seems ultimately inexplicable – *why* all this effort and bother and worry?

I reserve that question for the next chapter. Here I am concerned with the prior question of how they are made to matter – how, routinely, they are brought off live and in real time as that which they are meant and intended to be. In a moment I will look at what happens, shot by shot, when goals are scored in international soccer matches. But in order to understand *how* this happens, I must first sketch in the production process involved in the coverage of a soccer event. It would be tedious and maybe unnecessary to describe in detail a single live television production and all its technical and technological complexities, the many and varied skills and expertises of all involved in the production process and the ways in which it all comes together to yield the televisual experience of the match itself. But it is very important at least to acknowledge all this if we are to have a due and proper respect for, and understanding of, the making of things, how they are made to happen.

Suffice it, then, to note that the day before a match the mobile production units, all relevant equipment and peripheral necessities will arrive at the stadium which is rigged with cameras. For an international match, up to two dozen cameras will be strategically placed to produce shots, from many and varied angles, of the stadium, the match and all who are there – the players, their managers and the fans of both sides. A whole battery of state-of-the-art equipment is deployed around the ground. Behind the goals at either end several cameras are rigged (some operated manually, some by remote) to provide instant replays when goals are scored. Super-slow digital cameras can now drastically slow down the movement of a ball in flight without any loss of focus, making visible what is undetectable to ordinary sight. Most cameras are fixed in place, but touchline steadicams allow for smooth, flowing mobile ground-level shots both of the match and of the crowd without loss of focus and without any distracting camera joggle. Two key cameras are rigged at the half-way line at a height of about 30 feet. The so-called 'prime camera' (hereafter C1) provides most of the coverage in any game: it is strategically positioned to produce optimum visual coverage from end to end of the pitch and follows continuously the action around the ball. Beside it, a companion camera (C2) produces a tighter, closer shot on the action, keeping the player with the ball in frame. In the course of the game the match director will cut between shots from these two cameras. For really big matches, a blimp is hired with its small crew to produce the occasional bird's-eye view of the stadium itself and its surroundings.

Live coverage on the day has three distinct production components. There is the management of the on-site studio overlooking the stadium, in which a panel of experts (usually former players and/or current team managers) discuss the game beforehand, at half-time and after the final whistle. A standard studio camera set-up is deployed, managed by a separate producer. In the main mobile production unit, from which the coverage of the match is managed, there are two distinct operations. There is the moment-by-moment coverage of the game itself, the joint responsibility of the match director who calls the shots, his or her vision mixers who bring them up on-screen and the voice-linked camera operators around the ground who provide a continuing menu of shots from which the director will call. There is also a separate small instant-replay unit, whose main responsibility is to ensure the recording of the unfolding game on all cameras and to set up the replays when goals are scored. This unit also puts together a mini-package of the game as it progresses to be played at the very end of the transmission as the edited highlights of the match. Technicians attend to the monitoring of all the complex electronic equipment in use.

Television coverage of sporting events has, as its overriding concern, a commitment to providing the best access to the occasion. Viewers are to have, as far as possible, direct, clear and interference-free visual access to the game-in-play and the event-as-a-whole. To achieve this, the production process must not intrude upon the attention of viewers. It must conceal itself. Trade manuals on multi-camerawork production emphasize invisible camerawork as the cardinal consideration of the whole operation:

> As multi-camera television deals with uninterrupted action in a time-scale created by the nature of the event covered, 'real' time has to be

continuously covered in a mixture of shot sizes, camera development and
matched shot sizes to allow invisible cuts between cameras. . . . Multi-
camera operators have to provide cutting points either pre-rehearsed or by
monitoring what the rest of the camera crew are providing. Idiosyncratic
personal composition by a camera operator will remain unnoticed only if
s/he is responsible for the whole of the visual production. It will immediately become apparent in multi-camera work if [. . . idiosyncratic] work is
intercut with standard camera technique provided by the rest of the crew.
Multi-camera work remains invisible provided it conforms to certain criteria. These standard conventions are inherited by everyone working within
live or multi-camera recordings. (Ward 2001: 14–15, 16–17)

Multi-camera live production depends upon team work. Individual
idiosyncrasies are not wanted and every camera-operator must produce
shots that will match up unobtrusively with all other shots on offer. The
whole live-and-in-real-time process has been gone through many times
by the crew, all of whom know what is expected of them. The procedures
are standard, routine and formulaic. The prime camera on the half-way
line will provide viewers with a privileged 'best seat in the house' access
to the game. From its midway position, it pans right and left to cover the
action from one end of the pitch to the other. In any actual game, most
of the coverage is shown through the prime camera, which anchors the
visual narrative, establishing and maintaining the visual 'axis of action'
for the duration of the event. Soccer is, as they say, a game of two
halves. In each 45-minute half, the game is mostly a mid-field struggle
between the sides to press into the opposing half and advance upon the
goal-area. Much of the routine coverage of a live soccer match simply
follows the action through C1 and C2, with occasional cutaways to the
touch-line steadicams for close-ups on particular players when injuries
and fouls occur.[5] Fouls and near misses often occasion a quick replay.
But the coverage mostly is designed to hold in focus where the action is
and to allow the commentary and the ambient sound to convey to the
viewer a sense of how the game is going. It is only when goals are scored
that television's visual coverage moves into a different gear. It no longer
follows the action. It produces its own visual narrative:

The visual format of goals

Germany/England, Munich: 01.09.01
Steven Gerrard's goal (47th minute)
1. Midshot. Gerrard scores from 30 yards
2. MCU Gerrard
3. MCU A smiling Sven-Göran Eriksson

4. MCU English players piling on Gerrard
5. Midshot Jubilant English fans
6. (as 4) English players piling on Gerrard
7. 1st replay
8. 2nd replay
9. 3rd replay.
10. MCU Gerrard (reverse of 2 above)
11. Symbolic cross-wipe
12. Normal coverage resumed

This sequence, or a variation on it, is run through whenever a goal is scored. It is a visual format, a repertoire of stock shots from the image-hoard that is routinely set up and sequenced the moment the ball is in the net. There are two parts to the sequence. Shots 1–6 are live and in real time. Shots 7–10 are the replays when television creates its own doubled time, a magical then-and-now. We must consider what determines the sequence as a whole and then the relationship between one shot and another. First, if the object of the sequence as a whole is to produce the replays of the goal, then something needs to be done to fill the unavoidable small time gap that is necessary to set up the replays. Thus shots 1–6 serve to maintain continuous live coverage while the instant replays are set up. But more than this, they set in play a narrative of the goal which has two parts; first, immediate reactions, and then commentary and analysis.

1. Midshot. Gerrard scores from 30 yards [5.00 secs] / cut
2. MCU Gerrard [3.6 secs] / cut
3. MCU A smiling Sven-Göran Eriksson [3.8 secs] / cut
4. MCU English players piling on Gerrard [4.00 secs] / cut
5. Midshot. Jubilant English fans [2.00 secs] / cut
6. (as 4) English players piling on Gerrard [4 secs] / Symbolic wipe

The prime camera is covering the game 'as usual' when Gerrard scores from 30 yards. It keeps the scorer in frame for a second and then there is a cut to a medium close-up of Gerrard as he runs away from the camera to the far corner-flag going into a sliding victory dive along the grass. As he begins his dive, there is a cut to a smiling Sven-Göran Eriksson on his feet with the team coach. A cut to the English players piling on top of the prone Gerrard is followed by a brief cutaway to the English fans in the crowd and then

back to the English players still piling on the now buried Gerrard. The English crest (three black lions couchant in a white shield) set in a white football is used as a cross-wipe to signal the end of the sequence and the start of the replays.[6]

A goal in a soccer match is a highlight, a golden moment. It is, in effect, what the whole point of the event is about. People go to matches and watch television to see goals being scored.[7] No goals, no resolution; a point confirmed by the necessity of extra time and penalty shoot-outs when there is no result after 90 minutes in knock-out competitions. Goals generate, in the players and the attendant crowds, moments of high excitement, of elation and despondency, depending on which side scores. Television analyses the spontaneous response of those there at the game, resolving it into its component parts, organized in a hierarchy of relevance. Thus the first response is always, in this formulaic sequence, a shot of the goal-scorer himself, showing his immediate, ecstatic reaction. From the scoring of the goal to a shot of the goal-scorer; the 'what next?' motivation of these two shots in sequence is canonical. It is, in CA terms, an adjacency pair. But what follows is slightly less determinate and, in any sample of goals taken for analysis, it may be that the next shot is either of the scorer's team-mates or of the team manager. A minimal routine is as follows: goal > goal-scorer > team-mates and then into the replays. The full routine, as in this case, produces shots of all the most immediately affected parties: the scorer, the manager,[8] the team, the fans in their hierarchic order of relevance, their proximity to the significance of the goal that has been scored.

The sequence is closed by the cross-wipe whose pragmatic function is similar to Tony Blackburn's 'Right', serving to indicate an ending and a beginning. We now enter a very peculiar space and time, whose character was first disclosed by Stephanie Marriott's linguistic analysis of tense shifts in instant replays (Marriott 1995, 1996). In considering the replay sequence in terms of what we see and hear, in terms of its spatial and temporal characteristics, we begin to see that liveness is not inevitably an irreversible process. It is possible, 'in fact', to re-live the living moment, through the combination of the liveness of television broadcasting and its supporting recording technologies:

Germany/England, Munich: 01.09.01
Steven Gerrard's goal (47th minute)
7. 1st replay: The goal from behind the goal line
[C3: 9.5 secs]
TB. I hope he heh survives. What a strike this is.
It's a deliberate kick back from Rio Ferdinand.
Chests it down and it's in the net from the moment it
left his boot

/ mix to

8. 2nd replay: As 1 above. The original shot of the goal [C1: 9.5 secs]

TB. Watch Rio Ferdinand as it comes in. Look he deliberately knocks it back.

He knows he's there. Chests it down 'nd he's thirty yards out.

Zips off the sock.. What a strike from Steven Gerrard
/ mix to

9. 3rd replay. Shot unfreezes. From right-hand corner post,

the goal in slow motion[C4: 10.2 secs]

JM. First sightings I thought maybe it just brushed Michael Owen

as it went through but I don't think anybody did get a touch.

Barmby who nearly touched it
/ mix to

10. Gerrard, in slow motion, slides towards corner-flag [C4: 6.8 secs]

JM. But it's a goal for Gerrard. A goal for England.

And they lead Germany two-one

11. symbolic wipe

12. Normal coverage resumed

In the first part of the goal sequence, the visual shots have a self-explicating significance. The viewer, as an audience member, is presumed to have certain basic knowledge and a basic position in relation to the game. Since the coverage of the game is provided by the BBC, the viewer is taken to belong to a membership category that is 'British'. It is assumed that the viewer will recognise shot 3 as showing the English manager and shot 5 as one of the English fans. The implicature, in each case, is of the same order as that identified by Sacks in his discussion of the child's story. It is not necessary to state that the man in the shot is the manager of the England team, nor that the crowd members shown are supporters of the English team. Both those facts are implicated in their reactions as shown. And those reactions are determined by the temporal priority of the goal that has just been scored, just as the mommy's reaction is determined by the temporal priority of the baby crying.

In the second part of the sequence – the replays of

the goals – we enter into a different determinate relationship between what is shown and what is said. The significance of the shots – the replays – is treated as something to be interpreted, by an expert, on behalf of non-expert viewers. The comments on shots 1–6 are provided by John Motson (Motty to his many fans), the BBC's star football commentator. In the commentary box beside him is Trevor Brooking, an ex-footballer who played for England many times. As we move into the replay sequence, Brooking takes over from Motson to explicate for the 'non-expert' viewer just how the goal was scored. Shots 7–9 are at least twice the duration of shots 2–6. They show the goal from three different perspectives: from behind the goal line (7), from the original prime camera, now replayed (7) and from a touch-line camera on the other side of the pitch (8). The temporality of the first two shots is exactly the same; they both pick up the action from exactly the same moment, Beckham's delicate chip to Rio Ferdinand which sets up the goal. The third shot, a fraction later, starts with Beckham's shot in mid-air to Ferdinand.

What the cameras show in shots 7 and 8 is Beckham's chip, on the near side, into a ruck of players in the centre of the pitch just outside the goal-mouth area. His shot is picked up by Rio Ferdinand who rises to head it back, away from the goal, directly towards the incoming Steven Gerrard, who receives the ball at chest height, knocks it down and, on first strike, scores from 30 yards out. The viewer knows, from the previous play, that it is Beckham who sets the whole sequence in motion (he had just taken a free kick and the ball has come back to him). What s/he does not recognize is Ferdinand, to whom the ball is fed, nor his deliberate skill in picking out the incoming Gerrard to whom he directs his header. Brooking's commentary makes clear the skills of the three players whose interactions combine to set up and produce the goal. Shot 7 from behind the goal-line provides the 'money shot' of the ball slamming into the bulging net at the back of the goal, conclusive visual proof of the fact of the goal. Less clear is the sequence of events that produced it. The next shot (8), a replay of the original C1 coverage of the goal, shows how the goal was set up. Brooking tells the viewer what to look for: '*Watch* Rio Ferdinand as it comes in. *Look* he deliberately knocks it back.' But what is the point of saying this? Does it need to be said? Or to put it slightly differently, does the viewer see what Brooking sees? It is surely, in the eyes of the ordinary (non-expert) viewer, counter-intuitive in such a situation for a player to head the ball away from rather than towards the goal. But Brooking directs us to see that Ferdinand does this *deliberately* (it was not unintentional; the ball didn't accidentally come off the back of his head). Why? 'He [Ferdinand] knows he's there [Gerrard] chests it down.' The referents of the deictic pronouns are quite clear to the viewer. Brooking is speaking directly to what the viewer is seeing. But what Brooking sees is something more than the viewer. He sees how Ferdinand skilfully sets up a shot for the incoming Gerrard. His comments do not confirm what we are watching at this moment, but explain and enrich what we are seeing.

The third replay has a different function. Unlike the first two, it starts from a freeze frame and is in super-slow motion. It picks up Beckham's chip shot in mid-air. It does not show Ferdinand's header towards Gerrard, but highlights Gerrard chesting the ball down and dispatching it towards the goal. In slow motion we see the flight of the ball towards and into the net. The first two replays attend to what produces the goal. The third attends to the goal itself. Motson takes over from Brooking in providing the running commentary. What he attends to is the passage of the ball to the goal from the moment it leaves the boot of Gerrard. 'First sightings I thought maybe it just brushed Michael Owen' . . . The first two 'sightings' have made it clear how the goal was set up, but have not conclusively shown who scored the goal. Perhaps another player got a touch to the ball in its flight towards the goal. This shot, slowed down, shows two players identified in order by Motson; Owen, the English striker who sways to avoid contact with the ball and Barmby, an English defender. Neither touches it. It is, conclusively, Gerrard's goal.

The next shot elegantly wraps up the whole sequence. It is a match-on-action mix from the previous shot in which we saw Gerrard strike the ball goal-wards. As the ball heads in that direction, Gerrard himself goes out of the picture and runs towards the corner-flag. The mix picks him up as he does so, raising a clenched fist in a gesture of triumph and then diving towards the corner-flag. The shot is the exact reverse of shot 2. Shot 2 is the first reaction shot of the goal-scorer, and shows Gerrard running away from camera towards the far corner-flag. The shot ends as Gerrard, back to camera, begins to throw himself forward into his sliding dive. Shot 12 gives us the reverse shot of this and picks up where it left off. It shows what shot 2 could not; the delight in Gerrard's face and his whole body as, in slow motion, he goes into his victory dive. Thus, the last shot returns to the beginning of the whole sequence, neatly repeating the first reaction shot from a different perspective and thereby achieving narrative closure. We start and end with the joy of the scorer of the goal that elicited the whole subsequent narrative sequence. The cross-wipe that closes the shot signals the end of the sequence (Right) and the return to the real-time event and its normal coverage.

Events and their moments

Thus far I have been concerned with the management of liveness, emphasizing what is at stake when the performance is the event; the event, the performance. In order for a live performance to come off (whether it is an epic poem, a three-hour live-to-air DJ programme or television coverage of an international soccer match), a common set of techniques are required in order to ensure an effective performance, not now and then, but every time. Since live performance is intrinsically risky (there is always the wild possibility that it might go wrong), its techniques are negatively designed to minimize the risks involved. The formatting of routines in one respect can be thought of as making the performance 'safe'. But this is by no means enough. The task of live performance is to bring something to life, to make it alive. If this is so, we must enquire as to how it is done and, indeed, what it means. In any event – a musical performance, a play, a movie or a soccer match – there will be stretches of time when nothing much seems to be going on. No performance can sustain the same level of intensity throughout. There will be variations in tempo, in mood. There will be highs and lows, dull patches, even moments of poor performance. Yet at the end of the day, and looking back on it, one will remember the high points, the memorable moments, and forget the rest. What I want now to attend to is the meaning of 'the moment' in relation to the event. In soccer, as I have tried to show, a goal is 'a moment' and marked as such by the formatted narrative routines of television. Not all goals, however, have the same significance. Some are more significant than others, as we shall see in considering the goal scored by David Beckham in the match that followed the Germany-England game in the qualifying rounds of the 2002 World Cup.

Going into the game against Germany, there was little expectation of victory. At that point in the qualifying process England were lying second, six points behind Germany, although with a game in hand. The pre-match discussion and analysis tended to assume that England would finish second in their group and thus would fail to qualify automatically. They would probably have to go into a playoff with a runner-up from one of the other European qualifying groups. Gary Lineker, *Match of the Day*'s presenter, greeted viewers with the observation that the game could be 'an uncomfortable watch' and offered a couple of statistics. England had not won in Germany for 36 years and the Germans had only lost one World Cup qualifying round, *ever*. The studio discussion was cautious. Germany had not lost a game in their Munich stadium in 28 years. It was 'the hardest place in world football to come to and get a result'. England *might* win; *could* get a result. But the general view was that it would be 'a really difficult game'.

These expectations were, in the next 90 minutes, stood on their head. Gerrard's goal, right on half time, gave England a 2-1 advantage going into the second half. A fine goal by Michael Owen within three minutes gave England a 3-1 lead. Owen went on to complete a hat-trick and England won 5-1, an outstanding and wholly unexpected result. After England's fifth and final goal Motson exclaimed in a voice that was a mixture of triumph and disbelief: 'Listen to this! Germany 1. England 5!!' In the closing minutes, the losing team, whose grit and resolution had been emphasized in the pre-match discussion, had become 'a bedraggled Germany' and the cameras picked up shots of German fans streaming out of the stadium before the final whistle – 'walking out in disgust', according to Motson. 'England have re-written the history books', he declared with three minutes to go. The post-match analysis now anticipated a rather different scenario. If England were to beat Albania, who they were to play in the next week, they would be level on points with Germany, but leading the group since their 5-1 victory gave them a much better goal-difference. England duly beat Albania, so it was all down to the last two games both to be played on the same day and at the same time: Germany against Finland in Gelsenkirchen, and England against Greece at Old Trafford.

Expectations were therefore running high, and it is fair to say that the nation (and even those parts that normally didn't care a fig) was agog on the day of the match against Greece. Pre-match discussion was not *whether* England would beat Greece, but by how much. After all, they had already beaten Greece quite comfortably in Athens, and the Greek team had the poorest record in the group. But even so, there was some anxiety in the BBC studio at the stadium. It was a big occasion, but 'one of those twitchy ones', because 'everyone is like expecting really just us to trounce them, off the back of Germany everybody just thinks teams like Greece and Albania we're expecting just goals upon goals'. However, Ian Wright went on, 'personally I think it's not going to be that easy but I think we should nick it two three nil'. Alan Hansen concurred: 'The problem is that everyone expects them to play like world beaters and it doesn't happen like that; it's going to be difficult. The Greeks have got men behind the ball but you've got to be patient. England have got a great team now . some great players. One bit of magic could set them up. It could be great for them if they get an early goal but if they nick it one nil then everyone will be happy.'

It is in the nature of occasions that they come invested with an ontology of expectations which are both prospective and retrospective, part of the historicality of any situation; its before-and-after. Before the German game, British expectations were modest. After it they were high. The Greece match carried with it the cumulative baggage of all

that had gone before. Going into it, and based on recent past performance, England was now expected to win and thereby qualify for the
World Cup finals in Japan and South Korea. It thus came as a dismal
surprise that, at half time, England was a goal down. There was agonized discussion in the studio. 'Why oh why do we always have to be put
through this', moaned Gary Lineker opening things up. England were
'diabolical', 'hopeless' in the words of Alan Hansen. The more optimistic Peter Reid thought the good thing was that it could only get better.
There was certainly general agreement that it could not get much worse.
A report from Tony Gubba, covering the other match, confirmed that
Germany was not doing much better: 'Finland look dangerous and as
likely to score as Germany but nil nil at half time.' 'There's no point
in beating Germany five one away to come here and get beaten', Alan
Hansen concluded. Handing back to Motson and Brooking, Lineker
hoped that 'perhaps since we've given them a bit of stick at half time it
might inspire them for the second half'. As the game re-started Motson
declared it 'a big 45 minutes this for the England team, for Sven-Göran
Eriksson, for the nation if you like. So sit tight.'

Perhaps it could not get worse, but it did. A header by Sheringham
in the 67th minute put England level, but Greece scored again within
three minutes to go 2-1 up. After 90 minutes England were still a goal

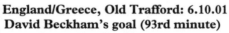

down. There were four minutes of injury time. In the 93rd
minute of the game, England was awarded a free kick just
outside the penalty area. This was it. The lonely moment of
the last chance had arrived. If England scored they would
qualify – the Germany-Finland game was about to finish in a
goalless draw. If they missed (there was barely a minute left),
Germany would go through and England would still face the
agony and uncertainty of a further play-off to make it to the
finals. Everything depended on a single kick:

England/Greece, Old Trafford: 6.10.01
David Beckham's goal (93rd minute)
  1. **Long shot. Beckham comes up to take the kick [2 secs]**
     JM. It's a free kick 25 yards out
     / cut to
  2. **MCU. Beckham places the ball on the spot. [3 secs]**
     In what is probably the penultimate minute of the game
     /cut to
  3. **MCU. An anxious English fan, hands joined as if in**
     prayer [2 secs]
     / cut to
  4. **Long shot. Beckham prepares for the kick. Magic**
     circle displayed[9] [10 secs]

Everybody bar the Greek supporters praying for a goal
Beckham to take
/ cut to

5. **MCU. Beckham starts his run up [2 secs]**
The 93rd minute at Old Trafford
/ cut to

6. **Long shot. He strikes the ball and scores [3 secs]**
Beckhaa::aaM YES YES
/ cut to

7. **MCU Beckham begins his victory run [5 secs]**
HE'S DONE IT FANTASTIC
/ cut to

8. **MCU Beckham gestures to the fans. English players
rush up to embrace him [10 secs]**
Its 2-2 and England may still be going to the World Cup
automatically
It's a fantastic ending to a very very poor performance
/ cut to

9. **MCU. Sven-Göran Eriksson from behind. Hand on
shoulder of team coach [2.5 secs]**
And he's a lucky manager
/ cut to

10. **MCU. Beckham running back to take up position
[4 secs]**
And he deserves the goal
Because Beckham
/ mix to

11. **1st replay. Overhead directly behind the goal [4 secs]**
has virtually played Greece on his own
What a curler
/ mix to

12. **2nd replay Overhead directly towards the goal [4 secs]**
Right in the corner. Trevor Brooking
TB. Well what a goal
/ mix to

13. **3rd replay Close up, ground level. Behind the goal
[6 secs]**
Absolutely fantastic
He's chased himself all over the pitch.
He's won tackles. He's taken free kicks
/ mix to

**14. MCU Sven-Göran Eriksson, rising from his seat
[8 secs]**
>And look at that reaction
>That is a top class free kick on goal
>Wonderful wonderful stuff
>/ cut to

**15. Long shot. The game has restarted and the ball is in
the English half [C1]**
>And he thoroughly deserves it
>Now let's concentrate on the back for goodness sake
>**(game continues)**

The format of the coverage is the same, though there are some noticeable differences from Gerrard's goal. This time the narrative begins before the goal is scored, because it results from a free kick rather than the game-in-process. The interval between the kick being awarded and its being taken allows the edited continuity sequence to begin beforehand. Thus, a crowd reaction shot comes before rather than after the goal and serves to indicate something of the tension in the seconds before the kick is taken (cf. Motson's comment, shot 4). The length of each shot and the total time of the post-goal sequence (7–15) is considerably shorter than for the Gerrard goal. The Beckham sequence lasts 44.5 seconds compared with 63.5 seconds for Gerrard. The length of each of the three replays is half that of those in the Gerrard sequence. Two reasons suggest themselves. Firstly, Gerrard's goal came right on half time and the whistle went after it was scored. Although Beckham's goal comes at the very end of the game, there is still a little bit of further play (no more than half a minute) before the final whistle. Thus the Gerrard sequence has more time to show the goals (there's nothing else happening; the players are leaving the pitch), whereas the Beckham sequence must get back to the game, which it does so quickly and without the small adornment of a *Match of the Day* cross-wipe. Brooking switches instantly from the goal to the game (15): 'Now let's concentrate on the back [the ball is with the English defenders] for goodness sake.' But, perhaps more to the point, the second goal is less complex and viewers have had plenty of time beforehand to see how it comes about. Whereas the Gerrard replays go back to before the moment the goal is struck in order to show and explain the three-move combination that produced it, the Beckham replays simply feature the shot itself. No prior explanation is needed, either from the cameras or from Trevor Brooking. Anyone can see how brilliantly it is taken. 'What a curler' (Motson). 'What a goal . . . Absolutely fantastic . . . Wonderful, wonderful stuff' (Brooking).

'Oh ye of little faith!' exclaimed Gary Lineker. 'It was never in doubt. Not for a heheh second.' But it was not for the 'faint-hearted'. 'They had their hearts in their mouths and their fingernails virtually down to the bone there until the 93rd minute', said John Motson over shots of the ecstatic English fans after the final whistle. 'What a story. What a headline [. . .] You couldn't have written a better script. Here at Old Trafford. The English captain. In the very last minute.' 'One of the great performances of all time.. unbelievable... awesome.. you'll never never get a better finish', were some of the views from the studio in the final post-match analysis . . . 'A fantastic piece of skill'.

Beckham's goal is a perfect example of the relationship between events and their moments. The event as a whole bore no comparison with the game in Germany where England played *as* a team and were effortlessly superior to their opponents. Here, they did not deserve to win, and there was some doubt as to whether they really deserved the free kick at the end that clinched their place in the World Cup finals. There was little pleasure in watching the game, and increasing anxiety as it went on. Pre-match expectations were dashed. It looked as though England would lose and Germany would go through. All this served only to ratchet up the tension and pile on the pressure as the game went into injury time. The goal, when it came, struck like a flash of lightning. There and gone in an instant. And yet everything was now transformed – an electrifying moment which had everyone leaping from their seats, jumping for joy, punching the air in triumph. The  goal itself took less than a second. It was the most perishable of things and yet imperishable: a never to be forgotten moment of pure, ecstatic delight.

Moments and their magic

Why else do we watch football games if not for that 'one bit of magic' which, as Alan Hansen presciently observed in the pre-match discussion, was all that was needed on this occasion? In our ordinary understanding an event 'goes on' from moment to moment. An event is made up of moments. But this is to think of moments as the fractional components of ordinary time, like the tick and tock of the movement of a clock. What, then, is the moment of magic if not a moment out of time, the moment when time stands still? Proust thought of 'the moment' as time regained. It is 'brief as a flash of lightning', 'a fragment of time in its pure state'. It is a moment 'freed from the order of time' in which we ourselves are free from time and necessity. Such a moment is 'death-less'. 'Situated outside time, why should [we] fear the future? (Proust 1996: 224–5). For Proust, art performed the essential, redemptive act of recreating, out of the past, the living moment in which we are freed to encounter what it is to be. My analysis has tried to show something of the same order; how television recreates moments in which time is reversed and we live again – not once, but twice and three times over – a moment in its absolute purity.

Such a moment is unique to television. It is not the same as the moment experienced by the crowd there at the match. What those in the crowd get to experience is being there with others; a shared collective memory to which each individual can lay claim: 'I was there, when Beckham scored that goal.' In discussions about going to the match compared with watching it on television with my students (on both sides of the Atlantic), a number of points come up regularly. Going to the match has a ritual character to it in which anticipation of what it will be like to be there is important. On the plus side what you get (which you cannot get from seeing the game on television) is the atmosphere, the mood in the ground, the sheer physical presence, in every way, of the crowd. You 'live' the experience with everyone else who is there. You are there as a 'fan', a supporter of one of the teams. You experience solidarity with other fans, and join in the rituals of pumping up support for your team and of jeering at the opposition fans and their team. On the down side, the weather may be foul, your view of the game may be impeded and, if it is a dull game or your team loses, you may feel let down.

Match of the Day began in 1964 and showed recorded highlights, later in the evening, of First Division games played earlier in the day. In many ways, as Chris Horrie points out, it was more attractive than watching a whole game, much of which could be boring. 'The editor of the programme at the time said that making it was simplicity itself: "You just cut out all the rubbish, point the camera at the most crowded part of the ground and turn up the sound level" . . . At a time when youngsters in particular could hardly see anything unless the ground was half empty or they stood on a soap box, the games on television looked much better and exciting than they often were in cold reality' (Horrie 2002: 23). Half a century later and the technology of television today can do things undreamed of in the 1960s. It is no longer just a case of pointing the camera and cutting out the boring bits. Television no longer merely points and shows. It narrates. It puts together a story, even as it is happening, whenever a goal is scored. Not just the fact of the goal itself but its before and after; how it came about and the reaction it elicited. It thus captures, *live*, the essential temporal structure and dynamic of the living moment (its past-present-future) and instantly displays and analyses this. The moment of the goal is 'all-at-once'. All at once, simultaneously, *now* the ball hits the net, the player begins his victory run, the team-mates rush up, the manager is on his feet, the crowd roars in delight. When you are there you do not, cannot, see all this. You are simply part of it, caught up in it, carried away by the moment. You *live* the moment.

The television viewer, who is not there, gets to *re-live* the moment, captured in a double movement. First there is the narrative sequence that flows effortlessly from the moment of the goal, the narrative of what-comes-next. The all-at-onceness of the reactions there, at the ground, of all those most immediately touched by the moment now just gone, is analytically deconstructed and reconstructed into a rapid visual sequence with a strict temporal order of significance. This is done in real time, live, allowing the replays to be set up. When they commence, we enter into a temporality specific to television. Time is now reversed and slowed down. The 'then' (the goal that was) has entered into the 'now', creating a then-and-now. Marriott drew attention to how this doubled time is there in a heard but unnoticed way. In television's now, we see the replays, and the commentators speak to them; that is, they speak in the present of the moment just gone. However, in the event's now, the game is continuing even as they speak, and the background ambient sound is part of that on-going reality. Viewers hear but do not attend to the background sound because they are listening to the foregrounded commentary which addresses a different moment. What we see displays the moment gone – the visual (not the sound) recording of the goal. What we hear captures the magic doubled moment: the now of the background ambient sound of the on-going game in real time, and the then of the visually displayed moment just now past to which the foregrounded words of the commentator speak. The equipment deployed in live sports coverage routinely produces an impossible temporal doubling, the effect of being in two different times (the 'then' and the 'now') at one and the same time. Sight and sound, inseparable 'in reality', are deconstructed via the communicative technologies of television that simultaneously transmit and record live events. They are recombined to create a multi-dimensional spatiality and temporality for viewers.

Television does not create the moments, the goals, which are the event's raison d'être. But it is ready for them and when they come they are, in one and the same instance, shown-and-recorded and instantly narrated in the two-part story format discussed above. The now of the event has a determinate priority to which television responds in producing its now. But the now of the event is not somehow more real or genuine than the now of television. Modern communicative technologies, as Ian Hutchby has argued, create new communicative affordances, new possibilities of communicative action and interaction (Hutchby 2001). These possibilities are realized in the interplay of the form of the technology and its application and use. Radio and television were, originally, live-to-air communicative technologies and recording devices came later. In each case, sound and video recording were sought for not in order to replace live broadcasting but to give it greater flexibility, more communicative affordances. Instant replays are one such affordance out of the repertoire of what can be done with recording devices for television (this chapter is another!). By virtue of the double process of broadcasting live events and simultaneously recording them, new communicative possibilities, hitherto impossible, are afforded viewers. One such instance – the visual replay sequence – has been considered here, in a little detail, in order to make explicit how it is that we get to live and re-live the magic of David Beckham's decisive goal in the dying moments of the England-Greece game on 6 October 2001.

11

Being in the moment: the meaning of media events

The question of experience

I am concerned to justify the *possibility of the experience* of television: that it really *is* possible to have an experience watching television and thus that television does indeed, really and truly, furnish us with access to the public world that lies over and beyond the immediate life world of, in each case, my immediate experience. That is what Heidegger got to experience watching a football game on television and what he denied in his public talk to the people of his home town, Messkirch. It is time now to consider the meaning of the momentary now of Heidegger's spilt teacup. He had raised the question of the now himself, in his lecture on 'The concept of time' to the Theology Department at Marburg half a life time earlier in 1924:

> What is this now, the time now as I look at my watch? Now, as I do this; now, as the light here goes out for instance. What is the now? Is the now at my disposal? Am I the now? Is every other person the now? Then time would indeed be I myself, and every other person would be time. And in our being with one another we would be time – everyone and no one. Am I the now, or only the one who is saying this? With or without any explicit clock? Now, in the evenings, in the mornings, tonight, today . . .
> (Heidegger [1924] 1992: 5E)

To that battery of questions let me add one more: What is this now – the time *now* as I watch television? That was the question posed and addressed by Daniel Dayan and Elihu Katz in their celebrated study of *Media Events* whose subtitle is 'The live broadcasting of history'.

Eventful television

The germ of the idea for what became eventually the book, was Katz's perception of the importance of what he called 'festive' television, its 'high holidays', when ordinary television is momentarily suspended and something extraordinary takes its place – the funeral of John F. Kennedy, the wedding of Lady Diana Spencer and the Prince of Wales, the journeys of Pope John Paul II and Anwar el-Sadat to Israel, the TV debates of 1960 between Kennedy and Nixon, Watergate, the revolutionary changes of 1989 in eastern Europe, the Olympics and others (Dayan and Katz 1992: 4). This initial indicative check-list is a rather mixed bag that includes a few unexpected happenings and more strictly political events along with the great occasions that Dayan and Katz are mainly concerned with – its French title, *La Télévision Cérémonielle* captures the book's focus more exactly. For this is a book about television with 'a halo', auratic television we might call it with a nod in the direction of Walter Benjamin. The aura of the extraordinary event shines brightly as its stands out from the ordinary, the humdrum and routine. The occasional event comes with (creates and generates) a sense of occasion, a moment out of the ordinary. Normal routines are suspended as whole populations take time-out from the ordinary complexities and animosities of daily life (ibid.: 152). Collective attention is monopolized by and focused on the event which is covered by television *en direct*, live and in real time as it really happens. The time of the event, the time of television and the my-times of countless viewers all converge in the experiential, living enunciatory now of the event as it unfolds in a shared, common public time.

This was, at the time of its publication, a dazzlingly original topic. Katz came upon it after a decisive moment in his career when he had been instrumental in establishing television in Israel. He thus had experience of broadcasting from within, from the side of the industry, understood its industrial practices and saw it as a real-world phenomenon with real-world effects. And that is the most striking feature of *Media Events*. It is a study of television that properly acknowledges and accepts its *worldliness*; that does not approach it as if it were a *problem*, a social disorder or pathology in need of critical academic diagnosis and corrective treatment. It is wonderfully accepting and non-judgemental, taking the essential worldliness of television in its most striking manifestations and attempting to account for them. For the simple amazing fact of huge television audiences on rare occasions remains true to this day and for the foreseeable future. Now and then and on occasion everything does indeed come to a stop and everyone turns to television.

Dayan and Katz did their work in the 1980s, before the technological transformations of the 1990s kicked in to yield the astonishing globally mediatized world we inhabit today. Television, as an object of study in the eighties, was largely thought of as *national* television within the frame of the politics and culture of particular nation-states. Their book is one of the first to break out from that conceptual strait-jacket. Dayan and Katz's object of study is the impact and significance of television worldwide; not this or that television but television as the truly global phenomenon it was just then becoming. In that respect they were ahead of the game in 1992. At all points Dayan and Katz remain firmly focused on real events in their actuality *and* in their coverage by television. They were not the first to attend to this, but they were the first to do so systematically and without prejudice.

In trying to figure out how to analyse televised events, Dayan and Katz had little to go by. Their topic scarcely existed in the emerging academic study of television in Europe and North America and the title of their book identified and named something new; new that is, to the field and its then current preoccupations. Dayan and Katz were keenly aware of the kinds of objection that were likely to greet them, and in their preface they cheerfully and robustly anticipate and fend them off:

> The live broadcasting of history? Don't they know that history is process, not events? Certainly not ceremonial events! Don't they know that media events are hegemonic manipulations? Don't they know that the royal wedding [in 1981, of Lady Diana Spencer and the Prince of Wales] simply blotted out the ethnic rioting that had occupied the streets of London the day before? Haven't they read Daniel Boorstin's *The Image*? (Dayan and Katz 1992: vii)

They knew full well that they were taking a very different stance to most if not all current academic orthodoxies. They took issue with the historians and their dismissal of what Fernand Braudel had dubbed *histoire événementielle*; with the critics of 'the society of the spectacle' from Boorstin to Debord; with Cultural Studies and its hegemonic preoccupation with 'the political'; with the social and political scientists – notably Gladys and Kurt Lang. They parted company with the Frankfurt School luminaries, including Walter Benjamin. They were at odds with all those, who one way or another, were dismissive of public life as theatre and television as its publicity agent.

Thus they refused to accept that ceremonial occasions were what Daniel Boorstin called 'pseudo events' ([1962] 1992) and the tormented Guy Debord, following in his wake, inflated into a full-blown theory of the spectacle as the commodification of experience by global capitalism – 'the very heart of society's real unreality' (Debord [1967] 2004: 13). They acknowledged but begged to differ from the standard

Left critique of public ceremony as 'a theatre of power' enacted before but not for the masses (Habermas [1962] 1989: 8) – a cynical distraction to blindside them to what was really going on. They took on board Benjamin's influential concept of fake aura; the aestheticization of politics through the spectacular mass event but were not persuaded by it. There might be some truth in the perception of ceremonial occasions as forms of hegemonic control imposed from above on those below – and yet there was more to events than this.

A deflationary view of events refuses to acknowledge the possibility of the greatness of occasions. It will always see through that aspiration and find a way of puncturing it. As Dayan and Katz freely admit, the kinds of event that they wish to focus on are, if that's how you choose to see them, hegemonic. You could say they contribute to the reproduction of the existing order of things, the powers that be, the authority of church and state or whatever. From this perspective, the inflationary role of television makes it therefore an active supporter of (as they used to say) the status quo. It is an old objection that has recently been revived by Nick Couldry in his 'critical approach' to media rituals. Couldry is determined to take Dayan and Katz to task for their un-political view of media events as the affirmation of shared experience. Media rituals are, in his view, *really* exercises in 'the management of conflict and the masking of social inequality' whose function is to confirm an established social order as somehow natural and beyond question (Couldry 2003: 4). If this is so, it follows that media events are no more than a theatre of power whose intention is to deceive the masses or, at least, to reconcile them to their fate. This is, in some circumstances, a relevant and necessary critique: totalitarian regimes have in the past exploited the politics of mass spectacle to bind the masses to the party and the state. Fascism aestheticized politics, as Benjamin pointed out. But ceremony and spectacle have always been part of public life in any society, and objections to them are as old as the events themselves. Puritanism has an iconoclastic dislike of conspicuous public display which offends its austere worldview. Utilitarianism grumbles that such things are a waste of time and money, both of which could be better spent on less idle and more practical things. By any cost-benefit analysis, ceremonial events are irrational. They are neither useful nor necessary. To be sure, issues of power and inequality are centrally important concerns in any society and any politics. But now and then, societies choose momentarily (as all of us do), to take time out from the grittiness of ordinary life and celebrate. Media events are precisely not to be judged by the usual political criteria and if they are, they will simply slip through your fingers like butter. *Any* political interpretation of media events is deflationary. What is it, then, about media events that the political optic does not and cannot see?

For an ontology of occasions

For the last 12 years I have taught, in England and the USA, an undergraduate course on media events, inspired by Dayan and Katz's book. Each year I begin with a little exercise in free association to establish what the class thinks it is about. I ask the students to jot down quickly what comes to mind when I toss a phrase at them: – 'events in my life', 'historic events', 'sporting events', 'media events'. 'Events in my life' always includes the following mix: birthdays, Christmas, Thanksgiving Day (USA), weddings, funerals and (for American students) commencement (or graduation) day. Historic events are mainly wars, battles, deaths and disasters (natural and human). Media events overlap with them to some extent and have included the moon landings, the death of Diana as well as, more recently, leading 'reality' shows – *Pop Idol*, *American Pop Idol* and (in the UK) *Big Brother*. Sport includes the Olympics, the World Cup, Wimbledon (UK), the Rose Bowl and Superbowl in the USA. These results are, year on year – allowing for variations between the USA and the UK – almost entirely predictable. The class has mapped its shared, common-sense, ordinary understanding of the meaning of (the word) 'events'. We begin the course by raising the question of the relationship between worldly events and events in our own lives; public and private occasions.

If we consider what the students think of as events in their lives, we find that they relate to the human life course and to the calendar. A birthday spans both: on the one hand, an intimately personal thing, on the other hand, a date on the calendar. Your birthday is something that matters when you're young. There is a *big* difference between being five and six (as my grandson knows) and it means something getting to double figures, getting into one's teens and then getting out of them – these are benchmarks in an unfolding individual existence when getting older is something to look forward to. Some days stand out from the routine character of the ordinary and the everyday. Key days for children (and their parents) include those when they go back to school and those when the holidays begin; days whose approach brings childish dread and happiness and similar feelings, though perhaps inversely, for parents. The eventful day shows up against the backdrop of unmarked uneventful days. The occasion is occasional and marked in private diaries and on the calendars of public life as something to be noted in advance. Occasions always come with an ontology of expectations. They are to be talked about before, during and after their occurrence. They never just happen. They must always be made to happen. But why? Why do we take occasional time out from routine, uneventful existence if not in order to give ourselves an experience?

Experience comes to us in two ways. There is firstly the slow incremental process of *becoming* experienced. An experienced parent or teacher gets to be so in the course of time, through the day-to-day business of coping and managing and dealing with their own children or a classroom of them – and children, of course, reciprocally, become experienced in dealing with their parents and teachers. *An* experience, however, stands out from the unremarkable, unnoticed, incremental accumulation of life experience. It is by definition an occasional, now-and-then occurrence; a singularity, a one-of-a-kind sort of thing.[1] For it to be such it must be made to be distinct from the everyday. Not every day is a birthday or Christmas or Thanksgiving. We make such days remarkable by doing remarkable things: things we must think about, plan and talk about in advance. Presents, cards, dressing up in special clothes and celebratory food and drink are all tokens of that thoughtfulness which marks the special nature of the occasion – and all for the sake of creating the possibility of an experience.

The phenomenology of mood is one of Heidegger's most brilliant insights in Division One of *BT* (Heidegger [1927] 1962: 172 ff.).[2] Human beings, of course, have all sorts of moods which we learn to recognize in ourselves and others, but so does every human situation and occasion. What was it like? It was: boring, exciting, thrilling, frightening, annoying, sad, wonderful, funny, solemn . . . tick the words that apply. Whatever it was or wasn't, any event is defined by its mood. Mood is not some value added to occasions. It is their raison d'être, their reason for being, that for the sake of which they were made to happen. If the occasion is to be festive, its sought-for mood is fun and enjoyment and there are standard ways of securing such effects. Parties require mood-enhancing devices which their organizers take care to lay on in advance: jellies, ice-cream and cake for children; wine, beer and finger food for grown-ups. If the occasion is to be solemn, there are prescribed ways of securing that effect too. As it is in private events, so it is with their public equivalents. In either case they are meant to be memorable. The hope is that, on the day, all the advance preparations for it will happen as they were meant to happen so that the occasion turns out to be that which it was meant to be, whether festive or solemn, a *great* occasion, a cherishable moment in time; something worth remembering, something to look back on with pleasure. Yes, it *was* a good wedding. The bride was radiant. Her wedding dress was beautiful. The church service went off without a hitch. The wedding feast was appreciated by all the guests. The speeches were not disasters. All the anxious care that preceded it and all the expense were worth it if, in the end, all can say, looking back, yes it *was* a great day. The *care-structure* of the occasion has worked to produce it really and truly as that which it was meant and intended and so found in the end to be. Whether it was one of countless private weddings or the rare public wedding of a prince, there was an experience to be had, an occasion to be remembered:

> No feeling could seem more childish than the enthusiasm of the English at the marriage of the Prince of Wales. They treated as a great political event, what, looked at as a matter of pure business, was very small indeed. But no feeling could be more like common human nature as it is, and as it is likely to be [. . .] All but a few cynics like to see a pretty novel touching for a moment the dry scenes of the grave world. A princely marriage is the brilliant edition of a universal fact, and, as such, it rivets mankind.

Not a commentary on the princely weddings of 2011 or 1981, watched around the world on television, but Walter Bagehot, a brilliant political journalist, commenting on the wedding of a rather earlier Prince of Wales (the future Edward VII) in March 1863 (Bagehot [1867] 1963: 85).

It is not just the Brits who like a good royal wedding. Every country with a monarchy makes a splash when the heir to the throne gets married, and even countries that don't have monarchies (such as Germany) get excited when one of their own marries into royalty. A survey by the Institute for Social Research at Frankfurt explored public attitudes to the wedding of Crown Princess Beatrix of the Netherlands to Claus von Amsberg, a German diplomat, in March 1966. Its findings were discussed in an essay on 'Free time' by an ageing Theodor Adorno ([1977] 1991) in which he reiterated the negative critique of leisure under capitalism that he and Max Horkheimer had begun to articulate some 30 years earlier. And yet, he now conceded, the results of the survey cast doubts on their assumption that 'the culture industry utterly and totally dominates and controls both the conscious and the unconscious of those at whom it is directed'. One set of questions showed that 'people enjoyed it [the wedding] as a concrete event in the here and now quite unlike anything else in their everyday life'. However, another set of questions probed the significance that the interviewees attached to 'the grand event'. To Adorno's evident surprise, many of those interviewed suddenly showed themselves 'to be thoroughly realistic, and proceeded to evaluate critically the political and social importance of the same event, the well publicized once-in-a-lifetime nature of which they had drooled over breathlessly in front of their television sets' (Adorno [1977] 1991: 169–70). Adorno detects in this 'symptoms of a split consciousness' in the masses. It comes as news to him that ordinary people are quite capable of enjoying an occasion such as a royal wedding while knowing full well that it is politically insignificant.

Meaningful time

The loss of meaningful experience is a recurring theme in critiques of life under industrial capitalism. This was what early audience studies in the USA claimed to have found; that radio was a substitute for actual experience in the lives of people void of meaningful experience (Herzog 1941, Merton [1946] 2004). An undifferentiated existence is one in which nothing ever happens – in which the most exciting thing is something you hear on radio rather than anything in your own life. It should not be thought that this was merely the experience of the poor who toiled under the dull yoke of economic necessity. In his scintillating study of Charles Baudelaire, Benjamin takes the collapse of meaningful experience to be a defining characteristic of the passage into modernity and a crux for the very possibility of lyric poetry. In its early modern rein-carnation as Romanticism, lyric poetry turned from the emergent new industrial order to Nature as a redemptive alternative. Wordsworth's *Lyrical Ballads* is exemplary. But this was a poetics in retreat into the margins of actual experience, as the dominant experience of life in the nineteenth century came to be defined by factory capitalism and urban working life. Two European authors who most closely engaged with the emergent order of modern experience were Dickens and Baudelaire, each of whom took metropolitan life, in London and Paris, respectively, as his central subject matter – two great European cities at the epicentre of the experience of modernity, the shock of the new.

The collapse of tradition under the impact of societal modernization in the nineteenth century, a central motif in Benjamin's writings, was a commonplace theme of that century's thought and experience. To say that meaningful experience is a sharable common public phenomenon means that it must be a historical phenomenon which endures in time, held in place as tradition by the central institutions of any society.

> Experience is indeed a matter of tradition, in collective existence as well as in private life . . . Where there is experience in the strict sense of the word, certain contents of the individual past combine with material of the collective past. The rituals with their ceremonies, their festivals [. . .] kept producing the amalgamation of these two elements of memory over and over again. They triggered recollection at certain times and remained handles of memory for a lifetime. (Benjamin [1939] 1973: 159, 161)

Modern man has been cheated out of his experience (p. 182) and it is this that gives a sense of measureless desolation to Baudelaire's verse. 'For someone who is past experiencing, there is no consolation' (p. 186). Baudelaire is 'the poet of no experience'; his lyric poetry the expression of this loss.

The man who loses his capacity for experiencing feels as though he is dropped from the calendar. The big-city dweller know this feeling on Sundays; Baudelaire has it *avant la lettre* in one of the *Spleen* poems:

Des cloches toutes à coup sautent avec furie	Explosively the bells begin to ring
Et lancent vers le ciel un affreux hurlement,	hurling their frightful clangor towards the sky,
Ainsi que des esprits errants et sans patrie	as homeless spirits, lost and wandering,
Qui se mettent à geindre opiniâtrement.	might raise their indefatigable cry.[3]

The bells which were once part of holidays have been dropped from the calendar, like the human beings. They are like the poor souls that wander restlessly, but outside of history . . . Baudelaire [. . .] holds in his hands the scattered fragments of genuine historical experience. (Benjamin [1939] 1973: 186–7)

Fleurs du Mal was published in 1857, at exactly the same time that Dickens was publishing *Little Dorrit* in monthly serial parts (1855–7). Here is his memorable opening description of London on Sundays:

> It was a Sunday evening in London, gloomy, close and stale. Maddening church bells of all degrees of dissonance, sharp and flat, cracked and clear, fast and slow, made the brick-and-mortar echoes hideous . . . In every thoroughfare, up almost every alley, and down almost every turning, some doleful bell was throbbing, jerking, tolling as if the Plague were in the city and the dead-carts were going round . . . Nothing for the spent toiler to do, but to compare the monotony of his seventh day with the monotony of the other six, think what a weary life he led, and make the best of it – or the worst, according to the probabilities. (Dickens [1855–7] 2009: 31)

As he listens to the maddening bells, Arthur Clenham, a central figure in the novel, reflects upon the dreary Sundays of his childhood, and 'a legion of Sundays, all days of unserviceable bitterness and mortification' pass slowly before him in his mind (ibid.: 33). In nineteenth-century London and Paris, Sunday has lost its meaning and there is absolutely nothing to do on the weekly day of rest. *Ennui* has become the century's secular equivalent of medieval *accidie* or sloth, spiritual boredom, dry-rot of the soul. The old religious calendar has collapsed with nothing to replace it, and Sundays are experienced as empty time, days drained of meaning in which nothing happens. Of all the vices in Baudelaire's dreamy, druggy garden of evil, Boredom is the worst:

C'est l'Ennui! L'oeil chargé d'un pleur involontaire,	Boredom! He smokes his hookah while he dreams
Il rêve d'échafauds en fumant son houka.	Of gibbets, weeping tears he cannot smother.
Tu le connais, lecteur, ce monstre délicat,	You know this dainty monster, too, it seems,
Hypocrite lecteur, – mon semblable! – mon frère!	Hypocrite reader! – You! – my twin! – my brother![4]

Ennui is the curse of empty time, the waste of time in which there is nothing to do, the experience of no experience: the twin effect of the repetitive drudgery of dull economic compulsion on the one hand and on the other, the existential void of the so-called day of rest. Time drained of meaning – this structure of feeling was a leitmotif of mass society; the experience of an undifferentiated existence in which there was nothing to do but work and nothing to look forward to except more of the same.

David Cardiff and I have argued in earlier writings that a key function of early broadcasting was to gather up what Benjamin calls 'the scattered fragments of genuine historical experience' and work them into an annual calendar of events (Cardiff and Scannell 1987: 157–73; Scannell 1988: 15–31; Scannell and Cardiff 1991: 277–303). This work was begun by the BBC in the 1920s as it transformed itself from a network of local stations into a centralized national institution, broadcasting to the whole of the United Kingdom. The components of a national culture were beginning to converge in early twentieth-century Britain, but their full convergence, their synthesis as elements of a single corporate national life available to all, awaited the establishment of broadcasting in its applied social form and the quite new kind of public – the *general* public, a public commensurate at times with the whole of society – that it brought into being. From the early years of broadcasting through to now, this general public has been most strikingly manifest in what Dayan and Katz call 'media events'. The BBC's National Programme, a service from London aimed at the whole country, began in 1930. In the review of the Corporation's activities for that year, it was noted that 'the broadcasting of ceremonials appeals, it would appear, to a very wide circle of listeners: it is perhaps the only activity of the BBC to attract an audience drawn equally from all grades of the listening public' (*BBC Yearbook* 1930: 82).

In the course of time, a recurring calendar of annual events was put in place first by broadcast radio and later television. It was a mix of the secular and the sacred, religious and state occasions; a wide variety of sporting events with their seasonal fixtures and climaxes; a medley of cultural events (the Proms, for instance); festive programming for public holidays, commemorative programmes on solemn days of national remembrance. Much of this was delivered, live and in real time by OB (outside broadcasting) units and much of it was routine. Its impact was gradual and unobtrusive, but what emerged was a modern, secular equivalent to the old religious calendar which the broadcast calendar replaced. The calendar is based on natural temporal cycles – the lunar month, the solar year – and is a means of regulating, in the long term, the manifold purposes of religious and secular existence. It not only organizes and coordinates social life, but gives it renewable content, anticipatory pleasures, a horizon of expectations. As Anthony Giddens has pointed out, it is one means whereby 'the temporality of social life is expressed in the meshing of present with past that tradition promotes, in which the cyclical character of social life is predominant' (Giddens 1979: 201).

Media events are embedded in the public calendars of whole societies (nations) and marked up on the private calendars of individual lives. They are (can *only* be) delivered by what Dayan calls 'television of the center', broadcasting institutions with the reach and resources to provide coverage of events from where they are taking place, live and as they happen, to whole populations (Dayan 2009). Big media events are not hosted by small, local or community broadcast services. They emerged in the course of time as broadcasting, which began everywhere on a local basis, developed into centralized national institutions that provided services for whole populations. By the time Dayan and Katz took note of the phenomenon of 'media events', they had become global in their reach and impact. Even in the era of national televisions, certain kinds of event found ways of overcoming the technical restrictions of their times. Recordings of the coronation of Queen Elizabeth II in 1953 were flown immediately to the USA and shown on network TV the following day. It is not immediately obvious as to why on earth Americans should care to watch an event that contradicts the very foundations of their constitution – but they did. It remains genuinely strange why the British monarchy should matter to anyone other than the British themselves and yet royal coronations, weddings and deaths have been amongst the greatest of media events in their worldwide impact and reach. The death of Diana, Princess of Wales, was a truly strange experience that gripped an entire nation and riveted the attention of the rest of the word for a whole week, from the moment the story of her death broke to the moment her body was finally laid to rest after a funeral service that the whole world had watched.

Die Augenblick

I began this chapter by raising the question of experience as a way into the meaning of events. I have suggested that it is a distinctive aspect of our common humanity that we can and do arrange to *give* ourselves experiences in order to have them – this is the fore-givenness, the gift, of experience. In making things happen in order to have an experience, we voluntarily submit to the pre-planned occasion for the sake of the experience of it – the sought-for mood that defines the kind of event that it is. In doing so, we get to *own* the experience. For this to happen, we must be open to the possibility of the experience that the event may promise but not necessarily deliver (the game may turn out to be boring; the wedding, a disaster). Those who dismiss events have closed themselves off from this potential. To be open to the event means to allow oneself to be possessed by it; not simply 'to enter into the spirit of the occasion' as they say, but also the reverse – to let the spirit of the occasion (which we can and do sometimes resist) enter into one's self. To own an experience (to possess it) is to have been possessed by it. These are uncomfortable notions for those who prefer to think of possession as a feature of ritual cults in pre-modern societies. But experience, in its absolute purity, is momentary ecstasy – an even more uncomfortable idea.

Heidegger, who dismissed television on the one hand and was carried away by it on the other, thinks of the authentic 'now' as the *Augenblick*, the ecstatic moment of vision, the twinkling of an eye in which everything is transformed:

> That *Present* which is held in authentic temporality and which thus is *authentic* itself, we call the '*moment of vision*'. This term must be understood in the active sense as an ecstasis.[5] It means the resolute rapture with which Dasein is carried away to whatever possibilities and circumstances are encountered in the Situation as possible objects of concern . . .
> (Heidegger [1927] 1962: 387)

Heidegger will later insist that 'Ecstases are not simply raptures in which one gets carried away' (p. 416), but even so, that is one of the things they are. What then is the ecstatic now? I take it to be what Heidegger experienced when he knocked over his teacup watching a soccer match on TV at a friend's house. It is embedded in everyday life and ordinary, routine, humdrum existence. Heidegger is watching television *and* having a cup of tea. The game goes on in ordinary time, marked by the presence of the clock and the minutes ticking away on screen in present-day soccer coverage. It can be tedious, the play may be dull, but at any moment it may be transformed by the scoring of a goal – the most fleeting and transient of things which comes and goes in the twinkling of an eye. Professional soccer is a routine, weekly event during its season; most games are not overburdened with expectations, nor heavily invested with significance by those for whom they matter. But the game that Heidegger watched and the one that I discussed above were pregnant with significance for those who cared to watch them either at the ground itself or on television. They were extraordinary occasions within the world of soccer and much was at stake for those who watched: a place in the final of the European Cup for Hamburg and automatic qualification for the finals of the World Cup for the England team.

Broadcasting has been implicated in sport since it began, and its commitment has been, through to the present, to make sporting events available for listeners and viewers in such ways that they might be experienced for what they are by those who are not there (Whannel 1992, 2009). Sport is not a necessary thing and its occasions are situated mainly in weekends freed from weekday toil. They are located in time freed from necessity. Television, whose existence presupposes a world no longer dominated by necessity, has helped to expand the availability of sport as something to be watched at one's leisure in all parts of the world. Soccer has a classic event structure that fits the schedules of broadcasting and the leisure time of modern societies. Ninety minutes of continuing action with occasional goals as highlights makes it perhaps *the* premium sport of the global television era. Television's technical coverage of soccer, as I indicated, has been driven by continuing innovation whose aim has been to enhance the viewing experi-ence. The technical coverage of the game watched by Heidegger 50 years ago was primitive in comparison with the games I discussed above. Today's TV coverage of international soccer is an exemplary instance of the superfluities of a world of material abundance in which there is always more than is ever necessary. Does soccer coverage *need* the deployment of two dozen cameras to produce the game as something to be watched by absent viewers?[6] Of course not. The blimp shot, deployed in big matches, is quite pointless and unnecessary, so why is it there? It is there because television does indeed work to inflate the occasion, to make something of it, to enhance its mood, to make the big match into a potentially great occasion. It is but one little instance of what Frances Bonner calls television's transformative 'gift of attention' (Bonner 2003: 127). The overhead blimp shot (like the icing on a cake) is either a pointless waste of money, or else it is one small way in which the significance of a big occasion is unobtrusively underscored in the way that television covers it. Whether you prefer a deflationary or inflationary interpretation of this particular shot does not negate the opposing view that you reject. Both are true.

If the blimp shot is unnecessary, the narrative format that clicks in automatically when goals are scored is perhaps even more superfluous to requirements. It is indeed inflationary. And yet it is truly wonderful, an extraordinary, unobtrusive display of the unique capacity of television both to *be* in the moment while simultaneously recording it, and instantly to retrieve the moment just now gone in replays from different angles whenever goals are scored. It is, as I say, essentially awesome and mysterious, when you come to think of it. What's the point of this little narrative that kicks in when a goal is scored? Is it part of TV hype? I don't think so. That is to say that I do not think that the narrative format that I have analysed is something externally superimposed on the moment of the goal in order, as it were, to make more of it than it merits. Rather it seems to me to be a small, uncalled for gift that is true to the inner meaning of 'the moment', working to realize its authenticity.

In comparing the moment of a goal with Proust's discovery of time regained in the previous chapter, I was not (I hope) making a false comparison between great things and small. The meaning of the 'moment' is a recurring motif in the arts, literature and philosophy of the modern era. Vermeer's paintings of a maidservant in the scullery pouring milk into a bowl, of a young woman absorbed in making lace or reading a letter transform insignificant moments of everyday life into surpassing works of art. Wordsworth's *Prelude*, an autobiographical meditation on the formation of the artist, contains several beautiful accounts of what he calls 'spots in time' – moments of unsolicited and unexpected pure experience ('surprised by joy') that provide the essential impulse to poetic expression.[7] The *Augenblick* – the authentic moment of vision that comes and goes in the twinkling of an eye – is central to Heidegger's notoriously difficult meditations on time in Division Two of *BT*. Time, for Heidegger, is the horizon of our being, disclosed as such by death. It is not just that death is, in each case, the termination of the life that is mine. It is rather disclosive of life as such, for it is that which gives life the very condition of its possibility. Death is not life's end but the precondition of its everlasting renewal. It is that wherein and whereby *being and time* appear. It is that which yields the existential temporal structure of birth > life > death as the everlasting cycle of regeneration, which constitutes the one-and-only life-sustaining world of all living things as utterly distinct from the boundless, lifeless, timeless eternity of the universe. The temporality of *the* moment is existence bounded in a nutshell, contracted to an ecstatic *now!*, in which we encounter the aliveness of being (our being alive) as pure unalloyed experience. That is why, as They say, the moment is 'to die for'. It is a little death, *une petite mort* as the French put it. In its utter transience and perishability, it is nevertheless a moment out of time, never to be forgotten by those who experienced it. It is no longer art alone that redeems the moment of ecstasy as time regained. Through the liveness of television, we get to have experiences from afar and through its recording technologies we get to relive them – time and time again (Marriott 1995, 1996).[8]

12

Catastrophe – on television

News disaster narratives

When disaster strikes, it seldom comes with its meaning branded on its forehead.[1] An immediate issue for broadcasters is to establish, as quickly as possible, what in fact has happened and what in fact it means. News coverage, ordinarily, has a retrospective character. The original event has already taken place 'off-stage' and the resources and narrative strategies of television newsrooms are committed in the first place to catching up both with what has happened and the immediate consequences for those most nearly and fatefully caught up in it. On 11 September 2001 the original event – the first plane crashing into the north tower of the World Trade Center – did indeed take place 'off-stage' from television but it was, within minutes, brought live into morning news programs in the United States. It instantly became a catastrophe that unfolded 'live-to-air' on television screens around the world. At first it was utterly incomprehensible but, by the end of the day, the situation had been accurately analysed and correctly understood. Immediate action had been taken and future courses of action predicted and assessed.

In what follows, I attend to both these moments – the breaking news story at the beginning of the day as shown on CNN, and retrospective accounts and analyses at the end of the day, in the BBC's main nightly news programme at 10 pm. These two moments have different temporalities; the *forward moving present* of live-and-in-real-time coverage of an unfolding event as it happens and, on the other hand, the *retrospective present* of nightly news as it looks back on the events of the day. Summary accounts of CNN and BBC news coverage are followed by a brief discussion of what they reveal about the role of broadcast news when disaster strikes.

I

CNN live coverage

It is a normal day on CNN's rolling early mornings news program, *Live at Daybreak*.[2] At 8.45 am, Eastern Time, the studio has a live-to-studio report on a New York fashion show of clothing for pregnant women. It

is a light-hearted piece with the CNN reporter at the venue interviewing three very pregnant models and the designer of the outfits they are wearing. There is playful banter between the female studio anchor, the reporter and the interviewees.

As the item is wrapped, the programme cuts out to advertisements and then back to a short report on business news followed by promotional ads for the Station's corporate business sponsors. Coming out

of the ads, what is displayed next is a shot of a skyscraper with smoke billowing from its upper storeys against the backdrop of a clear, blue morning sky. Across the bottom of the screen is the strapline:

**BREAKING NEWS CNN
LIVE**

For the next 50 minutes, CNN continues to hold on screen static shots of the World Trade Center, nearly all from the same camera position, about two miles away from the buildings and showing only their upper section. Advertisements are scrapped and coverage is continuous. Over images of the towers (and it is not easy to distinguish one from the other) there is what has, in effect, become a voiced-over radio commentary from the news program's two anchors, Leon Harris and Carol Lin:

CNN: 11.09.01: 8.50 am[3]
Lin: Yes .
This just in.
You are looking at obviously
a very disturbing live shot there.
That is the World Trade Center
and we have unconfirmed reports
this morning that a plane has crashed
into one of the towers of the World Trade Center
CNN center right now is just beginning
to work on this story obviously our sources
and trying to figure out exactly what happened
But clearly something relatively devastating happening

this morning there at the south end of the island of Manhattan.
That is once again one of the towers of the World Trade Center
Harris: Well you can see these pictures
It's obviously something devastating has happened
and again unconfirmed reports
that a plane has crashed into one of the towers there
We are efforting more information on this subject
as it becomes available to you

In retrospective news stories, the newsroom informs its uninformed audiences of what it knows. There is an asymmetry of knowledge between the producers and tellers of the news and those for whom it is produced and to whom it is told. But in this breaking story, the CNN news team knows no more than viewers about what they are looking at on screen. Moreover, in retrospective news coverage the boundaries of the event are apparent, precisely because it has already happened and is now over. It is available as a whole and, as such, can be narrated, discussed and assessed. But again, at this moment and for the next few hours, the boundaries of what is happening cannot be foreseen. Indeed, at a certain point (when the newsroom is trying to cope with the attack on the Pentagon as well as the World Trade Center and then the collapse of the two towers) the most terrifying aspect of the unfolding chain of events is that there is no apparent limit to it. It seems to be a spiralling disaster without end.

Throughout all this, the two CNN presenters fronting the live coverage maintain their professional focus. The disaster is treated, without hesitation, as a *story* right from the start. Everything that follows is work on discovering what the story is, done live-to-air. The overriding concern is to establish what, precisely, is happening and, beyond that, how it *could* have happened. Desk-bound in the newsroom, as viewers are bound to their TV sets, the production team searches continuously for witnesses who can testify to what has happened and what is now going on. Thus the most immediate thing to establish, as a matter of fact, is that it was indeed a plane that crashed into the building (and which one) and this is confirmed within seconds by the first over-the-phone witness who actually saw the plane go into the World Trade Center.

CNN: 11.09.01: 8.52 am
Lin: Right now we've got Sean Murtagh
He is a CNN producer
On the line
Sean what can you tell us about what you know?
Murtagh: This is Sean Murtagh

I was just standing on the (.)
aahh vice president of finance
Harris: Sean?
Murtagh: Vice president of finance for CNN (.)
Harris: Sean we're on the air right now
What can you tell us about this situation?
Murtagh: (.) Hello?

Harris: Sean we're on the air right now
Go ahead what can you tell us?
Murtagh: I just witnessed a plane that appeared to be cruising
Slightly lower than normal over New York city
And it appeared to have crashed into
I don't know which tower it is
But it hit directly in the middle
of one of the World Trade Center towers
[Interview continues for two more minutes]

In spite of the monumental catastrophe he has just seen, this first eyewitness is more concerned at first to correct his interviewer and establish just who in fact he is – no mere producer, but the vice president of finance for CNN. With exquisite politeness, Harris reminds Mr Murtagh that he is on the air and coaxes him to tell what he just saw. The ensuing phone conversation (the viewer never sees any of the speakers – Lin, Harris or Murtagh) is resolutely low key. What kind of a plane? A passenger jet? Was it in difficulty? Was there any smoke or flames coming out of the engine? Is it embedded in the building still? Are there any sirens going, any ambulances, any sort of response to this yet? Murtagh's responses are cautious and factual. He sticks to what he saw but points out that the plane was not on a normal flight path. As a frequent business flyer he knows that domestic flights seldom go directly over Manhattan but usually come up over the Hudson River, heading north and passing alongside the island of Manhattan.

In a lecture on 'Doing "being ordinary"', Harvey Sacks draws attention to the ways in which people maintain the ordinary perspective on what's happening, even in the direst situations. He cites newspaper reports in which airplane passengers caught up in hijacks give their version of what happened:

I was walking up towards the front of the airplane and I saw the stewardess standing facing the cabin and a fellow standing with a gun in her back. And my first thought was he's showing her the gun and then I realized that couldn't be, and then it turned out he was hijacking the plane.

It really is remarkable, Sacks remarks, to see people's efforts to achieve the 'nothing happened' sense of really catastrophic events. Just imagine, he continues, rewriting the monumental events of the Old Testament with ordinary people having gone through them (Sacks 1995, Volume II: 220). As we will shortly see, accounts of eyewitnesses on the ground close to the World Trade Center and of a survivor who escaped from one of the towers are ordinary in just the same way. But in the special case of journalism, the resolute maintenance of the 'ordinary perspective' as a taken-for-granted professional stance has the effect of holding in place the intelligible, meaningful character of what is happening, however horrific, confusing and inexplicable it may appear to be. Natural reactions of anguish, shock or panic are avoided. A coherent flow of news-talk is maintained. The news-anchors make clear, at all times, the status of what they say; whether or not it is confirmed, and by whom. They refuse to speculate. Even in the direst moments the situational proprieties of news routines are maintained.

In the next ten minutes or so, CNN, while always holding on screen shots of the smoking towers, cuts away to live reports from two of its affiliates, WNYW and WABC. Both stations provide live-to-air interviews with a succession of eyewitnesses who establish that it is the north tower that has been hit at around the 80th floor. At 9.02 am the WABC anchorman is talking, from the studio, to a downtown eyewitness, Winston Mitchell, who confirms that the plane went 'totally into the building' and lodged in it. He is then asked if there is a lot of debris:

CNN 11.09.01: 9.02 am
Static shot of the top half of the north tower
from a WABC traffic-monitoring helicopter
Winston: No because it looked like it inverted with the impact
everything went into the building. The only bit that came out
was a little bit of the outside awning,
but I'd say the hole is
(.) just let me get a better look right now
WABC: OK go ahead
Winston: The umm (.) I'd say the hole takes about
six or seven floors were taken out
A plane comes into frame for a split second and disappears behind the tower.
The image cuts out for a moment and then returns to show a

fireball mushrooming out of the side of the building
And there's more explosions
hold on people are running hold on
WABC: hold on just a moment we've got an explosion inside the

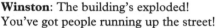

Winston: The building's exploded!
You've got people running up the street!
I don't know what's going on
WABC: OK just put Winston on pause there for just a
moment
Winston: The whole building just exploded
the whole top part of the building's still intact
people are running up the street . . . Am I still connected?
Another full screen shot of the north tower
WABC: Winston this would support what Libby[4] and
you both said
that perhaps the fuselage was in the building

that would cause a second explosion such as that
Winston: Well that's just what's happened then
WABC: That would certainly (*background sounds of
shouting in the studio*)
We are getting word that perhaps
Winston: OK hold on
the people here are
everybody's panicking
**Zoom to close-up of the tower. Shot obscured by
helicopter boom**

WABC: Alright (.) you know Winston
let me put Winston on hold for just a moment
Winston: I dunno how long I'm gonna be here
I'm inside of a diner right now
WABC: Well Winston you know what
if you could give us a call back (.)
I just don't want panic here on the air (.)
Let's just take some of our pictures from our news
chopper seven
Cut to long distance shot

Now one of our producers said perhaps a second plane
was involved
let's not let's not even speculate to that point
but at least put it out there that perhaps that may have
happened
(0.2)

ermmm
(.) the second explosion which certainly backed the theory
from a couple of eyewitnesses that the plane fuselage
perhaps stayed in those upper buildings

**Cut to close-up shot in which both towers can now clearly be seen
with smoke and flames coming out of them**
Now if you look at the second building
there are two both twin towers are on fire
now this was not the case – am I correct? – a couple of
moments ago.
This is the second twin tower now on fire (.)
and we're gonna check on the second flight if perhaps
this happened.
This all began at about 8.48 this morning.
Again, what we know, in case you're just joining us.
A small plane not a Cessna type
**Cut to full-screen shot that focuses on flames
coming from the second tower**
or 5 or 6 seater but instead perhaps a passenger flight
ran into the north side of the World Trade Center
As you can see the second explosion that you're looking
at now,
the second twin tower has spread much debris,
much more debris than the first explosion or accident
Aah if there is
is Winston still on the line with us?
(0.2)
OK he's not there
Do we have – I'll just talk to my producer – do we have an eyewitness
that perhaps sees better than we do from these pictures?
Again you can see that there is debris falling off
OK we actually have an eyewitness news reporter
Dr Jay Adelberg who was downtown at the time
and he is on the phone with us live.
Dr Jay what can you tell us?

At the moment that the second plane crashes into the south tower, the ABC anchor, focused on his live-to-air eyewitness interview, fails to see what is clearly, but only for an instant, visible; a plane coming in low from the right-hand side of the television screen and disappearing behind the north tower. It is not immediately obvious that it has, in fact, crashed into the south tower. Winston responds immediately: 'The building's exploded . . . the whole building just exploded.' The anchor interprets this to support the point that Winston and an earlier witness have established; that the first plane is embedded in the north tower and hence may have caused a secondary explosion – an assessment accepted by the eyewitness. What is in vision on screen is hard to interpret because the two towers are not clearly distinguishable from each other. Now, as in all the early minutes of the unfolding catastrophe, there is a continuing demand for 'an eyewitness that perhaps sees better than we do from these pictures'. The instantly upcoming interviewee, Dr Jay Adelberg, confirms that a second plane came in, moments ago, at a low altitude and appeared to crash into the World Trade Center. This is followed by a sequence of replays of the plane going behind the north tower and, after a fraction of a second, a spectacular fireball exploding from the side of the barely visible south tower.

Thus far, all interviews have been with ordinary people who are on air simply because they have either a better line of vision on what is happening than the newsroom (and viewers) or else actually saw the planes going into the buildings. Next up is the first expert witness, Ira Furman, a former National Transportation Safety Board (NTSB) spokesman. In the course of a lengthy discussion, Furman makes it plain that it is inconceivable that two planes could accidentally crash into the towers given the perfect flying conditions and that, in the case of the second plane, the smoke billowing from the first stricken tower marks it out as a visible disaster area to be avoided. Harris concludes the phone interview with a thanks and the observation that 'the longer we talk the less convinced many will become that this was an accident'.

From now on there is an incremental accumulation of information from varied sources, including the major press agencies – Associated Press and Reuters – that begins to flesh in the background to the thus far inexplicable disaster that fills the television screen. An AP report talks of 'a possible plane hijacking'. An FBI official tells CNN that the possibility of terrorist acts is being investigated. Rescue operations are under way. A further AP report describes the plane crashes as acts of terrorism. Reports come in that President Bush will shortly make a news statement from Saratoga where he is visiting an elementary school. At 9.29 am, 50 minutes into the breaking story, the President's brief press statement is chromakeyed on screen in a small framed box but with the stricken towers still the dominant visual image. Bush speaks of 'a national tragedy' and 'an apparent terrorist attack on our country'.

At 9.40 the strapline across the bottom of the screen changes to 'reports of fire at Pentagon'. The newsroom catches up with this new

headline within a minute via a phone interview with CNN's Chris Plante in a car near the Pentagon. Reports are coming in that the White House is being evacuated. At 9.45, for the first time, the smoking towers in Manhattan are displaced by a shot from WUSA (a Washington CBS affiliate) of a huge plume of smoke behind buildings in the foreground. Again the initial on-screen picture is far from clear (the strapline reads: 'Fire on Washington mall') and there is an immediate off-screen search for clarification of what is happening. The flow of background information increases as the volume of separate incidents rises. The Federal Aviation Authority has grounded all flights in the USA. John King, CNN's senior White House correspondent in Washington, reports from there that everything that's happening is being treated as a terrorist attack and that the initial assumption, according to an unnamed official source 'was that this had something to do or at least they were looking into any possible connection with Osama bin Laden. The administration recently released a warning that they thought Osama bin Laden might strike out against American targets.'

CNN now has a third anchor, Aaron Brown, established in the open air on a rooftop with a clear and unimpeded panoramic view of the two smoking towers standing high above the Manhattan skyline. He continues the commentary live to camera against this backdrop. At 9.58 CNN cuts to a full-screen shot of what is not so obviously the Pentagon engulfed in a huge black cloud of smoke.

Voiced over this is a down-the-line report to Brown from Jamie McIntyre, CNN's senior Military Affairs Correspondent at the Pentagon:

CNN 11.09.01 9.58 am
Full screen shot of Pentagon from WUSA
MacIntyre: Again it appears that an aircraft of some sort
did hit the side of the Pentagon.
The west part which faces sort of towards Arlington National Cemetery.
It's a corridor where a lot of army officers are located
Brown: Wow! Jamie Jamie I need you to stop for a second.
There has just been a hu::ge explosion
Cut to tight close-up of a side of the still standing north tower
and behind it a great cloud of smoke. The camera begins to pull back

We can see a billowing smoke rising
and I'll tell you that I can't see that second tower.
But there was a cascade of sparks and fire
Cut to Brown on rooftop against the Manhattan skyline
And now this it almost looks like a mushroom cloud an explosion.
This huge billowing smoke in the second tower

this was the second of the two towers hit.
And I you know I cannot see behind that smoke
Cut to panoramic shot of Manhattan, smoke rising
high above
and behind the north tower and rising below and
all around it,
enveloping all buildings in the area
Obviously as you can't either (background sound of
sirens)
the first tower in front has not changed
and we see this extraordinary and frightening scene behind us
of the second tower (.) now just encased in smoke
What is behind it I (.) I cannot tell you (.)
But just look at that.
That is about as frightening a scene as you will ever see
Again this is going on in two cities.
We have a report that there is a fire
at the State Department as well and that is being evacuated
So we've got fires at the Pentagon (.) evacuated
The State Department (.) evacuated
The White House (.) evacuated
on the basis of what the secret service described
as a as a credible terrorist threat
We have two explosions (.)
we have two planes hitting the World Trade Center
here in New York
And what this second explosion was
that took place about (.) a part of that would be
the south tower has apparently collapsed

In the live coverage of breaking news, as time moves on implacably, the newsroom is journeying forwards into the unknown, while looking back over its shoulder in a continuing effort to catch up with and make sense of what has just-now happened. Continuously aware that, from moment to moment, new viewers are joining the program, the presenters regularly re-cap and summarize what has thus far happened and what is thus far known about what has happened. Along the way, incoming bits of information are added to the snowballing narrative. But even so, fragments of data, which will later turn out to be hugely important may, in the first instance, appear to be no more than straws in the wind. Barely an hour after the first plane crashed into the World Trade Center, the name of Osama bin Laden has been mentioned by CNN's Washington correspondent in connection with what is happening. But at this moment, it appears to be no more than an incidental detail, a passing conjecture that is instantly blown away and lost in the onrushing whirlwind of events.

II

BBC end-of-day news coverage

In the UK, ten o'clock at night has long been the time-slot preferred by the national broadcasters, the BBC and ITN, for their main end-of-day news program precisely because by then the events of the day have 'settled' and there has been time for the newsroom to gather, assess and organize data from all available wide and varied sources. Breaking news, urgently seeking informa-tion from moment to moment, accesses incoming data along the way, and transmits it with hedges and cautions precisely because there is no time to check and confirm its evidential status. Retrospective news, by contrast, enjoys the benefit of hindsight that only time can give. There has been time to sort and sift, to check and cross-check, to pick the most telling moments and the most incisive quotes. Above all, there has been time to sort out the event and its telling and present it within an interpretative frame and a story format: the frame is 'terrorism', the story format is 'disaster', the narration is direct, authoritative and without qualification:

BBC News, 11.09.01: 10.00 pm
Peter Sissons, BBC news anchor:

Sissons, in studio, direct to camera
Terrorists attack the heart of America with catastrophic loss of life

The second plane crashes into the south tower
Hijacked planes smash into and destroy New York's tallest buildings

Close-up of the top of the north tower as it begins to collapse
Both towers of the World Trade Center collapse with thousands trapped

The Pentagon wreathed in clouds of smoke
Another plane explodes on the Pentagon, mocking America's defensive might

Crowds in Manhattan fleeing an approaching dust cloud
In the streets panic, and the certainty that casualties are horrendous

Prime Minister Blair about to make a press statement
Tonight Britain imposes drastic security measures as Blair
condemns the terrorist barbarism

These are the top-of-the-news headlines, read out before the signature music and captions that lead in, each night, to the ten o'clock news. The first and last headlines set the overall frame of 'terrorism' within which the catastrophe flagged in the four intermediate headlines is to be understood. The overall frame is political. The disaster is not. Those most immediately caught up in the disaster, those who suffer – the dead and dying, the injured, their relatives and friends – demand immediate attention *because* of their suffering, irrespective of any question of their causes.[5] The narrative format of news disaster stories has a structure whose logic is determined by a hierarchy of temporal relevance in which the imperative issue is always the nature and scale of the disaster and its fateful impact on human life. Thus the first half of the BBC news programme on the night of 11 September recapitulates the sequence of events, assesses the scale of their impact in terms of human suffering and attends to the rescue efforts in their immediate aftermath. Only after this has been dealt with does the news turn to the wider political implications of the disaster as a deliberate act of terrorism.

First the precise chronology of events is set out under the banner headline: AMERICA UNDER ATTACK. The first detailed report 'on the day that terrorism struck at the heart of the world's most powerful nation' is from the BBC's diplomatic correspondent, James Robbins. It is a brilliantly edited sequence that draws on the most powerful visual images and most telling eyewitness accounts taken from the huge stock of footage available hours later to the newsroom. The live-and-as-it-happened images available to CNN as the story broke were visually of poor quality, static and low in information; the visuals in the end-of-day report are riveting. There are spectacular shots of the second plane going into the south tower both in close-up and from a distant panoramic shot (an amateur video clip) across the bay with the whole of Manhattan in view. The shots of the towers going down are simply heart-stopping as are the images, moments beforehand, of the doomed souls trapped in them, hanging out of windows, waving in vain for help. Intercut with shots of the buildings are sequences from hand-held, mobile cameras at ground level, that graphically capture the panic on the streets as the police try to control and direct the fleeing crowds. The ambient sound of running footsteps, of shrieks and cries powerfully evokes what it was to be there caught up in the disaster zone. None of this was available in the first hour of CNN's morning coverage. The eyewitness interviews again are in sharp contrast with those used in the breaking story. Those consisted largely of people looking out of their windows at the World Trade Center and describing, over the phone, what they saw. The interviewees were in the same position as the newsroom and the television viewers: observers, onlookers at a distance. The straight-to-camera interviews with men and women on the streets in the disaster zone have a direct and compelling character:

BBC News, 11.09.01: 10.04 pm
Eyewitnesses, New York:
Man: I wuz just standing here watching the World Trade Center
after the first after the first plane hit.
I just saw a second plane come in from the south
and hit the whuh south . tower
half way between the bottom and the top of the tower
its gotta be a terrorist attack
I can't tell ya anything more th'n that.
I saw the plane hit the building

Man: Well big explosion happened.
some guy came out . his his skin was all off
I helped him out . that's him all over.
There's people jumpin outta windows
I seen at least fif fourteen people jumpin outta windows
its its its horrific.
I can't believe this is happening

Woman: We heard a big bang
and then we saw smoke coming out.
everybody sort of running out.
'nd we saw the plane on the other side of the building.
and there was smoke everywhere
people were jumping out of the windows.
they were jumping outta windows
I guess because they're tryna save (?) themselves
I dunno

To re-live a moment such as this testifies to the *pain* of witnessing. The anguish in the face and voice, in the whole body of these anonymous men and women 'in the street' as they tell of what they have just now seen is all caught in the recordings. The first speaker's assessment of what he saw is immediate, certain and precise. It has to be a terrorist attack. It is the only interpretation that makes any sense of what, no matter how many times one watches it, is simply unbelievable – a plane flying into a world famous landmark out of a clear blue sky. The final shot in the report, from across the broad and shining expanse of the bay, of the Manhattan skyline, the towers gone and the whole area involved in a drifting shroud of smoke, is unforgettable.

Robbins's report, towards the end, touches briefly on the rescue efforts in the aftermath of the collapse of the second tower. This is the focal concern of a follow-on report from Niall Dickson. The numbers of the dead are beyond calculation, but they will be 'more than any of us can bear' says Mayor Giuliani of New York, leading the rescue response, in a hastily organized press conference. The hospitals are stretched to breaking point, dealing with more than 2,000 injured. A call for blood goes out as the hospitals are running out, and improvised centres take donations from a host of volunteers. The scenes of the rescue services picking their way through the dust and rubble of the ruined heart of the city are eerily quiet. The report attends to the fatalities at the Pentagon, and the support for the wounded. Again no precise figures can be given. The one exact figure, at the end of the report, is that 266 people died in the four aircraft; the two that went into the World Trade Center, the one that went into the Pentagon and the one that came down later in a field near Philadelphia.

The scale of a disaster is always measured in terms of its fateful impact on the lives of human beings. In terms of this event, its immediate impact and consequences were immeasurable, and initial responses registered stunned shock, astonishment and disbelief. A middle-aged man talks to camera of how he escaped from the north tower before its collapse:

BBC News, 11.09.01: 10.07 pm
Eyewitness, New York:
.uhh big boom.
come down the steps
everything fine till we get to the basement
then everything just fell in.
I wuz got trapped under there with another guy.

crawled out.
kept getting hit on the head.
bashed all around
finally we crawled our way out over the rubble.
we did alright

It is not what he says but the sight of him standing there, in the debris –
his head and face covered in blood and dust, his clothes in tatters – that
confirms the enormity of what has just happened to him. For the victim
himself, the significance of what has happened, at this point in time, is
beyond the reach of words.

What is not beyond the reach of words is the strategic significance of
what has happened, to which the news now turns, having dealt with the
events and their immediate aftermath. 'Terrorists attack the heart of
America with catastrophic loss of life' were the first words of the whole
programme, but who the terrorists might be is neither mentioned nor
dealt with until half way through the programme:

BBC News, 11.09.01: 10.20 pm
George Eakin, BBC reporter: [Photo 84]
And it's this wealthy Arab fundamentalist
the Americans are already naming as an immediate
suspect.
Osama bin Laden.
He controls and finances al Qaeda.
an umbrella network of Islamic militants
and he's vowed to destroy the United States

The report gives further details of bin Laden's activities against the US. It notes that, while the possibility
is not excluded, no-one is suggesting that it could be (like the Oklahoma
bombing) an act of domestic terrorism. It further considers the possibility of a 'rogue state' being behind the attack, but reports that initial
US responses think this unlikely. Following on from this, Peter Sissons
goes to a live interview with the BBC's World Affairs Editor, John
Simpson, in Islamabad, who was in Afghanistan the previous week.
He is asked whether bin Laden could have done it, and replies that he
certainly could: 'he's got the fanaticism, he's got the followers, he's got
the money and he's frankly got the imagination'. Sissons then asks, if
the United States wanted to go after bin Laden, how difficult would that
be?

BBC News, 11.09.01: 10.24 pm
John Simpson:
Well it's easy enough to hit at Afghanistan
and I do think it important to draw the distinction
between the Taliban government in Afghanistan who are
bin Laden's hosts.
not perhaps all that willingly his host.
and the man himself.
I think frankly it's going to be extraordinarily difficult
for the Americans to hit him.
He's got his own peculiarly difficult and complex system of communications
which they simply can't break into (.)
er I think frankly they'll they'll if they're going to attack
if they decide that the attacker came from there
they'll hit Afghanistan very hard.
They'll hit the hosts
but frankly I doubt if they'll get the guest.

Towards the very end of the programme in a studio interview, the BBC's Diplomatic Correspondent, James Robbins (who compiled the lead story on the events of the day) confirms the assumption that there will be retaliation on a massive scale from the Americans against bin Laden. He is then asked whether heads will roll in America's intelligence community who failed to see this coming:

BBC News, 11.09.01: 10.40 pm
James Robbins:
I think that's also a very distinct possibility.
It is extraordinary that both the CIA and the FBI failed
to detect a threat
and failed to prevent four separate concerted and synchronized attacks . . .
[..] It's very hard to believe
that the American intelligence establishment can escape
the blame.

Now, years later and with the wisdom of hindsight, we know that Simpson has been proved right. The Americans did, indeed, hit the host but missed the guest. And it did begin to emerge, months later, that American intelligence had picked up on the imminent possibility of terrorist hijacks in the USA in the weeks before September 11th. That, in turn, gave rise to questions as to why the Bush administration apparently did nothing about such reports in the weeks leading up to September 11th.

III

The politics of the present

In his splendid study of *Distant Suffering*, Luc Boltanski asks 'What reality has misfortune?' (Boltanski [1993] 1999: 149–69). How can 'the moral spectator'[6] believe the accounts of human suffering that he or she reads about in newspapers or sees on television? At the heart of this question is the problem of witnessing (Peters 2001). To be a witness is to be present at an event of some sort and thereby to have direct and immediate access to what is taking place. A witness 'has' (owns) the experience of 'being there' and thereby has moral and communicative entitlements. Witnesses have the moral entitlement to evaluate and pass judgement on what they witnessed (they are entitled to their opinions on the matter), whereas others who were not there have no such rights. Arising from this moral right, witnesses have further communicative entitlements. In particular, they have the right (indeed the duty) 'to bear witness'. They can, and must, speak to others of what they saw. Such speech, no matter how banal, has a compelling truth for those who were not there.

We, television viewers, were not there on New York's day of wrath. The structures and routines of news are designed to produce effects of truth in such ways that we can believe what we are told and shown. It is precisely because news narratives, told in the third person by a news presenter, lack the force of first-person narratives by those who are there, that broadcasting institutions invest such high-cost technical and human resources in order to establish first-person accounts and evaluations of 'news'. The camera crews who are 'there', the reporters who are 'there', the eyewitnesses who are 'there', the correspondents and analysts who are 'there' all combine to furnish compelling evidence as to the primary facticity of what has happened and is still happening. All of them, in their different roles, act as witnesses to the truth of the event, not on their own behalf, but for the sake of absent audiences for whom they show and speak of what is happening. They do this so that anyone and everyone who watches will 'own' the experience and thereby be entitled to have and to speak their opinions on the matter.

Boltanski wishes to defend a politics of direct and immediate response to disasters. While others sit at home in their armchairs and criticize, humanitarian aid, at least, is there trying to do something, dealing with the situation, bringing relief and comfort to the suffering. 'Ultimately what justifies the humanitarian movement is that its members are on the spot. Presence on the ground is the only guarantee of effectiveness, and even of truth' (Boltanski [1993] 1999: 183). There has to be room for a politics of the present, one that is responsive to what is happening now: 'to be concerned with the present is no small matter. For over the past, ever gone by, and over the future, still non-existent, the present has an overwhelming privilege: that of being real' (ibid.: 192).

And this applies, with equal force, to broadcasting. It is part of the familiar critique of 'the media' not merely that they are parasitic on events, but that their presence distorts them and their accounts misrepresent them. Dayan and Katz's pioneering study of media events began to correct that view (Dayan and Katz 1992) as does the foregoing brief discussion of news on 11 September 2001. Television coverage on the day established the truth of what was happening and of what was being done. In its responses to the unfolding events of that day, the whole world witnessed, through the mediations of television, the immediate, instinctive repair work to the torn and damaged fabric of everyday existence. In such rare moments, the politics of the present achieve a transcendent character. And this is something that we get to see and understand through the power of live broadcasting, whose ordinary, worldly news routines shore up, on behalf of us all, the meaningful character of existence even as it appears to be collapsing in ruins before our disbelieving eyes.

13

Television and history

Television today is routinely experienced everywhere as part of the ordinary life-world of members of modern societies, and watching it is just one of those things that most of us do in the course of an ordinary day.[1] As part of that routine, in daily news services the world over, audiences experience, as a commonplace thing, their situated connectedness with what's going on elsewhere in the world. In exceptional moments people the whole world over are glued to their television sets as witnesses of celebratory or catastrophic events. In all this, broadcasting has accomplished something quite unprecedented. It routinely makes visible the working through of history, day by day, on a worldwide basis. Through it we see the manifest truth of the claim that human beings do indeed make history; their own histories, the history of the country in which they live, the history of the world. But what is much harder to see is how to account for and understand these interlocking historical processes which are all embedded in each other. I will try to unpick them from three perspectives: the ways in which television has itself entered into history, thereby becoming historical; the historicality of television itself (its role in the making of history in the immediacy of the here and now) and, in the end, how this 'politics of the present'[2] discloses the nature of the human situation at the site of history.

Television in the past: the past on television

Academic engagements with the study of media have for the most part been absorbed in and by the politics of the present; the endless pressure to keep up with what's going on in the world right now – this, after all, is what, at every level, the human situation amounts to. The two foundational moments in the academic study of radio in the USA in the 1930s and of television in Britain in the 1970s were both concerned with the impact of then very new forms of mass communication. Both moments assumed that the new medium had a powerful impact on individuals and social groups and both were characterized by anxiety about their effect on the average American or British citizen. In each moment there was a flurry of interest and attention that lasted no more than a couple of decades after which the sociological interest in the impact of radio and TV declined in the USA, and Cultural Studies' interest in the media, strong in the 1970s and 1980s, began to fade thereafter. Today these now 'old' media are thought, by some, to be losing their political and cultural centrality: they no longer have the social and moral authority they once possessed. And yet these old media, television particularly, are new by any historical reckoning. It is only now that television has begun to appear as a historical phenomenon because it has only recently begun to have a past. The notion of history means *having* a history, a past. New things don't have histories. The internet does not yet have a history (though it will, in the course of time) because it has not yet quite entered into the historical past. The study of the media is mostly preoccupied with what's new. From the historian's perspective of the *longue durée* (Braudel [1969] 1980), television is still a very new thing. It is only now that it begins to have a history, because it only now begins to have its own visible past.

When does the present become the past? – a teasingly difficult question that points to the elusive historical phenomenon of generational time, the work of re-generation through the time of generations. Assistant professors belong to the up-and-coming generation of scholars; associate professors are the next generation; and full professors the senior generation in the institutional life of American universities. When you start off as a graduate student, you have no academic history (the publication record in your CV is empty). Years pass and, by the time you get to be the distinguished professor you once hoped to be, your *publication record* runs to pages, and stretches over 30 or 40 years or more. Television's past is its *program record*: the silent bedding down, year by year, of its broadcast output. This accumulates in time and only becomes visible with the passing of time. TV in the USA and Britain has being going since the end of the Second World War and there is now a cumulative repository of old programs going back to the fifties, some of which still show up on TV today in endless repeats out there in cable land.

How should we think of radio and TV as *archives*, historical resources (Robertson 2011)? Firstly, the archive is the totality of available recorded output across all genres at any time. All program genres are of equal historical interest and weight: it would be an elementary error to think that the only properly historical part of the record were 'serious' factual programs; news and documentaries. 'Trivial' output in general and fictional entertainment in particular is every bit as relevant and interesting as 'serious' factual output and no less historical for being fiction. Things that were previously unhistorical, for there was no record of them, have now entered into the historical record by virtue of recording technologies developed by the industry for quite different purposes. In written archives one reads inscribed and printed texts. In television archives one reads looks and glances, tone of voice, apparel, bearing and demeanour, actions and interactions. We monitor and evaluate people in public in the same ways that we evaluate the people we interact with in our own private lives because we now have access to public persons in the same way. The spatial and temporal proxemics of tele-technologies has brought this about. Whole new historical possibilities are opened up in this: longitudinal studies of continuities and change in voice, talk, looks and gestures – micro-studies of the performed self-in-everyday-life made possible by the new regime of publicness brought into being by broadcasting and preserved, for the record, by its technologies.

Any engagement with radio and television from a historical perspective encounters, with unusual force I think, the complexity of the relationship between past and present – perhaps the fundamental concern of historiography. Traditionally history has been intimately connected with writing. It is not merely that the work of historians is understood as *historiography* – the art, or practice, of writing history. It is also, and in the first place, that the writing of history depends upon the existence of a written record that professional historians draw on to produce their written accounts. Prehistoric time, in common parlance and dictionary definitions, is time *before* written records and accounts. Historical societies are those with permanent written documentation and records. The act of writing comes after the event of necessity, because written texts are not produced at first go, 'just like that'. Writing (like making a movie) is a laborious, discontinuous process of stops and starts – of crossings out, revisions and corrections – in order to produce an edited, final 'clean' text that is free of spelling mistakes and grammatical errors while maintaining fluency and coherence. Writing is a slow process and itself takes time, a point famously underlined by Lawrence Sterne's eponymous hero, Tristram Shandy, as he tried to write the story of his own life. The more he wrote, the more time it took up and thus, as he found, he could never catch up with himself and bring his life-story up to date. The novel stops – it doesn't come to an end – four years before Tristram's birth. The very act of writing his life story produced it as a receding narrative that moved away from its fictional narrator even as he wrote. There is, of course, a further time-lag, between the act of writing and the printing and distribution process. The tremendous technological developments of the nineteenth century produced the national daily press designed to overcome as far as possible the time-space constraints of the production circuit of gathering, writing, printing and distributing news; but even news 'hot' from the press reaches us hours after the event. In short, the medium of writing produces not merely narratives of the past, but the past as something that recedes from the present. With radio and television, however, the time of the event and the time of its telling coincide. Both exist in the same real time now.

Television in the present: the meaning of the 'now'

Live broadcasting inhabits two orders of time, I have argued; the punctual and the phenomenal now. Each expresses a way of being-in-time that is indicative of the fundamental difference between beings (ontology A) and being (ontology B). The difference between digital and analogue time shows up in the difference between traditional news on radio and television and the more recent 24/7 news that began in 1980 when Ted Turner founded Cable Network News (CNN).[3] The 'meaning' of events and history is concealed and revealed in the different temporalities of these two kinds of news and the ways in which they now intersect. Traditional news, on televisions of the centre, is broadcast at certain times of day. It is embedded in a daily broadcast schedule. As such, each newscast has a before and after – the programs that precede and succeed it – as well as being embedded in the time-of-day, the days of the week, the months and seasons of the year. Programs that are part of a schedule of mixed programming – the classic content of national broadcast services from their start-up to the present – are embedded in the recurring calendar that makes up the broadcast year. This news is always embedded in a convergent order of temporalities that combine to 'give' the situated now in which and to which it 'speaks'. As such, it has a before and after and is thus the sum of three temporalities – the historic, immediate and future present that come together in and as the enunciatory now from and to which it speaks. The *historic* present is that which has just now happened while the *future* present is that which is just about to happen. One moves away from, while the other moves towards, the *immediate present*, the now that attends and speaks to both. In so doing, the news unobtrusively reproduces the primordial structure of the time of day while disclosing its existential narrative arc.

We have recently begun to live in globalized 24/7 time, to which news dedicated channels are oriented. This news exists in the perpetual *now* of the breaking news story. The presenters in the news studio are endlessly in response to what has just now happened, to what is emerging as 'a happening' in the happening now. In this perpetual punctual now of breaking news, there is neither past nor future. To be sure, news stories disappear as they are overtaken by newer news. But where do they go? Into the past? Who can say? They simply vanish. Where did they come from? Again, who knows? They are happening somewhere now, and that is the immediate matter to hand. Such news has lost its situated relationship to other kinds of programming in the daily schedules and the orders of time in which all are embedded. Live news is always in response to what is happening now, but what that means can never become apparent until it has achieved closure; until, that is to say, it has passed – until it leaves the present to begin to become the past wherein its shape, structure and significance begin to come into focus. History is made in the present but what it means becomes apparent only with the passage of time as the historical event recedes into the past. A news service that exists *only* in the immediate present (the zero point of the punctual 'now') is trapped forever in a discourse of conjecture about possible motives, meanings and explanations beyond which it can never proceed. Ordinarily this generates more noise than light. On rare occasions – such as September 11, 2001 – it serves to hold in place the possibility of meaning when meaning itself seems to be collapsing.

Scripted and unscripted news discourse

I have argued for a conversational turn as a communicative affordance of all tele-technologies: telephone, radio and television. I have shown how *unscripted* talk was introduced and managed on radio and with what effects back in the 1940s. It was then found preferable to *scripted* talk at the microphone and has remained ever since the normal, normative way of producing talk in the studios of radio and television and between broadcasters and audiences in most live-to-air contexts. News remains the outstanding exception to this general development. From the beginning to the present, news has been dependent on the news script and this continues to be the case in traditional news bulletins. 24/7 news is, however, predominantly unscripted. Scripted and unscripted news discourses point up the temporal difference between scheduled news programs and 24/7 news. While both discourses are transmitted live-to-air, the script speaks of that which has already happened as the unscripted speaks to that which is happening in the unfolding now. The differences between the written and the spoken in broadcast news begin to take us close to the enigmatic heart of the meaning of *live*. What begins to be disclosed, in the intersection of the two kinds of news and their different temporalities is the nature of the always fore-given situation that constitutes the terms of our existence.

> Yes . This just in.[4]
> You are looking at obviously
> a very disturbing **live** shot there.
> That is the World Trade Center
> and we have unconfirmed reports
> this morning that a plane has crashed
> into one of the towers of the World Trade Center

At the start of this day, when the story breaks into morning news, it is not possible to say any of the things that end-of-day news will say. What in the end has become known started off as an unknown. The things that are known are so either because they have already happened or are known to be about to happen (an upcoming presidential speech later in the day) as part of the knowable future. But, at any moment, on any day, the unexpected may happen, and when it does, it does not come with a script. The script presupposes either a known known (that has happened) or a known unknown (that is going to happen). It cannot handle a Rumsfeldian 'unknown unknown' that comes out of the blue. Yet news, of course, is on perpetual standby for that very possibility and has well established routines to cope with it. The care-structures of 24/7 news are like those of auxiliary emergency services who in normal times remain on standby for the next calamity waiting in the wings of history to make its appearance. The studio anchors will front a continuing unscripted discourse about what is unfolding while backstage there is frantic activity to get some purchase on what is happening.

> CNN center right now is just beginning
> to work on this **story** . obviously . our sources
> and trying to figure out exactly what happened.
> But clearly something relatively devastating happening
> this morning there at the south end of the island of Manhattan

This discourse is characterized by uncertainty, hesitancy, and ambiguity all of which speak truly to what the discourse confronts and all of which mark it as unscripted.[5] It could not be otherwise, for what it confronts is radically 'off-script', and yet there is confidence, from the beginning that there is a story to be found, a story to be told. From the very start, viewers are assured that the institutional apparatus of CNN is working to that end.

It is extremely rare for news to be in the situation of the CNN studio on the morning of September 11, 2001, when broadcasters knew no

more than viewers about what was happening. News discourse characteristically speaks authoritatively because it knows what it is saying; it
knows because what it speaks of has already happened and therefore the
essential parameters of the event have begun to emerge:

- Terrorists attack the heart of America with catastrophic loss of life
- Hijacked planes smash into and destroy New York's tallest buildings
- Both towers of the World Trade Center collapse with thousands
  trapped

These bulletin headlines at the start of the BBC's end-of-day news
have a directness, fluency and lack of hesitancy all of which are effects
of the authority of the script and the 'scriptedness' of the discourse
that is animated by the newsreader. What was just beginning in the
morning of that day is now over and can be spoken of, with certainty, as
that which has now happened. In retrospective news that speaks from
the historic present, the headlines are characteristically written in the
historic present tense[6] that has the effect of bringing the past events of
the day into the enunciatory now. Speaking to the news script, live and
in real time, and addressing the viewer directly via auto-cue, the studio
anchor is the visible front-of-house spokesperson and representative of
the news-producing institution that has gathered, confirmed, written
and warranted what s/he is saying. The believability of news is no small
achievement: the full script of the bulletin (not just what is said, but the
running order of news items, the feeds, the links, the reports – the whole
narrative structure and all its component parts) is where the massive
invisible off-screen labour process of news gathering comes together as
a hidden care-structure transformed into an on-screen live-to-air public
discourse.

The authority of news, then, is carried by its institutionally authored,
authorized and warranted script. Within the script, however, as Martin
Montgomery has shown, there is an increasing tendency to turn to
unscripted talk in order to 'liven' things up, to heighten the impact and
immediacy of news. It is important to note, though, that unscripted talk
is subordinate to scripted news.[7] It always comes after, never before,
the scripted news presentation of the studio anchor and/or the scripted
news package that reports and elaborates on the headlines news. The
so-called 'live two-way' is a significant recent innovation in broadcast
news journalism. It is standard practice for a news item to be established from the studio and then reported on in an edited recorded news
package put together from the scene of the story. These are often now
followed by a live-to-air two-way interaction between the anchor in the
studio and the reporter at the scene of the action. In this unscripted talk

between the studio and the remote location, the function of the reporter
moves from accounts of what is happening to comment and evaluation.
As Montgomery points out, the live two-way is a singular example of
the technological capacity of information gathering and reporting today
'to collapse the deictic spaces between the "there-then" of action and
the here-now of its enunciation' (2007: 120). It also highlights a shift
from an older concern with the informative function of news to a newer
preoccupation with its communicative relationship with viewers. The
priority of 'classic' television news was the facticity and truth of what it
reported – its informative role. But in recent years, faced with declining
audiences and the rise of 'tabloid television', televisions of the centre
have increasingly been concerned to enliven news by making it more
dynamic, lively and interactive for news audiences who expect more
than just the austere delivery of 'facts'. Broadcast news journalists today
still have a commitment to accurate, truthful news reporting, but now
they also comment on, evaluate and criticize their reports. This is not
without its dangers. Things may be said in the unrehearsed unscripted
moment with unpredictable and fateful consequences:

BBC Radio 4, *Today*
29 May 2003: 6.07am
Gilligan: What we've been told
By erm one of th::e . senior officials in charge of . erm
Drawing up that dossier
Was that erm . actually the government probably . knew
That that forty five figure was . wrong
Even before it decided to put it in
(Montgomery 2007: 130)

This little fragment from a live two-way between John Humphrys
(anchor) and Andrew Gilligan (reporter) on the BBC's national
morning radio news programme led directly to a government inquiry,
the suicide of the unnamed 'senior official' who was Gilligan's source,
and the resignation of the BBC's two top personnel, its Chairman and
Director General, following the publication of the Hutton Report. It
was the notorious allegation that the British government had knowingly
'sexed up' an official dossier it had recently made public which pur-
ported to prove that Saddam Hussein's regime not only had weapons of
mass destruction but could deploy them within 45 minutes of an attack.
Montgomery describes the extraordinary, unravelling consequences of
this scrap of talk. The Hutton enquiry honed in on BBC news practices
and concluded that 'the editorial system which the BBC permitted was
defective in that Mr Gilligan was allowed to broadcast his report at 6.07
a.m. without editors having seen a script of what he was going to say and

having considered whether it should be approved' (Montgomery 2007: 134). It was, however, not a report, but a live-to-air two-way with John Humphrys that Gilligan was involved in at the time and, as he himself admitted, under cross-examination:

> It was a mistake. It was the kind of mistake that does arise in live broadcasting . . . it was a live broadcast and once the words are out of your mouth, the – you know, I did not go back and look at the transcripts. (Montgomery 2007: 134)

It was the *kind of mistake that arises in live broadcasting*. I have shown what is at stake in the management of live-to-air transmission on radio and television; that in a fundamental way, *all* its management and production practices in all live genres are designed to minimize the possibility of technical failure and human error in the living enunciatory moment of transmission. If something goes wrong, the best you can do is damage limitation for once the words are out of your mouth they are in the public domain and they cannot be unsaid. There is now a subgenre of items on YouTube of things indiscreetly said by public figures who think the microphones are off when they're not. The script in news is a fail-safe device. But that is not all it is. It is the source of the validity of news, its warranty and guarantee. What is being said now has already happened, has been checked, confirmed and authorized. The truth conditions of news depend upon its scriptedness.

Events, news and history

At the heart of news, at the heart of history, is the relationship between events and their telling, speech and action. I have proposed a simplest taxonomy of events based on the crucial distinction between the things that happen to us and the things that we make to happen. I have called the former *happenings*, the latter *occasions*. From this we can extrapolate four kinds of event:

- Happenings
- Occasions
- Happenings > occasions
- Occasions > happenings

I have made case studies of all four: disasters (whether from natural or human causes) are happenings – a tsunami, a hurricane, a car, train or plane crash. I have treated the attack on the World Trade Center as an utterly unexpected and inexplicable disaster because that is how it first appeared and was treated as such, until it became crystal clear (the moment the second plane hit the north tower) that it could not possibly be an accident. Sporting events, coronations, weddings, funerals are all occasions and it is as such that I discussed the meaning of 'the moment' in an international soccer match. Elsewhere, I have examined the two possible variants on the happenings/occasions distinction. The death of Diana began as a 'meaningless' accident (a car crash) and was transformed into a great occasion by her funeral service, watched live and in real time around the world: a classic example of the transformation of a happening into an occasion (Scannell 1999). Events that begin as occasions and turn into happenings are rare, but there is one well established class of such occasional happenings; the protest march which turns into a massacre. The event known as Bloody Sunday is one of the more recent examples in a genre of historic events that includes the massacres of Peterloo (Manchester), England, 1819; Amritsar, India, 1919; Sharpeville, South Africa, 1960. On 30 January 1972, a march took place in the city of Derry (Northern Ireland) organized by the Catholic minority in the province as a protest against the policy, newly imposed by the British government, of internment without trial. Marches and parades in the province had been banned at this time by the British government. The troubles in Northern Ireland were by now a focus of international media attention, and TV news crews from around the world were there in anticipation of a confrontation between the marchers and the British army whose troops were on the street in large numbers to control and contain them. The confrontation took place and, as expected, tear gas and water cannon were turned on the angry crowd. But no-one expected that the army would use live ammunition against the protesters. At the end of the day, 13 Derry men and boys were dead. What had started as a known and expected occasion had transformed into an unexpected massacre in the turmoil and confusion of the unfolding event (Scannell 1997).

Happenings and occasions stand in a dialectical relationship to each other as auguries of Fate and History. Their crucial difference is that the former are not meant to happen while the latter always are. Happenings begin as apparently meaningless accidents, while occasions from the start are meant as meaningful. No-one knew to begin with why a plane had crashed into the World Trade Center. It appeared to be an inexplicable accident, while the actual explanation was too bizarre to imagine. No matter how many times you watch the heart-stopping images of the second plane going into the north tower, you cannot believe that it is done deliberately. And yet that is the only possible explanation.

The first plane might have been an accident. The second plane could not possibly have been so. When you have eliminated the impossible, only the improbable remains. The meaning of disasters has to be found and this is the work that news performs on behalf of all of us. The task of finding and telling the story is the work of narrative. The automatic assumption in the CNN studio that what was happening had a story to it is the foundational basis of news.

All stories have a narrative format. News stories are not, as the social constructivists would have it, a fabrication of journalists invented and imposed by them upon events. The story formats of news are discoveries. They are *found* in events because they are immanent in them. The event's story structure is its meaning structure, what makes it narratable and thereby intelligible and meaningful. Events are messy; stories are coherent, John Durham Peters reminds us (Peters 2009: 44). To find and tell the story of the unexpected disaster is to reconfigure it as a meaningful event. The disaster format requires attention in the first place to establish what exactly is going on: *Was* it a plane that went into the building? *Was* it an accident – or not? As the essential facts begin to emerge, attention turns to the fate of those immediately involved: the dead and injured, the scale of the disaster, what is being done on behalf of the suffering. In news, effects always come before causes, rightly and properly so. Only when these have been attended to, does the disaster format turn to possible causes (retrospective) and possible consequences (prospective). Looking backwards and forwards, the politics of blaming begins. Who or what was at fault? Who will be held accountable? What can be done to ensure that it does not happen again? Every story has a moral. The moral that news draws from every disaster is that it should not happen again (if human) or the next time it does (in the case of inhuman fate) we should be better prepared. The victims of the disaster will not have died in vain. Hope will be salvaged from it for the future. Life (and the news) moves on. This, as they say in Media Studies, is the work of meaning-making. And it presupposes the phenomenal, historical now of experiential time, rather than the ever-present punctual now of numbered time.

Journalists are the historians of the present, academics the historians of the past. But journalism always comes first because the present precedes the past, as effects in news always come before their causes. To study news and news-making is to engage with what history is, how it is made and under what conditions. Events make news, not journalists. 'Journalists do not create hurricanes or tornadoes, elections or murders. They do not create Christmas, or rock concerts or the Olympics', Michael Schudson pointedly remarks. How news organizations and their practices respond to, act upon and interact with events is, he argues, the challenge that confronts the sociology of news today. Schudson has come round to the view that news, whatever it is, cannot be reduced to social, economic, political or cultural explanations, separately or together (Schudson 2005: 173).[8] Journalists do not 'manufacture' news out of nothing:

> They act on 'something' in the world. The 'something' they work on are events, happenings, occurrences in the world that impress journalists and their audiences with their importance or interest, their remarkableness, their noteworthiness. (Schudson 2005: 173)

News is driven by events. 'Journalists confront the unexpected, the dramatic, the unprecedented, even the bizarre' (Schudson 2005: 173). That is how they understand their job and they do it routinely, on behalf of us all. They are a crucial part of our frontline defences against the accidents and disasters of Fate, the radical contingency of human existence. Each of us lives with the background knowledge that disaster can strike at any time, when least expected and with devastating effect. Any day could be our last. Any day can start as a perfectly ordinary, normal day and end in ruin, as the events of 11 September 2001 made horrifyingly clear. *In extremis*, the existential-historical role of news is to salvage meaning from meaningless happenings, thereby holding the world in place for all of us in the bewildering uncertainty of the immediate happening now.

For Braudel, the academic historian, the time of events was no more than the heat and smoke of the moment viewed from the perspective of the *longue durée*:

> Traditional history, with its concern for the short time span, for the individual and the event, has long accustomed us to the headlong, dramatic, breathless rush of its narrative [. . .]: an event is explosive, a *'nouvelle sonnante'* ('a matter of moment') as they said in the sixteenth century. Its delusive smoke fills the minds of its contemporaries, but it does not last, and its flame can scarcely ever be discerned. (Braudel [1969] 1980: 27, 28)

The time of events is 'the time of individuals, of daily life, of our illusions and our hasty awareness'. Above all it is 'the time of the daily newspaper', the time of journalism. It is 'the most capricious and the most delusive time span of all' (Braudel [1969] 1980: 27, 28). In his own life, Braudel was overwhelmed by events. When war broke out in 1939, he enlisted, was captured by the Germans when they overran France, and spent five years (1940–5) as a prisoner of war in an internment camp. In those difficult years, he tells us,

Rejecting events and the time in which events take place was a way of placing oneself to one side, sheltered, so as to get some sort of perspective, to be able to evaluate them better, and not wholly to believe in them. To go from the short time span, to one less short, and then to the long term (which, if it exists, must surely be the wise man's time span) and having got there, to think about everything afresh and to reconstruct everything around one: a historian could hardly not be tempted by such a prospect. (Braudel [1969] 1980: 47–8)

During his imprisonment he spent his days laboriously putting together on scraps of paper, without any books or documents, and relying only on his prodigious memory, a draft of the work that would make him famous, *La Méditerranée et le Monde Méditerranéen à l'époque de Philippe II*, published in 1949. Who, in such circumstances, would not be tempted to withdraw from the overwhelming present into the tranquillity of the past? But a historian of broadcasting cannot escape the noise of history, the life and times of the present, the here and now of daily life, the eventful world as routinely displayed in the totality of radio and television output. *Pace* Braudel, we must see the event as the starting point, the driver of both news and history. No events, no news, no history – in that precise temporal order.

The politics of the present

It is, however, and this is Braudel's point, extremely hard if not impossible to get a perspective on what is happening in the heat of the moment. We all of us live our lives caught up in the immediate now of concern, the politics of the present. We cannot stand back from this. We have no vantage point outside of this. There is no time out from the existential situation we are in. We cannot stop the clock of history or our own life. Still less can we turn back the clock, rewind the tape and re-edit things, though we all might wish, at times, that we could. Do we understand what's happening in our lives and in our lifetime? Does anyone? These are not academic questions. They matter in our own individual lives and at the level of nation-states and global politics. Each of us commits to fateful life-choices: this particular kind of work, this particular person, these children that we chose to have – or not. As we commit to these life-defining choices, we have no idea how they will work out. The world is in an economic recession right now. No-one really knows exactly why it happened (it was not *meant* to happen), nor can anyone say for sure what the right way out of it is.

This – crudely, grossly – is what I take to be the nature of our existential situation and our existential predicament which we encounter always only and ever in the enunciatory now – the moment of the event, of the speech-act, of news. Instead of thinking of news in the first instance as an institution, we might think of what news *means* in our lives: of what it is to *have* news (to be *bursting* with news that one is *dying* to tell), to *long* for news, to be thrilled, shocked, amused or scandalized by it.[9] From this perspective the human interest story is a primary definer of the meaning of news and of news values – what we value in news is what is humanly interesting, because to be human is an intrinsically interesting thing and a matter of no little concern.[10] The death of Diana, Princess of Wales, was a tremendous news story of no political significance whatever, and the attack on the World Trade Center, though full of political consequences, was, in the first place, a tragedy of epic proportions that will echo down through the millennia like the sack of Troy . . . *urbs antiqua ruit, multos dominata per annos.*[11]

A phenomenology of news does not yet exist. Were there to be one it would be centrally concerned with its production care-structures, with how news manages to do what it does in response to and in the grip of the exigencies of the immediate present which defines its tasks and of which it seeks to give good accounts.[12] The institutions of news, phenomenally understood, are designed to be always already ahead of the news of the day that we and it are 'in'. There could be no news today without institutions that are always already before and always already after the day today. In its institutional being-towards-the-future, news routinely functions to hold in place a normative sense of normality for all of us, wherever we are. We mostly scan the news to check what's going on and if we find there is no news (of interest to us) we are reassured. News is an ongoing daily reality check, 'a source of security in a disturbing world' (Berelson [1949] 2004: 261a). Barbie Zelizer writes of journalists as 'the creators and conveyors of views about how the world works' (Zelizer 2005: 208). They work to produce and hold in place the ordinary world in the face of the unexpected and extraordinary; a view of the world as ordinary, the pre-condition of everyday existence as such for everyone.

The sociology of institutions, from Max Weber onwards, has thought of them in terms of a politics of power. A phenomenology of news institutions would try to understand them as working to hold the world in place, day by day, through the time of *longue durée*. The long term is as much, if not more so, the limitless future as the endlessly receding past. What intersects in the enunciatory now, the living moment, the affair of news, is the past, present and future in their *now-becoming*: the future becoming present, the present becoming past as they encounter each other in the experiential phenomenal now.

Well it's easy enough to hit at Afghanistan
and I do think it important to draw the distinction
between the Taliban government in Afghanistan
who are bin Laden's hosts.
not perhaps all that willingly his host.
and the man himself.
I think frankly it's going to be extraordinarily difficult
for the Americans to hit him.
He's got his own peculiarly difficult and complex system of communications
which they simply can't break into.
er I think frankly they'll they'll . if they're going to attack.
if they decide that the attacker came from there.
they'll hit Afghanistan very hard.
They'll hit the hosts
but frankly I doubt if they'll get the guest.

This is the informed assessment towards the end of end-of-day news, of the BBC's John Simpson, an experienced, widely travelled news journalist, much respected by his peers and the public, as he tries to assess the future in the light of what has happened. The discourse markers indicate that an unscripted professional personal view is being put forward (frankly) with considerable hedging and disfluency as he formulates his punch line – 'They'll hit the hosts but frankly I doubt if they'll get the guest.'[13] It remains quite extraordinary how, in the direst circumstances and starting from scratch, by the end of the day, news had accounted for what had happened, laid the blame in the right quarter and correctly prophesied the intermediate if not the long-term outcome of the events of that unforgettable day (it took America ten years to 'hit' bin Laden).

The historical process, the day-by-day making of history, depends on human actors and human actions. These actors *must* act without guarantees of the rightness of their words and deeds or the success of their outcomes. Life does not come with a script. That is in the nature of what Luc Boltanski calls the politics of the present, the only real actually existing politics with which broadcast news is concerned each and every day. This politics, the politics of real life in which we are all caught up, is quite distinct from what academics often think politics *ought* to be. For I take the situation of news to exemplify the situation of *live* broadcasting in general and both to be formal indications of our own situation, the human situation at the site of history, the enunciatory *now* of speech and action, words and deeds. It seems to me that live radio and television are really and truly disclosive of our existential situation as such and its politics – the politics of the present. To see them in this way, however, requires a momentary suspension of the play of that politics, a change of focus, a different emphasis, the elaboration of which has been the care and concern of this book.

Notes

Acknowledgements

1 Details of the history of the group and the topics discussed at its annual meetings since they began in 1992 at the beautiful Ross Priory on the banks of Loch Lomond can be found at its website: ross-priory-broadcast-talk. com

Preface

1 Back in the 1970s, there was a great debate in the emerging field of cultural studies in Britain about what determined social life. It focused on a 'problematic' in Marxist sociology, formulated by Louis Althusser: within a whole social formation, whose structural elements consist of the economic, the political and the ideological-cultural, which is determining? The orthodox answer was 'It's the economic, stupid!' But this was regarded as too simplistic, and elaborate arguments were put forward to justify the 'relative autonomy' of the cultural. This little storm in an academic teacup now seems long ago and far away, but it illustrates my essential point. The question of determinations was raised as a problem within 'the social'. The crucial question 'But what determines the social?' was simply not raised. The 'outside' of the social was recognized as 'nature', but it was simply understood, following Marx, as the raw material of the social. See the opening (two and a half page) paragraph of Hall (1977) for the then standard account of the transformation of nature into society and culture.

2 The human situation is distinct from the human condition. The question of determination is again at stake. What determines what? To be – not as an abstraction but 'in fact' – is unavoidably to be alive and living in a real-world situation of some sort whose irreducible components are persons, place and time. Pragmatics examines these as distinctive linguistic phenomena under the rubric of deixis. Spatial deixis ('here'/'there'), temporal deixis ('now'/'then') and social deixis ('me'/'you') separately and together are

formal indications that any speech act/event is unavoidably in a situation
which the act of speaking presupposes in the form of its utterance(s) and as
the condition of its possibility (for a brief sketch of pragmatics, see Scannell
2007: 179–84). The situation, then, is unavoidably what we each and all are
in. But what gives the existential situation? The conditions of human existence are twofold: the first and most fundamentally determining, which we
share with all other living species (call it D1), are the terms upon which life
is, in each case, given at birth. The implacable realities of birth and death,
the irreversible trajectory of the life span (from infancy through adulthood
to old age and death), our racial sexual and species-given differences, are
fundamentally determinate and determining facts about ourselves with
which each and all of us must come to terms and make of them what we
can in the course of an unfolding life. The second determinant of the conditions of human-specific existence (D2) is historical and social, as Marx so
clearly understood. In this book, I am concerned to clarify the determinate
existential nature of our human situation (D1) whose historically 'given'
conditions of existence (D2) are in fundamental ways determined by
technology – the material world, the built environment of humanly made
things, what is referred to in BT as the umwelt.

3 The two 1949 Bremen lectures are reprinted in Figal (2009: 253–83). The
   second lecture on 'The Ge-stell' is centrally concerned with technology. It
   was reworked and given as a lecture called 'The question of technology' to
   the Bavarian Academy of Fine Arts in 1953. See Safranski (1998: 390–4)
   for the circumstances of both occasions. The Bremen lectures begin with a
   brief but sweeping denunciation of radio, film, television and air travel as
   destructive of temporal and spatial distance (Figal 2009: 253–4). Today,

> everything is swept into the distance-less uniformity. How? Is the
> convergence into the distance-less not more uncanny than everything
> blowing apart? We stare at what could be coming with the explosion
> of the atomic bomb. We do not see what has long already arrived, and
> indeed has happened, of which the atomic bomb and its explosions
> are only the final eruptions – to speak nothing of the one hydrogen
> bomb whose detonation could suffice, in the furthest of possibilities,
> to extinguish life on earth. What is this helpless fear still waiting for, if
> the dreadful has already arrived? [. . .] What is that which is dreadful?
> It shows itself and conceals itself in the way that everything comes to
> presence, namely in the way that, despite all overcoming of distances,
> the nearness of what is remains lacking' (Figal 2009: 254; text slightly
> modified).

4 Two benchmark early texts are Feuer (1983) and Rath (1988). Feuer's
   much cited article treats live news broadcasting as exemplifying the 'ideology of immediacy', while Rath's brief (and largely overlooked) think-piece
   raises the question of live broadcasting as 'a generator of events in everyday
   life', anticipating themes taken up by Dayan and Katz (see also Rath 1989).

Jerome Bourdon's article on live television starts with the supersession of live broadcasting by recorded content, yet liveness, he claims remains an immanent possibility of the medium and is central to its understanding (Bourdon 2000). New life was breathed into that possibility by the rise of Reality TV, the subject of a special issue of The Communication Review a few years later (2004, 7:4). See Peter Lunt's introduction ('Liveness in reality television and factual broadcasting') and key articles by Corner, Couldry and Roscoe. There are several monographs related to the topic. Auslander (1999) focuses on liveness in the performing arts (theatre and music especially) and Marriott (2007) deals with live television. Montgomery's study of television news has much to say about its liveness (Montgomery 2007). The growing interest in the question of technology is reflected in Andrew Crisell's recent study of liveness and recording in radio and television (Crisell 2012).

5 My understanding of technology in all that follows draws on Heidegger's analysis of how we encounter everyday things in daily life as equipment – as zuhanden, as to-hand and handy things-for-use (Heidegger [1927] 1962: 95–122). I discuss how we encounter television in this way in chapter 5.

Prologue: Heidegger's teacup

1 On Heidegger's background and childhood, see Safranski (1998: 1–15).

2 Discussing hospitality, 40 years later, Derrida is equally suspicious of 'those new technologies, the telephone, the television, the fax or email, the Internet as well, all those machines that introduce ubiquitous disruption, and the rootlessness of place, the dis-location of the house, the infraction of the home' (Derrida 2001: 90–1).

3 When exactly, during the game, Heidegger spilt his teacup is (like the songs of the Sirens) beyond conjecture, but it was by all accounts a gripping, memorable match. Hamburg, the home team, was not well known outside Germany, while Barcelona was beginning to be mentioned in the same breath as Real Madrid, its historic rival, and, at that time, the uniquely dominant club team in European football (Real had won the cup five times in succession at that point – every year, in fact, since the European Cup began in 1955). In the semi-final of the 1960–61 season, Hamburg, dominating throughout the match, was leading 2-1 when Barcelona scored in the last minute or so to force a replay. Barcelona won the replay and went into the final (having earlier knocked out Real Madrid) to be beaten, 3-2, by the leading Portuguese team, Benfica. All details from www.europeancuphistory.com.

4 I am most grateful to Amit Pinchevsky who drew my attention to this story. Kittler told it in the course of a rather extraordinary keynote lecture he gave in London in 2008 at the *Media Matters* symposium organized by The Tate. It was recorded and can be heard (*live*) at https://itunes.apple.com/us/itunes-u/symposia-2008/id497715043.

Chapter 1   What is phenomenology?

1 Sociology is a problematic term, more so in the USA than elsewhere. It is not the same as 'social science' since this term includes psychology and politics (political science), economics and other disciplines. Sociology today embraces social theory (in the European tradition from Marx, Weber and Durkheim onwards) and quantitative social science as developed in the USA from the 1930s. For a review of Goffman, Garfinkel and Sacks, see Scannell (2007: 145–68).
2 The meaning of (the word) 'life', and not The-Meaning-of-Life. Cf. 'The meaning of a word' (Austin 1961: 55–75).
3 It helps to understand what Heidegger means by 'being' to read it as always meaning 'being alive', the aliveness of being. Not all things that exist have life, as the fundamental distinction between ontology A (the universe of Things) and ontology B (the living world) makes explicit. This cardinal distinction between the lifeless infinite time-space universe, and the one-and-only living world is how I gloss Heidegger's foundational distinction between beings (ontology A) and being (ontology B). All living things inhabit both ontologies – they are both objective *things* and *living* things at one and the same time.

Chapter 2   Available world

1 For a short history of distributive justice from Aristotle to Rawls, see Fleischacker (2004).
2 *Ontos* is the present participle of the Greek verb *einai*, to be.
3 'Dasein' in colloquial German can mean 'everyday human existence', and so Heidegger uses the term to refer to human being (Dreyfus 1991: 13). *Dasein* emphatically does not mean the individual, the human subject – 'me'. Heidegger, attentive as always to the etymology of words, is mindful of its literal meaning – *da* (there), *sein* (being), 'being there'. What is the *da* of Dasein? It is the world in which it finds itself to be and in which it has its being. And what determines Dasein's being (here in the world) is time – hence the title, Being *and* time. The term is usually left untranslated in Heidegger studies. It is perhaps best read as indicating that common time-bound humanity that every individual has.
4 For a contemporary meditation on *The comfort of things*, see Daniel Miller's beautiful anthropological study of the contents of people's homes in one South London street (Miller 2008).
5 Heidegger discussed the experience of being in the lecture in his very first lecture after the First World War, in 1919. He talked about being in the lecture hall from his own and other viewpoints including those of a Black Forest farmer and a Senegalese negro (Figal 2009: 33–7).
6 On the 'time-geography' of everyday routines, see Giddens (1984: 110–16).

Chapter 3   Available self

1 See their discussion of how to translate the term: *BT*: 148n.1.

2 Heidegger, of course, constantly makes clear, in all his writings, that this is always possible if not inevitable. A recurring metaphor for thinking, in his writings, is that of the pathway, down which the thinker must go, following the track of a line of thought. At any point one may be side-tracked, or wander off track. One may end up in a clearing (in which one achieves clarity) or nowhere as one loses track altogether. On any life-journey one is liable, at any point, to take a wrong turn and maybe end up lost. Others may help one get back on track by pointing one in the right direction.

3 It might be objected that many people find the opposite; that they are not spoken to by this or that program or, indeed, by programs in general on mainstream radio and television. Such claims have been raised about the unrepresentative character of output by a range of social or cultural minorities. Nevertheless, in the very act of making such claims, they all take it for granted that they personally should be addressed as the persons that they are by radio and television. The 'politics of recognition' (Taylor [1992] 1994) presupposes what is here being argued for.

4 I have discussed in detail whether or not watching a TV program can be claimed as 'an experience' that gives rise to communicative entitlements (Scannell 1996: 93–116).

5 Benedict Anderson makes exactly the same point in respect of reading the newspaper, in the context of his overall thesis of nations as 'imagined communities' (Anderson [1983] 2006: 35).

6 This phenomenological three-part structure of 'the self' is implicated in the authorial 'I' deployed throughout the text. The 'I-that-speaks' in it is sometimes myself-as-anyone (any human being, any academic – my *impersonal* self) and sometimes myself-as-someone (with an individual life that is unique to me – my ownmost *personal* self). It can also be my 'anyone-as-someone' self – my ordinary everyday (non-academic) *sociable* self, with my particular tastes and opinions, likes and dislikes and so on. The application of Austinian principles and methods should clarify which 'I' is in play in any context in which it appears in the text.

7 Riesman ([1950] 2001: 18). Though Riesman emphasizes that he does not conceive of the inner-directed individual simply as a non-conformist Protestant, the way that he writes of this type throughout the book suggests that he is indeed an American WASP (White Anglo-Saxon Protestant). Weber's *Die protestantische Ethik und der Geist des Kapitalismus* was translated into English by Talcott Parsons, then Tutor in Economics at Harvard, in 1930.

8 Not a term used by Riesman, and I use it as a deliberate anachronism.

9 Thorstein Veblen had noted the emergence of what he called the 'leisure class' in America at the start of the twentieth century. The new rich were given over to a culture of conspicuous consumption which, in the United States served rather to encourage than (as in France, say) enrage the masses.

Their lifestyle was something to be actively pursued rather than passively envied. In the 1950s, it appeared within reach of ordinary Americans.

10 The emergence of bourgeois 'civil society' in eighteenth-century Europe is the locus for the formation of people oriented towards civil interaction with others in the contexts of everyday life.

Chapter 4   Available time

1 I might add that, if you want to find traces of Nazi ideology in *Being and Time*, the theme of authenticity is the place to look. A few years after publication, individual authentic resoluteness morphed easily into the altogether more sinister notion of the resolutely Authentic German People (*Volk*) and its world-historical mission and destiny. See especially Heidegger's notorious inaugural lecture as the elected rector of Freiburg University in May 1933, by which time he had joined the Nazi Party. It remains excruciatingly painful and embarrassing to read (Figal 2009: 108–16).

2 The punctual now and the phenomenal now (and indeed the two ontologies that each exemplifies) can be understood in relation to Zeno's paradox and Bohr's complementarity principle to account for the contradictions of wave-particle physics. Light can be thought of in two ways: as particles (photons) and as light-waves. There are classic experiments that observe and measure the properties of light-waves and particles. In the former, light is in motion. In the latter, it is static (caught in a frozen moment of time by high-speed photography). However, things cannot be static and in motion at one and the same time since they are opposites. Zeno's paradox of the arrow in flight long ago drew attention to this perplexity. It is paradoxical for something to be moving and static in the same instant of time, an impossible possibility, so Zeno argued. And yet both are real and true phenomena. The two ontologies are complementary in the same way as wave-particle theories in classical physics. They speak to different truths about the existence of things. They contradict but do not deny each other. They are not an either/or. Both are true.

3 See *BT*, 376n.2 for a discussion of the translation of *die Augenblick*, and p. 387 for its definition: 'That *Present* which is held in authentic temporality and which is thus *authentic* itself, we call "*the moment of vision*".'

4 It is possible to construe video as meaning TV and thus the difference would be between being there at the race and watching it on TV. But this is an odd construction in ordinary (English) English. One does not talk about watching something 'live' if one is there. It is redundant to say so. One speaks of watching something 'live' to indicate that it was seen at the time on TV as distinct from actually being 'there' (at the race).

5 I have borrowed this term from Jacques Derrida who uses it extensively in his later writings on television. See, for instance, Derrida (2001).

6 'Attunement' is an important motif in Division One of *BT* and is closely linked to the fundamental phenomenon of mood (Heidegger [1927] 1962: 172ff).

7 Speaking of radio and television recording technologies, Derrida remarks, 'Then there is *re*-production as re-*production* of life by itself, and the pro-duction is archived as the source, not as an image. It is an image, but an image that effaces itself as image, a re-presentation that offers itself as pure presentation. Life itself can be archived' (Derrida 2001: 71).

8 In Greek mythology Lethe was one of the five rivers that flowed through Hades, the underworld. Those who drank its waters experienced complete loss of memory of their past life in the world above. The word *lethe* thus meant forgetfulness or obliviousness. In classical Greek, a-lethe-ia meant literally un-forgetful-ness or unconcealment of what is covered over in oblivion. Heidegger increasingly felt, the older he got, that the question of being had been completely covered over in the modern world. Writing *Being and Time* was a work of unconcealment, of rediscovery or disclosure of something lost and forgotten. I share that conviction and concern and it motivates the writing of this book.

9 This is Dreyfus's preferred word for Heidegger's untranslatable *befindlichkeit* that has perplexed his English language translators and commentators (Dreyfus 1991: 168; Heidegger [1927] 1962: 172n.2). Alternatives might be responsiveness or openness. It means something like the capacity to be affected by and responsive to the world in the immediacy of the situation one is in, and is experienced as mood. Being happy, angry, cheerful, sad, bored, anxious, fearful, playful, etc., are all distinct and primary ways of being in response to (and affected by) the direct and immediate experiential encounter of the aliveness of the world and of one's own situated being in it.

Chapter 5   Turning on the TV set

1 Heidegger ([1927] 1962: 91–107). It is essential to note that the two ontologies (A and B) with their corresponding ways of being (present or ready-to-hand) are not an either-or. Both ontologies are constitutive of things and people and the world. But, and this is the crux, things (and persons) cannot *be* in both ontologies at the one and the same time. We switch back and forth from one to the other, but at any one time we are *in* one mode of being or the other. They are the two mutually exclusive con-tradictory dimensions of the truth-and-reality of things, persons and world.

2 Of course, today the television 'thing' or object comes in a variety of shapes and sizes: large, flat-screen and immobile (the fixed thing in the room); small and portable (laptop, tablet); miniature and mobile (iPhones). It is the first kind of object that is discussed here, but in principle the argument developed in what follows applies to all forms of the television-object-thing and what happens when it is 'turned on'.

3 Things in use, as Don Ihde notes in his commentary on Heidegger's analysis of equipment, no longer appear as objects to be seen but recede or withdraw from sight (Ihde 2007: 287). The hammer as an 'object' presents itself to our objective gaze. When we pick it up it disappears. We no longer 'see' it. We use it.

4 It is a useful exercise in 'linguistic botanizing' (as advocated and practised by J.L. Austin), to consider the differences between to see, to look and to watch by thinking of the situations and circumstances in which we might use these different verbs to describe our perceptions of television.

5 We regard our bodies in the same way as our domestic appliances, cars, etc. We are thankful that, in all their parts and as a whole, they 'work' and have no idea how they in fact do. Our own technological complexity is concealed from us (is black boxed, as it were) by our skin surface, in just the same way as the TV set. And if anything goes wrong with our bodies, we need the service of appropriate experts (dentists, doctors, etc.) as we do when our appliances break down. The design aesthetics of the human body and of humanly made things are homologous. It is not that we are like machines: *they are like us.*

6 For an account of this history in the United States, see Douglas (1987: 55–82). See plate 1, opposite p. 192, for a photograph that vividly captures this moment.

7 Adrian Forty describes three stages in the evolution of the first truly modern, mass-produced radio set in Britain; the Ekco AD65 receiver designed and manufactured by the E.K. Cole company and in the shops by 1934 (Forty 1986: 200–6; Scannell and Cardiff 1991: 356–62).

8 For an important historical discussion of the social applications of electricity and the design of domestic appliances, see Forty (1986: 182–221).

9 I don't think the components of the care-structure have the same 'weight' in relation to each other. Affordability and usability have fuzzy boundaries (they're 'more or less' affordable/usable). But the safety of an appliance is much less fuzzy. It had *better* be safe, period – not more or less safe. Reliable is also something an appliance had better be, and likewise durable (but how long do we expect a TV set, a car, a mobile phone to last – do we replace them because they're worn out, or because a newer, more sophisticated generation of MP5s, say, is on the market?). Attractiveness is hard to define and arguably as much in the eye of the beholder as the thing – but it is certainly the case that things are made to be attractive and are in part purchased because they are seen to be so.

10 This little trinity – faith, hope and trust – is a secular trace of the theological virtues of faith, hope and love. It constitutes the virtuous matrix of well-made things for general use – the structure of the care that produces them as *goods*. Moral philosophy treats the virtues as if they were aspects of persons. Here they are thought of as constituting the goodness of the material world of everyday things.

11 Making allowances for 'local' variations of course; left or right hand drive, manual or automatic gears for instance. The first time I tried to drive a car in the USA I was baffled by the absence of the hand-brake (standard in European cars) and it took me about twenty minutes to figure out that what I'd assumed opened the bonnet (hood) was in fact a foot-brake. I was very challenged by what appeared to be a computerized WC in the first Japanese hotel I stayed in, in Tokyo. It functioned the same way, basically, as all

WCs do of course, but a complicated looking keypad (with instructions in Japanese) implied that it could do lots of other things as well (warming the seat, providing music, sweet smells – who knows?) but I lacked the courage to experiment myself or seek advice. It remained a mystery to me!

12 Wenger spoke with his studio hosts through an interpreter. He was familiar with Japan and known to Japanese viewers. He had been the manager of Nagoya Grampus Eight from 1995 to 1996 before moving to London as manager of Arsenal, and I am grateful to Shaun Moores for pointing this out to me. The club, which plays in the J(apanese) League, was founded by Toyota, originally as its works soccer team. It is based in the city of Nagoya, the corporation's HQ, and gets its name from two well-known symbols of Nagoya: the two golden grampus dolphins on the top of the old castle and the *Maru-Hachi* (Circle eight: a mystical sign), which is Nagoya's official symbol (all details from Wiki).

13 The concept of communicative logic is adapted from H.P. Grice's fundamental analysis of the logic of conversation (Grice 1989: 22–41; cf. Scannell 2007: 171–97). Grice thought that the implicit logic of ordinary talk (the rational underpinnings that make it reciprocally intelligible in any interaction) extended more generally to logics of use in other practical everyday activities (see Grice 1989: 28). Here, I try to develop his fundamental insight in respect of ordinary talk and other everyday practical activities to everyday things as things-for-use. In a synthesis of Heidegger and Grice's thinking, I assume that there is (must be) a universal logic-of-use implicit in any and every everyday thing. The logical conditions of the intelligibility of talk (Grice) and of the everyday material world of things (Heidegger) are, and must be, for all practical intents and purposes, the same. These universal logical conditions are implicated in the practical usage and application of words and things.

14 In the USA, *The Jack Benny Show* (NBC 1932–9) discovered the same 'situation' format from very similar beginnings as a variety show, ahead of British radio, with even greater and more enduring popular success.

15 The distinction is a re-working of Heidegger's discussion of the apophantical (manifest) and 'existential-hermeneutic "as"' (Heidegger [1927] 1962: 201).

Chapter 6   Television and technology

1 The historical human world, in turn, is embedded in the evolving world of all living things, planet Earth, the source and home of life. This world – the one and only life-creating, life-giving, life-sustaining world – is outwith the concerns of this book. But it is always to be borne in mind that our human world is, in every conceivable and inconceivable way, wholly and utterly dependent on it.

2 Scannell (2007: 260–93). Here and in the next couple of paragraphs I'm following closely the summary of that argument in Scannell (2008).

3 Since time immemorial, the leisured classes (by definition, the rich: those

who can *afford* to be leisured) have employed slaves to do housework; in modern times, wage-slaves, a.k.a. domestic servants. Domestic service was the largest single category of employment in Britain before the Second World War. The domestic technologies of the 1950s made servants largely redundant. They were cheaper, more efficient, less troublesome and resentful and, all round, more reliable for the day-to-day running of a household than live-in human beings.

4 The classic study of television, domestic life and leisure in the USA in the 1950s is Spigel (1992). In the UK, David Morley's work on television as a domestic technology that exists in situ with other domestic electrical appliances is exemplary (Morley 2007).

5 Lucien Goldmann argues convincingly that Heidegger had read the essay which is referred to obliquely several times in *BT*. See his excellent introduction for a discussion of the basic similarities and differences in their thinking: Goldmann ([1973] 1979: 1–25).

6 The *Principles of Scientific Management* was published by Frederick Winslow Taylor in 1911. For a review of Lukacs, Horkheimer and Adorno's critique of Taylorism and the industrialization of culture, see Scannell (2007: 31–51).

7 Heidegger was 60 when he gave this public lecture in the town hall of Bremen, on 1 December 1949, to a non-academic audience. He had only just been declassified as a suspect Nazi and rubber stamped as 'fellow traveller. No punitive action'. It has become one of his best known later writings. Today technology is a recently emerging sub-division within the academic field of philosophy, and Heidegger's essay is a key text. In the view of the editors of the *Philosophy of Technology*, it 'is probably the single most influential – though by no means the most popular – position in the field' (Scharff and Dusek 2003: x; see pp. 265–338 for various responses to Heidegger).

8 The Obama Administration's policy, at the time of writing, in respect of nuclear weapons is to reduce and ultimately eliminate the stockpile held by members of the nuclear 'club' (essentially Russia and the USA who between them possess 96 per cent of the world's nuclear arsenal). The flip-side of this policy is to prevent the spread of nuclear technology and the manufacture of nuclear weapons in the rest of the world. Thus, in the interests of the whole world, post-modern global politics seeks to control and redress the harm of conflict-oriented modern technologies and politics geared to the interests of nation-states.

9 We all read, at the time, *The Postmodern Condition* (Lyotard [1979] 1986), *Postmodern Culture* (Foster 1985) and *The Condition of Postmodernity* (Harvey 1986), etc.

10 It would be too much of a distraction here to elaborate on this key point. But it is essential to acknowledge, for instance, that the things in our homes are, in all kinds of ways, transformed from being just 'things' into being *our* things, and in this way we make a house a home, an expression of our life. David Morley's work is especially good on just this crucial mundane matter

of the intimacy of everyday things as part of everyday real lives (Morley 2007: 275–91 and *passim*). See also Daniel Miller (2008).

11 This is perhaps an appropriate moment to acknowledge this chapter as partial homage to Raymond Williams's pioneering study: *Television: Technology and Cultural Form* (Williams 1974).

Chapter 7   The meaning of *live*

1 More exactly: immediacy (ontology A)/liveness (ontology B).

2 De-severance is the translation of the untranslatable *Ent-fernung* which means literally the abolition, the overcoming of distance or farness and thus making something close (as *zuhanden*: handy and within range) and as such available for use. See Macquarrie and Robinson's discussion of the translation issues: Heidegger ([1927] 1962: 138n.2).

3 'Experience' was a deeply contested term in the emergence of British cultural studies. There were bitter arguments over its centrality and relevance (or not) to the study of culture. For reviews of the disputes over 'the politics of experience', see Jay (2006: 190–215) and Pickering (1997). See Hall (1980) for a conciliatory discussion of the 'two paradigms', 'experience' and 'ideology', in cultural studies. It is an indispensible term, which I use *not* as a socio-cultural but as an existential term – the *experience* of being (alive and living) in the world.

4 For a fascinating and copiously illustrated account of Heidegger's hut at Todtnauberg, see Sharr (2006). It should be noted that the hut was indeed a retreat from 'the dominion of technology'. For many years it had no phone or electricity (added, Sharr tells us, at some point in the 1950s). Water was drawn from a well outside. It was here that Heidegger found peace of mind to contemplate the restless world of modernity below.

Chapter 8   How to talk – on radio

1 What follows is drawn mainly from Howard Thomas's accounts of the programme (Thomas 1944, 1977), which he treats as very much his own creation. The production files in the BCC Written Archives at Caversham (WAC) show that this claim, which Thomas vigorously asserted (demanding that the programme be billed as 'originated by Howard Thomas') was disputed within the Corporation partly because the original demand for a question/answer programme was handed to the production departments from programme planning, partly because Douglas Cleverdon was, from the beginning, the programme's co-producer and partly because of a corporate culture of anonymity. There was much conflict about all this at the time, but there is no doubt that *The Brains Trust* was Thomas's brainchild.

2 The Forces Programme was established in the Autumn of 1939 as a service for the army, billeted in France with nothing much to do – the European conflict did not begin until Spring 1940. This concern to provide entertainment for the troops is an early indicator of a concern for the welfare of the

rank and file, in stark contrast with the 1914–18 war. Britain was not a democracy in 1914. It was in 1939.

3 See Scannell and Cardiff (1991) for detailed accounts of the formation and development of these areas of production in the pre-war BBC.

4 Thomas worked in the London office of J. Walter Thompson (JWT) before joining the BBC. One of his clients was Radio Luxembourg, a European commercial radio broadcaster based in the Grand Duchy which broadcast popular radio entertainment in English aimed at Britain. Thomas made many programmes in the 1930s for Radio Luxembourg, in JWT's radio production suite. They were recorded on disc and flown to Luxembourg for transmission.

5 26 November 1940. BBC WAC (Written Archives, Caversham) 51/23/1. A variant on *The Brains Trust* format, called *Any Questions* began on West Region on 12 October 1948. It invited questions on current political issues from a live audience to be answered by a panel of four (of whom two at least were always MPs) through the programme's question master. *Any Questions* is still running on BBC Radio 4 today. Its companion programme on Radio 4 is *Any Answers* in which listeners respond on air to the issues raised each week in *Any Questions*. The format transferred to television in the 1970s and *Question Time* (BBC1) remains the BBC's long-running flagship programme for the weekly discussion of current affairs. Thus a format developed over 60 years ago is still alive and in use today as the BBC's preferred format for the discussion of politics on both radio and television.

6 The BBC had three different systems of studio recording at that time: on disc (the Marguerite Sound System), on steel tape (the Marconi-Stille system) or on film (the Phillips-Miller system). For details, see Pawley (1972: 178–94, 270–9). All were used simply to 'bottle' programmes 'live' as broadcast from the studio for purposes of record or (as in the case of *The Brains Trust*) for transmission at a later date. The possibilities of post-production tape editing awaited the development of lightweight cellulose-acetate magnetic tape (a 60-minute Marconi-Stille steel tape weighed 25 pounds; Pawley 1972: 385–6). This equipment was developed in Germany during the war, and picked up from the battlefield by the British and Americans after the invasion of Europe in 1944. It did not come into widespread use for broadcasting until the mid 1950s.

7 The BBC WAC press cuttings for the Forces Programme (1941–5) show how continuously newsworthy *The Brains Trust* and its three 'resident' performers became for the daily and weekly press. There was a photo-feature spread on the programme in *Picture Post* (3 August 1941), and *Illustrated* (3 November 1941) ran a cover story on 'Why Professor Joad plays hockey'. The front-page photograph showed the 50-year-old Joad in shorts surrounded by young women kitted up, apparently, for a game of hockey.

8 There were Agricultural Brains Trusts for farmers; Dig For Victory Brains Trusts for allotment holders and gardeners; Army, Navy and Air Force Brains Trusts; Women's Institute Brains Trusts, and even – on the BBC – a Religious Brains Trust called *The Anvil* which was not, however, a success.

'Made of tin, and they strike it with cardboard hammers' was the unkind description of it in the House of Commons (Thomas 1944: 10). See also *BBC Handbook* (1942: 72–3) for further details of the immediate impact of *The Brains Trust*.

9 In British society, at the end of dinner, women retired to the drawing room while the men remained behind and, thus separated, relaxed masculine and feminine conversations ensued in their separate spheres. In the brilliant salon culture of pre-revolutionary France, women were the organizers and facilitators of an art of conversation between the sexes – but it even so appears from Benedetta Craveri's marvellous history that, on the whole, men were the wits who sparkled and women their patrons and admirers (Craveri 2005).

10 It was a commonplace prejudice within an overwhelmingly male BBC at the time that women did not make good broadcasters. The characteristics described by Thomas are all attributable to the lack of confidence, exacerbated by lack of experience, which made women acutely self-conscious when speaking at the microphone.

11 The hugely influential concept of the political public sphere was established by Jürgen Habermas ([1962] 1989) and is fully discussed in the companion volume to this book (Scannell 2007).

12 Arthur Christopher Benson (1862–1925) had a distinguished literary and academic career. He was a prolific author of fantasy, poetry and essays. *From a College Window* was a collection of his occasional essays, the college being, presumably, Magdalene College, Cambridge, of which Benson was the Master. His ideas about conversation and its management doubtless came from his experience of presiding over the talk at a Cambridge college high table.

13 I have consistently resisted Habermas's thesis that the media have contributed to the refeudalization of public life in the late twentieth century, arguing that broadcasting has created real and effective forums for talk and discussion that enhance and deepen the meaning and practice of democracy (Scannell 1989, 1991, 1996).

14 Lazarsfeld, Herzog and Merton's work are all discussed in some detail in Scannell (2007: 9–30).

15 On these developments in the UK, see Scannell (1996: 58–74). For the USA, see McCracken (1999).

16 One should add, perhaps, the town hall meeting in the USA, which might seem to be an exception to what is being claimed here. But Michael Schudson has vigorously debunked the historical 'myth' of the town hall meeting as a model of participatory democracy, a Habermasian public sphere (Schudson 1998: 16–19) in which everyone spoke freely. For ordinary citizens even today, it is an intimidating experience to stand up and express your opinions in a town hall meeting and most prefer to stay silent while leading local figures (who are accustomed to speaking in public) hold the floor (Schudson 1997: 301).

17 This is how Hilda Matheson, the first Head of Talks at the BBC (1927–32),

discusses the matter in her seminal insider account of the impact of radio (Matheson 1933: 75 ff.) For a more detailed historical account of the management of talk on radio, see Scannell and Cardiff (1991: 153–80).

18 On the communicative affordances of technologies, especially in relationship to talk, see Hutchby (2001).

Chapter 9   How to talk – on television

1 Patrol Torpedo (PT) boats were fast attack craft armed with torpedoes used by the USA in the Pacific war against the Japanese fleet.

2 The Taft-Hartley Act was a federal law, passed in 1947, that imposed restrictions on the power and activities of the organized labour (trade unions) movement.

3 Her action (re-entering the room holding a football) generates an implicature that prompts a question: What's that (and furthermore, why on earth are you holding it)? The answer is not the obvious one (a football) but 'a wedding present' which explains *why* she is holding it. Mrs Kennedy had been talking about wedding presents before her exit. The thing she's holding on her return signals the resumption of where she had been in the conversation.

4 The show was taken out of the morgue and revived again by CBS in 2012. In its current reincarnation, exactly the same format is used but this time with two interviewers in the CBS studio looking at the magic window that takes them and viewers to the home of the celebrity interviewee. It is hosted by Lara Logan and Charlie Rose, 'two widely respected journalists who excel at the art of conversation' (www.cbsnews.com/8301-505383_162-57369701/person-to-person-new-life-for-legendary-tv-show). The new series opened on 8 February 2012 with George Clooney, a singularly appropriate first choice. Not only is Clooney perhaps the starriest male Hollywood celebrity today. He co-scripted, acted in, produced, directed and personally financed (mortgaging his home to do so) *Good Night and Good Luck* (2005), a film which recreated the legendary story of how Ed Murrow (played by David Strathairn), Fred Friendly (George Clooney) and the *See it Now* team at CBS took on and exposed Senator Joe McCarthy in the early 1950s. 'Good night and good luck' was Murrow's signature sign-off at the end of each *See it Now* broadcast.

5 Perhaps the most eagerly awaited *Person to Person* of all was with Marilyn Monroe in April 1955. Again Murrow fumbled the conversational ball. 'His questions were dreadful: "I saw some pictures of you the other day at the circus. Did you have fun?" "Do you like New York?" "Do you like Connecticut?" And to Mrs Green [the friend with whom Monroe was staying at the time] "Does she make her own bed?"' (Persico 1988: 351–2).

6 This custom was, by the time of the programme, the dying trace in Britain of the conventions of the French salon or the Italian *conversazione* cultivated by European polite society since the eighteenth century.

7 The performative pragmatics of doing 'being delighted' require that

you should be so without hesitation or qualification. Fisher responds to Dimbleby immediately but produces a hedge before and a slight pause after his expression of delight. The prefatory 'well' serves as a small qualifier (well maybe, perhaps . . .) to what comes next, while the follow-on 'more or less' violates the Gricean maxim of quantity (do not say more or less than the occasion requires). Saying 'more or less' appears to be having it both ways; a double violation of the maxim and in either case the implicature is clear – he is a bit less rather than more delighted with the situation he is in as he speaks.

8   A well-known English public school. Fisher became headmaster at the age of 27.

9   It was made, we learn, by women members of the Anglican Church in Japan and presented to Fisher by Bishop Yashiro at the Lambeth Conference of 1948.

10 Antony Giddens defines ontological security as 'Confidence or trust that the natural and social worlds are as they appear to be, including the basic existential parameters of self and social identity' (Giddens 1984: 375).

11 Trust in words and conversation was brilliantly tested in the 'breaching experiments' of Harold Garfinkel, who showed the devastating consequences of, for instance, the deliberate violation of the meaning of perfectly ordinary words – 'a flat tyre', for instance (Garfinkel [1967] 1984: 25–75; Scannell 2007: 152–6).

12 Implied meanings. The study of implicatures is a central concern in modern pragmatics as it developed from H.P. Grice's seminal work on the logic of conversation (Grice 1989). For a discussion, see Scannell (2007: 174–7).

13 All information in this paragraph is from a personal VCR copy of *Inside the News*, the first 25-minute episode in an invaluable documentary series about the rise of television news from its beginning through to and including the Falklands War (1982) made for and shown on BBC2 in the mid eighties, if I remember correctly.

Chapter 10   The moment of the goal – on television

1   The background research for this chapter was partially funded by a grant from the Hosu-Bunku Foundation to Professor Kazue Sakomoto, Ochanomisu University and myself, for a joint comparative study of Anglo-Japanese live television coverage of international soccer. I am grateful to Elif Toker and Aisling Grimes, who produced a complete transcript of the England-Greece match on which I have based my discussion of that game.

2   Blackburn speaks to the experiential now of ontology A, rather than the punctual now of ontology B.

3   There is a scattered literature on this topic. The essential ur-text is the 1975 BFI Monograph, *Football on Television* (Buscombe 1975), which contains useful by-now historical data on soccer coverage, plus short articles analysing the style of television coverage. Margaret Morse (1983) has a perceptive chapter – *Sport on Television: Replay and Display* – which focuses

on American football and its coverage, including some suggestive comments on the differences between the UK and the US coverage of soccer
and football, based on the Buscombe collection. Whannel (1992) is the best
introduction to the general issue of sport and the media, and I have drawn
on his discussion of how different sports are handled on British television.
Raunsbjerg (2001) is particularly recommended as a comprehensive and
up-to-date discussion of television coverage of live soccer. Dayan and Katz
(1992) on media events, is of course, a key background text to this topic.

4 Margaret Morse treats coverage of (American) football as conforming to
the rules and practices of Hollywood continuity editing. Its 'natural' *mise-
en-scene* – the playing field – with its clearly marked boundaries and sections
(the half-way and three-quarter lines, etc.) and its contained spaces of action
'seem tailor-made for continuity editing' (Morse 1983: 49). Unfortunately,
she offers no close analysis of how continuity editing, in fact, works in live
coverage of (American) football.

5 This aspect of coverage is dealt with in some detail in Tom Ryall's contribution to the BFI monograph, 'Visual style in "Scotland v Yugoslavia"'
(one of the matches in the 1974 World Cup). Ryall distinguishes between
the 'primary image', produced by the prime camera, and various kinds
of 'secondary image' or close-up (Buscombe 1975: 38–40). The primary
image produced by the prime camera 'is the "natural" view of football on
television and, generally, it gives way to the other [kinds of shot] only when
the action warrants it' (Buscombe 1975: 39).

6 The crest is worn on their shirts by the English team and the cross-wipe is
used only for English goals. Replays of the action during the game (a foul,
a near miss) are brought in and out with a cross-wipe of the programme's
logo, *Match of the Day* set within a white football. Both logos are promi-
nently displayed in the *Match of the Day* studio at the ground.

7 However, these are questionable assumptions. 'Compared to many continental cultures we [the British] subscribe to an orgasmic theory of football;
the foreplay only has meaning if it is climaxed with goals . . . this is not a
universal attitude to the sport; continental crowds appear to place just as
much value on the short passing skills of the build-up as on the brief ecstasy
of the goal. But it is a view that we tend to take for granted in television definitions of the game simply because it is so familiar to us' (Andrew Tudor in
Buscombe 1975: 60).

8 The significance of Sven-Göran Eriksson in the narrative of Gerrard's goal
(and also in the Beckham goal analysed below) should be accounted for.
He had only just been appointed as the English manager, after the previous
manager, Kevin Keegan resigned following England's 1-0 defeat, at home,
by Germany in one of their first World Cup qualifying matches. There
had been immense media interest and discussion of the pros and cons of
appointing Eriksson, the first non-British appointment to the job of managing the English team. Since taking over, Eriksson had begun to turn round
the fortunes of the English team. The return game against Germany was
by far the biggest game for England and for him since his appointment. If

he really was the answer to the hitherto disappointing performance of the England team, the game against Germany would deliver the proof, or not.

9 A computer-generated circle with a luminous green circumference is projected onto the screen showing the zone of exclusion outside which opposing players must stand so that they cannot immediately block a direct free kick. This technique was developed by Sky and subsequently picked up by the BBC.

Chapter 11   Being in the moment: the meaning of media events

1 This distinction has something in common with that, in German, between *Erlebnis* and *Erfahrung*, the former referring to special or meaningful life experiences, and the latter to the weight of incremental life experience. The former is immediate and unreflective; the latter accumulates in time and is reflective. For a discussion of these terms (especially in the writings of Walter Benjamin and Theodor Adorno) in the context of a sweeping historical survey of the category of experience as discussed in philosophy, theology, aesthetics, politics and history in Europe and North America from the eighteenth century to the present, see Jay (2006).

2 Heidegger focuses on individuals and their moods, notably fear, anxiety and boredom. But human situations also, and always, have their moods to which we always attend: the mood 'in the room' is something palpably felt and experienced by those who are there. My focus here is on occasions and their moods rather than as Heidegger discusses them. The key thing I take from him is that mood is a (if not the) primary register of human situated existence: it is that wherein and whereby our being in the world (our direct encounter with whatever worldly situation we are 'in') is experienced as such. In articulating mood (as being bored, being happy, being sad, etc.), we give expression to our encounter with the immediate reality of our human situation – our experience of it in particular and in general, in the short and the long term. The experience of mood is the interface between the living world life as encountered any where any time by the living.

3 Translation by Lewis Piaget Shanks (1931).

4 Translation by Roy Campbell (1952).

5 For a further gloss on the moment of vision as an ecstasis (time out of time), see Michael Inwood's invaluable Heidegger dictionary: Inwood (1999: 220–2).

6 The fundamental human necessity of the more than necessary is nowhere more starkly posed than in *King Lear*. Having foolishly given away his kingdom and divided it between his daughters, Lear naively thinks he can somehow retain the trappings of a king, which includes a personal retinue of a hundred knights. Goneril and Regan (who have to put up with them) demur. 'Do you really need that many?' they ask him. 'Why not twenty? Why not one?' Lear replies: 'O reason, not the need: our basest beggars Are in the poorest things superfluous. Allow not nature more than nature needs, Man's life's as cheap as beasts' . . . Of course he doesn't *need* a hundred

knights. But he does if he is to continue to be a king. As the consequences of his initial act of folly mercilessly unfold, Lear is stripped of everything; all the apparently unnecessary social and cultural trappings that made him what he was, until he is reduced to wandering on the bare heath, as a violent storm rages overhead, in the company of his Fool and a naked lunatic, Tom o' Bedlam (in fact Gloucester's son, Edgar, in disguise). Looking at 'poor Tom', Lear finally discovers the truth of humanity stripped of all superfluities: 'Thou art the thing itself: unaccommodated man is no more but such a poor, bare, forked animal as thou art.'

7 'The fine delight that fathers thought, the strong/Spur, live and lancing as the blowpipe flame/Strikes once and quenchéd faster than it came/Leaves yet the mind the mother of immortal song'. Thus G.M. Hopkins describes the *jouissance* of the moment of poetic inspiration in one of his last and most perfect sonnets.

8 I have a debt of gratitude to Stephanie Marriott that I wish, here in the end, to acknowledge. Her brilliant linguistic studies of television sports commentary, and especially what is going on in instant replays, opened up for me a line of thinking that has culminated in this chapter.

Chapter 12   Catastrophe – on television

1 The original version of this chapter was published in French (at the invitation of Daniel Dayan) in 2002 and in English two years later (Scannell 2002, 2004). It has been further revised and images added in this chapter.

2 The following account of CNN news coverage is deeply indebted to Paul Pheasey's undergraduate dissertation, 'Convention in Chaos. CNN's Search for Meaning on September 11th, 2001'. I have drawn extensively on his videotape and superb transcription of the first 50 minutes of CNN's live coverage of the breaking story, from 8.50 am onwards (Pheasey 2002).

3 All times given are for Eastern Time (ET), the time in New York.

4 An earlier interviewed eyewitness.

5 For a detailed discussion of this point, see Boltanski ([1993] 1999: 7–11) who links it to the parable of the Good Samaritan. The parable has a direct political significance in present-day France where individuals have a legal responsibility to come to the assistance of anyone in distress or danger. A key point of the parable is the provision of immediate aid *irrespective* of the identity and status of the victim and the wider politics of the situation. That is, immediate help should not depend on *who* the suffering individual is, nor wait upon clarification of the circumstances that caused the injury. All considerations of the factors that may have led to an attack on the injured, and any questions as to whether or not such an attack may have been justified or not must be set aside and immediate assistance given.

6 Boltanski derives this term from that eighteenth-century literary taste public discussed by Habermas ([1962] 1989) as the precursor of the critical opinion forming public of the late eighteenth century. Both note the signifi-

cance of two key early English magazines, *The Tatler* and *The Spectator*; the former constituting the reader as a gossip and the latter as one who gazes on the social scene. Boltanski stresses the importance of Adam Smith's *Theory of Moral Sentiments*, which includes a discussion of the spectacle of suffering and the moral sentiments it inspires in those who witness it (Boltanski 1999: 35–54).

Chapter 13   Television and history

1 On the ordinariness of television, see Bonner (2003).
2 This concept is introduced by Luc Boltanski as the final thought (on the penultimate page) of *Distant Suffering* ([1993] 1999). I hope to explore its meaning further in *Love and communication* – this book's successor.
3 For an excellent summary of the history of 24/7 news from CNN to the present, see Barnett (2011).
4 [.] = a micro-pause, a beat.
5 For a full discussion of the linguistic features that differentiate scripted and unscripted news discourse, see Montgomery (2007: 117–42) to whom I am deeply indebted for the clarification of this crucial distinction.
6 'Verbs in the "historic present" describe something that happened in the past. The present tense is used because the facts are listed as a summary, and the present tense provides a sense of urgency. This historic present tense is also found in news bulletins. The announcer may say at the start, "Fire hits a city centre building, the government defends the new minister, and in football City United lose"' (Language notes, BBC World Service; cited by Richard Nordquist, grammar.about.com/od/fh/g/histpreterm.htm).
7 The standard British manual on *Broadcast Journalism: The techniques of radio and television news*, by Andrew Boyd, was first published in 1956. The back-page blurb to the 6th edition (2008) promises that it is completely up to date in response to continuing technological innovation: 'Constant inter-activity between on-the-scene reporting and nearly instant broadcasting to the world has changed the very nature of how broadcast journalists must think, act, write and report on a 24/7 basis.' That said, the basics of journalism remain unchanged. The two fundamental abilities that any aspirant journalist must have are 'writing skills and an understanding of the needs of the audience' (Boyd et al. 2008: 4). Chapters 6–8 are about how to write the news. The first of these is called 'Conversational writing' (69–81) – write as if you are *talking* to an audience of one (71). This by now ancient mantra remains the first thing to be grasped about *writing* for radio and television in general. The art of news writing concerns the *presentation* of information and the *telling* of news stories with clarity, impact and immediacy for absent listeners and viewers addressed not as a collectivity but as individual persons.
8 Schudson's essay 'Four approaches to the sociology of news' first appeared in the 2nd edition of *Mass Media and Society* (J. Curran and M. Gurevitch, eds) in 1989. In the 4th and 5th editions (2005, 2010), its introductory

section has been revised to emphasize the importance of events as the determinant of news and what journalists do. The sociological literature overwhelmingly treats news as 'institution-driven' (p. 173), but for Schudson this is no longer adequate as an explanation either of what news 'is' or how it is produced. See also Schudson (2008) for further discussion of news coverage of catastrophic events.

9 People *like* to be scandalized, as Elizabeth Bird points out in a thoughtful contribution to *Media Scandals*, edited by James Lull and Stephen Hinerman (1997) – a fascinating collection that opens up a new line of enquiry into news and 'news values'.

10 The best study of news and the human interest story that I know of is by Helen McGill Hughes (1940), a forgotten gem from the classic period of American mass communication sociology (q.v. Peters and Simonson 2004).

11 Virgil: *Aeneid*, ii: 363. 'An ancient city is falling, dominant for many a year' ... so the Roman poet laments (in the historic present tense) the sack of Troy by the Greeks a thousand years earlier as if it were happening now as he tells the tale. John Durham Peters thinks I have misconstrued the Latin. *Dominata* modifies *urbs*, he argues and thus: 'The old city falls in ruins, dominated by many years.' I stood corrected by him on the matter of Postum (Scannell 2007: 65n.3), but here I stand my ground. In *The Iliad*, Homer tirelessly reminds his listeners of the might and power of the old city of Ilium (Troy), whose magnificent walls have withstood the assaults of the Greeks for nine war-weary years. It is still standing at the end of Homer's great epic and is only finally destroyed by guile (the Greek gift of the huge wooden horse) rather than force – as told in the Roman sequel, Virgil's *Aeneid*. Troy is, in every way, an old and mighty city (*urbs antiqua [et] dominata*) that has withstood the assaults of time and war *multos per annos* – through many a (long) year.

12 Philip Schlesinger's by now classic account of the culture of the BBC's television newsroom remains the best insight into the immediate pressures of time on everything journalists do (Schlesinger 1978: 83–105).

13 Note Simpson's constant shuttling between present and future tense. 'I think frankly' (twice) and 'frankly I doubt' are present tense precursors to evaluations of possible future outcomes ... 'they'll hit Afghanistan very hard', 'they'll hit the host', 'I doubt if they'll get the guest.' The intriguing use of 'frankly' as a modal qualifier of 'thinking' and 'doubting' means something like 'In my honest professional opinion'.

References

Adorno, T. ([1977] 1991) 'Free time' in J.M. Bernstein (ed.) *The Culture Industry: Selected Essays on Mass Culture*. London: Routledge, 162–70.

Adorno, T. and M. Horkheimer ([1944] 1979) *Dialectic of Enlightenment*. London: Verso.

Agacinski, S. (2003) *Time Passing: Modernity and Nostalgia*. New York: Columbia University Press.

Anderson, B. ([1983] 2006) *Imagined Communities: Reflections of the Origin and Spread of Nationalism*. London: Verso.

Anderson, P. (1969) 'Components of the national culture' in A. Cockburn and R. Blackburn (eds) *Student Power: Problems, Diagnosis, Action*. Harmondsworth: Penguin.

Ang, I. (1985) *Watching Dallas*. London: Methuen.

Atkinson, M. (1984) *Our Masters' Voices*. London: Methuen.

Auslander, P. (1999) *Liveness. Performance in a Mediatized Culture*. London: Routledge.

Austin, J.L. (1961) *Philosophical Papers*. J.O. Urmson and G.J. Warnock (eds), London: Oxford University Press.

Austin, J.L. (1962) *How to Do Things with Words*. Oxford: Oxford University Press.

Bagehot, W. ([1867] 1963) *The English Constitution*. Oxford: Oxford University Press.

Barnett, S. (2011) *The Rise and Fall of Television Journalism*. London: Bloomsbury Academic.

Barthes, R. (1984) *Camera Lucida: Reflections on Photography*. London: Fontana.

BBC (1930) *BBC Yearbook 1930*. London: BBC Books.

BBC (1942) *BBC Handbook 1942*. London: BBC Books.

Benjamin, W. ([1939] 1973) 'On some motifs in Baudelaire' in H. Arendt (ed.) *Illuminations*. London: Fontana, 155–201.

Benson, A.C. (1906) *From a College Window*. London: Thomas Nelson and Sons.

Berelson, B. ([1949] 2004) 'What missing the newspaper means' in J.D. Peters and P. Simonson (eds) *Mass Communication and American Social Thought, 1919–1968*. Lanham, MD: Rowman and Littlefield, 254–62.

Bird, E. (1997) 'What a story! Studying the audience for scandal' in J. Lull and S. Hinerman (eds) *Media Scandals*. Cambridge: Polity, 99–122.

Blanke, D. (2007) *Hell on Wheels: The Promise and Peril of America's Car Culture, 1900–1940*. Lawrence, KS: University Press of Kansas.

Boltanski, L. ([1993] 1999) *Distant Suffering* [*La Souffrance á Distance*. Paris: Editions Métailié]. Cambridge: Cambridge University Press.

Bonner, F. (2003) *Ordinary Television: Analyzing Popular TV*. London: Sage.

Boorstin, D. ([1962] 1992) *The Image: A Guide to Pseudo-Events in America*. New York: Vintage.

Bordwell, D. and K. Thompson (2001) *Film Art: An Introduction*, 6th edn. New York: McGraw-Hill.

Borgmann, A. (2003) 'Focal things and practices' in R.C. Scharff and V. Dusek (eds) *Philosophy of Technology: The Technological Condition*. Oxford: Blackwell.

Bourdieu, P. (1984) *Distinction: A Social Critique of the Judgment of Taste*. Cambridge, MA: Harvard University Press.

Bourdon, J. (2000) 'Live television culture is still alive: On television as an unfulfilled promise'. *Media Culture & Society* 22(5): 531–56.

Boyd, A., P. Stewart and R. Alexander (2008) *Broadcast Journalism: Techniques of Radio and Television News*, 6th edn. Burlington, MA: Focal Press.

Brand, G. and P. Scannell (1991) 'Talk, identity and performance' in P. Scannell (ed.) '*The Tony Blackburn Show*', *Broadcast Talk*. London: Sage.

Braudel, F. ([1949] 1996) *The Mediterranean and the Mediterranean World in the Age of Philip II*. Los Angeles, CA: University of California Press.

Braudel, F. ([1969] 1980) *On History*. Chicago, IL: University of Chicago Press.

Burke, P. (1993) *The Art of Conversation*. Ithaca, NY: Cornell University Press.

Buscombe, E. (ed.) (1975) *Football on Television*. London: British Film Institute.

Campbell, R. (1952) *Poems of Baudelaire*. New York: Pantheon Books.

Cantril, H., H. Gaudet and H. Herzog (1940) *The Invasion from Mars: A Study in the Psychology of Panic*. Princeton, NJ: Princeton University Press.

Cardiff, D. and P. Scannell (1987) 'Broadcasting and national unity' in J. Curran, A. Smith and P. Wingate (eds.) *Impacts and Influences. Essays on Media Power in the 20th Century*. London: Methuen.

Chambers (2011) *The Chambers Dictionary*, 12th edn. London: Chambers Harrap Publishers.

Corner, J. (2004) 'Television's "event world" and the immediacy of seeing: Notes from the documentary archive'. *The Communication Review* 7(4): 337–43.

Couldry, N. (2003) *Media Rituals: A Critical Approach*. London: Routledge.

Couldry, N. (2004) 'Liveness, "reality" and the mediated habitus from television to the mobile phone'. *The Communication Review* 7(4): 353–61.

Craveri, B. (2005) *The Age of Conversation*. New York: New York Review of Books.

Crisell, A. (2012) *Liveness and Recording in the Media*. London: Palgrave Macmillan.

Curran, J. and M. Gurevitch (eds) (1989) *Mass Media and Society*. London: Edward Arnold.

D'Acci, J. (1994) *Defining Women: Television and the Case of Cagney & Lacey*. Chapel Hill, NC: The University of North Carolina Press

Dayan, D. (2009) 'Sharing & showing: Television, attention, monstration' in E. Katz and P. Scannell (eds) *The End of Television? Its Impact on the World (So Far)*. London: Sage.

Dayan, D. and E. Katz (1992) *Media Events: The Live Broadcasting of History*. Cambridge, MA: Harvard University Press.

Debord, G. ([1967] 2004) *The Society of the Spectacle*. Wellington: Rebel Press.

Derrida, J. (2001) 'Above all, no journalists' in H. de Vries and Samuel Weber (eds) *Religion and Media*. Stanford, CA: Stanford University Press, 56–94.

Derrida, J. and B. Stiegler (2002) *Echographies of Television*. Cambridge: Polity.

Dickens, C. ([1855–8] 2009) *Little Dorrit*. New York: Barnes and Noble

Dimbleby, J. (1975) *Richard Dimbleby; A Biography*. London: Hodder & Stoughton.

Douglas, S.J. (1987) *Inventing American Broadcasting, 1899–1922*. Baltimore, MD: The Johns Hopkins University Press.

Douglas, S.J. (1994) *Where the Girls Are: Growing Up Female with the Media*. New York: Three Rivers Press.

Douglas, S.J. (2010) *Enlightened Sexism: The Seductive Message that Feminism's Work is Done*. New York: Times Books.

Dreyfus, H. (1991) *Being-in-the-World*. Cambridge, MA: MIT Press.

Feuer, J. (1983) 'The concept of live television: Ontology as ideology' in E.A. Kaplan (ed.) *Regarding Television: Critical Approaches*. Los Angeles, CA: American Film Institute, 12–24.

Figal, G. (2009) *The Heidegger Reader*. Bloomington, IN: Indiana University Press.

Fleischacker, S. (2004) *A Short History of Distributive Justice*. Cambridge, MA: Harvard University Press.

Forty, A. (1986) *Objects of Desire: Design and Society since 1750*. London: Thames and Hudson.

Foster, H. (ed.) (1985) *Postmodern Culture*. London: Pluto Press.

Foucault, M. ([1969] 1976) *The Archaeology of Knowledge*. New York: Harper and Row.

Galbraith, J.K. (1958) *The Affluent Society*. London: Hamish Hamilton.

Garfinkel, H. ([1967] 1984) *Studies in Ethnomethodology*. Cambridge: Polity.

Giddens, A. (1979) *Central Problems in Social Theory: Action, Structure and Contradiction in Social Analysis*. London: Macmillan.

Giddens, A. (1984) *The Constitution of Society*. Cambridge: Polity.

Giddens, A. (1991) *The Consequences of Modernity*. Cambridge: Polity.

Gill, W. and H. Jennings. (1939) *Broadcasting in Everyday Life*. London: BBC.

Goffman, E. (1981) *Forms of Talk*. Oxford: Blackwell.

Goldmann, L. ([1973] 1979] *Lukacs and Heidegger: Towards a New Philosophy.* London: Routledge and Kegan Paul.

Goodwin, R.E., J.M. Rice, A. Parpo and L. Eriksson (2008) *Discretionary Time. A New Measure of Freedom.* Cambridge: Cambridge University Press.

Grice, H.P. (1989) *Studies in the Way of Words.* Cambridge, MA: Harvard University Press.

Habermas, J. ([1962] 1989) *The Structural Transformation of the Public Sphere.* Cambridge: Polity.

Hall, E. (1966) *The Hidden Dimension.* New York: Doubleday.

Hall, S. (1977) 'Culture, the media and the "ideological effect"' in J. Curran, M. Gurevitch and J. Woollacott (eds) *Mass Communication and Society.* London: Edward Arnold.

Hall, S. (1980) 'Cultural Studies: Two Paradigms'. *Media, Culture & Society* 2(1): 57–72.

Hall, S. and M. Jacques (eds) (1989) *New Times: Changing Face of Politics in the 1990s.* London: Lawrence and Wishart.

Harvey, D. (1986) *The Condition of Postmodernity.* Cambridge: Polity.

Hayes, R. (1995) *Kate Smith: A Biography.* Jefferson, NC: Mcfarland & Co.

Hebdige, D. (1989) *Hiding in the Light: On Images and Things.* London: Comedia.

Heidegger, M. ([1923] 1999) *Ontology: The Hermeneutics of Facticity.* Bloomington, IN: Indiana University Press.

Heidegger, M. ([1924] 1992) *The Concept of Time.* Oxford: Blackwell.

Heidegger M. ([1927] 1962) *Being and Time* (J. Macquarrie and E. Robinson, trans.). Oxford: Blackwell.

Heidegger, M. ([1954] 1978) 'The question concerning technology' in D.F. Krell (ed.) *Basic Writings.* London: Routledge, 311–41.

Herzog, H. (1941) 'On borrowed experience. An analysis of listening to daytime radio sketches'. *Studies in Philosophy and Social Science* IX(1): 65–95.

Hoggart, R. ([1957] 1992) *The Uses of Literacy.* Harmondsworth: Penguin Books.

Horkheimer, M. ([1941] 1978) 'The end of reason' in A. Arato and E. Gebhardt (eds) *The Essential Frankfurt School Reader.* Oxford: Blackwell, 26–48.

Horrie, C. (2002) *Premiership.* London: Pocket Books.

Hughes, H.M. (1940) *News and the Human Interest Story.* Chicago, IL: University of Chicago Press.

Hutchby, I. (2001) *Conversation and Technology.* Cambridge: Polity.

Ihde, D. (2007) *Listening and Voice: Phenomenologies of Sound.* Albany, NY: State University of New York.

Inwood, M. (1999) *A Heidegger Dictionary.* Oxford: Blackwell.

Jay, M. (2006) *Songs of Experience. Modern American and European Variations on a Universal Theme.* Berkeley, CA: University of California Press.

Katz, E. and P. Lazarsfeld (1955) *Personal Influence. The Part Played by People in the Flow of Mass Communications.* Glencoe, IL: The Free Press.

Lazarsfeld, P. and R.K. Merton ([1948] 2004) 'Mass communication, popular taste and organised social action' in J.D. Peters and P. Simonson (eds) *Mass Communication and American Social Thought*. Lanham, MD: Rowman and Littlefield, 230–41.

Leavis, F.R. and D. Thompson (1932) *Culture and Environment*. London: Chatto and Windus.

Lefebvre, H. (1947) *Critique de la vie quotidienne*. Paris: B. Grasset.

Liebes, T. and E. Katz (1990) *The Export of Meaning: Cross-Cultural Readings of Dallas*. New York: Oxford University Press.

Lord, A. (1965) *The Singer of Tales*. New York: Athenaeum.

Lotz, A. (2006) *Redesigning Women: Television after the Network Era*. Chicago, IL: University of Illinois Press.

Lukacs, G. ([1922] 1983) 'Reification and the consciousness of the proletariat' in *History and Class Consciousness*. London: Merlin Press, 83–222.

Lull, J. and S. Hinerman (eds) (1997) *Media Scandals*. New York: University of Columbia Press.

Lunt, P. (2004) 'Liveness in reality television and factual broadcasting'. *The Communication Review* 7(4): 329–35.

Lyotard, J-F. ([1979] 1986) *The Postmodern Condition: A Report on Knowledge*. Manchester: Manchester University Press.

Marriott, S. (1995) 'Intersubjectivity and temporal reference in television commentary' in *Time and Society* 4(3): 345–64.

Marriott, S. (1996) 'Time and time again: "Live" television commentary and the construction of replay talk'. *Media Culture & Society* 18(1): 69–86.

Marriott, S. (2007) *Live Television: Time, Space and the Broadcast Event*. London: Sage.

Marx, K. ([1867] 1976) *Capital: A Critique of Political Economy. Volume One*. Harmondsworth: Penguin Books.

Matheson, H. (1933) *Broadcasting*. London: Thornton Butterworth.

McCracken, A. (1999) '"God's gift to us girls": Crooning, gender and the re-creation of American popular song, 1928–1933'. *American Music* 17(4): 365–95.

Merton, R.K. ([1946] 2004) *Mass Persuasion: The Social Psychology of a War Bond Drive*. New York: Howard Fertig.

Miller, D. (2008) *The Comfort of Things*. London: Polity.

Montgomery, M. (2007) *The Discourse of Broadcast News*. London: Routledge.

Morley, D. (2007) *Media, Modernity, Technology: The Geography of the New*. New York: Routledge.

Morse, M. (1983) 'Sport on television: Replay and display' in E.A. Kaplan (ed.) *Regarding Television: Critical Approaches*. Los Angeles, CA: American Film Institute.

Naas, M. (2012) *Miracle and Machine: Jacques Derrida and the Two Sources of Religion. Science, and the Media*. New York: Fordham University Press.

Nader, R. (1965) *Unsafe at Any Speed: The Designed-in Dangers of the American Automobile*. New York: Grossman.

Pattison, G. (2000) *The Later Heidegger*. London: Routledge.

Pawley, E. (1972) *BBC Engineering, 1922–1972*. London: BBC.

Persico, J. (1988) *Edward R. Murrow: An American Original*. New York: Dell.

Peters, J.D. (1999) *Speaking into the Air. A History of the Idea of Communication*. Chicago, IL: Chicago University Press.

Peters, J.D. (2001) 'Witnessing' in *Media Culture & Society* 23(6): 707–24.

Peters, J.D. (2009) 'An afterword: Torchlight red on sweaty faces' in P. Frosh and A. Pinchevski (eds.) *Media Witnessing: Testimony in the Age of Mass Communication*. Houndmills: Palgrave Macmillan, 42–8.

Peters, J.D. and P. Simonson (eds) (2004) *Mass Communication and American Social Thought, 1919–1968*. Lanham, MD: Rowman and Littlefield.

Pheasey, P. (2002) 'Convention in chaos. CNN's search for meaning on September 11ᵗʰ 2001'. Undergraduate dissertation, BA Media Studies, University of Westminster.

Pickering, M. (1997) *History, Experience and Cultural Studies*. London: Macmillan.

Proust, M. (1996) *Time Regained*. London: Vintage.

Rath, C-D. (1988) '"Live/Life". Television as a generator of events in everyday life' in P. Drummond and R. Paterson (eds) *Television and its Audience*. London: British Film Institute, 32–7.

Rath, C-D. (1989) 'Live television and its audiences: Challenges of mediated reality' in E. Seiter, H. Borchers, G. Kreutzner and E.-M. Warth (eds) *Remote Control: Television, Audiences and Cultural Power*. London: Routledge, 79–95.

Raunsbjerg, P. (2001) 'TV sport and aesthetics: the mediated event' in G. Agger and J.F. Jensen (eds) *The Aesthetics of Television*. Aalborg, Denmark: Aalborg University Press.

Riesman, D. ([1950] 2001) *The Lonely Crowd*. New Haven, CT: Yale University Press.

Robertson, C. (ed.) (2011) *Media History and the Archive*. London: Routledge.

Roscoe, J. (2004) 'Multi-platform event television'. *The Communication Review* 7(4): 363–9.

Sacks, H. (1995) *Lectures on Conversation*. Oxford: Blackwell.

Safranski, R. (1998) *Martin Heidegger: Between Good and Evil*. Cambridge, MA: Harvard University Press.

Scannell, P. (1988) 'Radio Times: The temporal arrangements of broadcasting in the modern world' in P. Drummond and R. Paterson (eds) *Television and Its Audience: International Research Perspectives*. London: BFI Publishing.

Scannell, P. (1989) 'Public service broadcasting and modern public life'. *Media Culture & Society* 11(2): 135–66.

Scannell, P. (1991) *Broadcast Talk*. London: Sage.

Scannell, P. (1996) *Radio, Television and Modern Life*. Oxford: Blackwell.

Scannell, P. (1997) 'Saying and showing: A pragmatic and phenomenological study of a television documentary'. *Text* 17(2): 225–40.

Scannell, P. (1999) 'The death of Diana and the meaning of media events'. *Rundfunk und Geschichte* 25(4): 218–28.

Scannell, P. (2000) 'For-anyone-as-someone structures'. *Media Culture & Society* 22 (1), 5–24.

Scannell, P. (2002) 'Quelle réalité du malheur?'. *Dossiers de L'Institut National de L'Audiovisuel* (special issue on 11 September 2001). Paris.

Scannell, P. (2004) 'What reality has misfortune?' *Media Culture & Society* 26(3): 573–84.

Scannell, P. (2007) *Media and Communication*. London: Sage.

Scannell, P. (2008) 'The question concerning technology' in M. Bailey (ed.) *Narratives of Media History*. London: Sage.

Scannell, P. (2013) 'The centrality of televisions of the center in today's globalized world' in M. Kraidy (ed.) *Communication and Power in the Global Era*. London: Routledge: 116–29.

Scannell, P. and D. Cardiff. (1991) *A Social History of British Broadcasting, 1922–1939*. Oxford: Blackwell.

Scharff, R. and V. Dusek (eds) (2003) *Philosophy of Technology: The Technological Condition*. Oxford: Blackwell.

Schiller, H. (1976) *Communication and Cultural Domination*. White Plains, NY: M.E. Sharpe.

Schlesinger, P. (1978) *Putting Reality Together: BBC News*. London: Routledge.

Schudson, M. (1997) 'Why conversation is not the soul of democracy'. *Critical Studies in Mass Communication* 14: 297–309.

Schudson, M. (1998) *The Good Citizen: A History of American Civic Life*. New York: The Free Press.

Schudson, M. (2005) 'Four approaches to the sociology of news' in J. Curran and M. Gurevitch (eds) *Mass Media and Society*, 4th edn. London: Hodder Arnold, 172–97.

Schudson, M. (2008) 'The anarchy of events and the anxiety of story telling' in *Why Democracies Need an Unlovable Press*. Cambridge: Polity, 88–93.

Searle, J. (1969) *Speech Acts: An Essay in the Philosophy of Language*. Cambridge: Cambridge University Press.

Shanks, L.P. (1931) *Flowers of Evil*. New York: Ives Washburn.

Sharr, A. (2006) *Heidegger's Hut*. Cambridge, MA: MIT Press.

Sperber, A.M. (1986) *Murrow: His Life and Times*. New York: Freundlich.

Spigel, L. (1992) *Make Room for TV: Television and the Family Ideal in Postwar America*. Chicago, IL: University of Chicago Press.

St. George, E.A.W. (1993) *Browning and Conversation*. Houndmills: Palgrave.

Taylor, C. ([1992] 1994) 'The politics of recognition', in A. Gutmann (ed.) *Multiculturalism: Examining the Politics of Recognition*. Princeton, NJ: Princeton University Press, 25–73.

Taylor, C. (1992) *Sources of the Self: The Making of the Modern Identity*. Cambridge: Cambridge University Press.

Taylor, F.W. (1911) *The Principles of Scientific Management*. New York: Harper and Brothers.

Thomas, H. (1944) *Britain's Brains Trust*. London: Chapman and Hall.

Thomas, H. (1977) *With an Independent Air*. London: Weidenfeld and Nicholson.

Thompson, J.B. (1995) *The Media and Modernity: A Social Theory of the Media*. Cambridge: Polity.

Tolson, A. (2006) *Media Talk: Spoken Discourse on TV and Radio*. Edinburgh: Edinburgh University Press.

Tunstall, J. (1977) *The Media Are American: Anglo-American Media in the World*. London: Constable.

Tunstall, J. (2006) *The Media Were American: U.S. Mass Media in Decline*. New York: Oxford University Press.

Ward, P. (2001) *Studio and Outside Broadcast Camerawork*. Oxford: Focal Press.

Weber, M. (1930) *The Protestant Ethic and the Spirit of Capitalism*. London: Unwin University Books.

Whannel, G. (1992) *Fields in Vision: Television, Sport and Cultural Transformation*. London: Routledge.

Whannel, G. (2009) 'Television and the transformation of sport', in E. Katz and P. Scannell (eds) 'The End of Television? Its Impact on the World (So Far)', special edition of *The Annals of the American Academy of Political and Social Science* 625: 205–18.

Williams, R. ([1958] 1965) *Culture and Society*. Harmondsworth: Penguin Books.

Williams, R. ([1961] 1965) *The Long Revolution*. Harmondsworth: Penguin Books.

Williams, R. (1974) *Television: Technology and Cultural Form*. London: Fontana.

Wrathall, M. (2011) *Heidegger and Unconcealment: Truth, Language, and History*. Cambridge: Cambridge University Press.

Wolfe, K.M. (1984) *The Churches and the British Broadcasting Corporation 1922–1956: The Politics of Broadcast Religion*. London: SCM.

Zelizer, B. (2005) 'The culture of journalism' in J. Curran and M. Gurevitch (eds) *Mass Media and Society*, 4th edn. London: Hodder Arnold, 198–214.

Index